In My Own Sweet Time

In
My Own
Sweet Time

AN AUTOBIOGRAPHY

Blanche Cooney

Swallow Press
Ohio University Press
OHIO

Swallow Press/Ohio University Press books ·
are printed on acid-free paper ∞

97 96 95 94 93   5 4 3 2 1

Library of Congress Cataloging-in-Publication Data

Cooney, Blanche.
  In my own sweet time : an autobiography / Blanche Cooney.
     p. cm.
  ISBN 0-8040-0966-X
  1. Cooney, Blanche. 2. Cooney, James, d. 1985. 3. Publishers and
publishing—Massachusetts—Haydenville—Biography. 4. Phoenix
(Woodstock, N.Y.) 5. Farmers—Massachusetts—Haydenville-
-Biography. 6. Bohemianism—United States—History—20th century.
I. Title.
Z473.C755 1993
070.5'092'273—dc20
[B]   93-16261
                                                                   CIP

FRONT ENDPAPER:
West Whately, summer view
looking south, 1976, by Gabriel Amadeus Cooney

BACK ENDPAPER:
Winterscape, looking west,
Morning Star Farm, 1977, by Gabriel Amadeus Cooney

Designed by Laury A. Egan

Acknowledgments

New England Monthly (May 1989)

Margin (March 1990)

Anaïs 9 (1991)

The Massachusetts Review (Summer 1992)

FOR JIMMY

Contents

(photo section follows page 120)

In My Own Sweet Time

Chapter One

BETTY AND JOE

– 1916-1917 –

THEY MET in 1916, on New York's Lower East Side. Betty stood in the doorway of her Rivington Street tenement, waiting for Ginger. Joe turned in her doorway, glanced at her as he brushed against her, and raced up the dimly lit stair. She followed him with her eyes, her dark, luminous, wide eyes. Ginger appeared, reliable Ginger took Betty's books, he gave her his arm, he walked on the curb side of the pavement. Ginger was becoming a real American: his English was almost without accent, he worked in a pharmacy all day, he led the chess club at the Henry Street Settlement in the evening, and he was always in the audience when Betty gave a dramatic recitation in her Elocution class. Ginger would probably ask Betty to marry him, but not until he finished law school. He was a sensible young man. Betty felt only sisterly affection for him, but in her thoughts he was her "little sweetheart," she so yearned for romance. Betty was a believer; she believed she was in the land of opportunity. Her hungry soul was fertile ground for the dedicated teachers of immigrant children. Music, art, literature: these were holy studies. When she considered that the body is the Temple of the Spirit, the peculiarly American courses in hygiene, nutrition, gymnastics, and domestic science were also vital. There was much to learn. It would be a pity, her teachers told her, if she did not go on to secondary school. She was so quick; no one in her class could recite stanza after stanza of Longfellow as Betty did, from memory, by heart. "By heart." Betty lingered over those words.

But she couldn't stay in school. Her sisters worked, and her widowed mother barely stretched the meager income; her family said they would find a way, but she wanted to do her part. Fourteen was the legal working age; for fifty cents Betty was able to get false papers from a notary. She put her hair up and found a job as an apprentice to a wholesale milliner. Betty thought the girls who worked in millinery were more intelligent, a cut above the clerks in Woolworth's. In the afternoons, to break the long workday in the dusty, airless loft, there were real performances. Dramatic monologues, operatic arias: elevating, enthralling diversions. Betty cherished those intervals, and even the bosses came out of their office to listen. Betty did go to high school at night, and she continued her faithful attendance at the Henry Street Settlement House where her modest talent and sweet earnestness gained the approval of teachers and the admiration of her friends. In time she led her own group; she had even had several conferences with Dr. Felix Adler, founder of the Ethical Culture Society. That was an honor. Now in 1916 Betty was twenty-three; she was an expert milliner and she had a secure job. Betty was of a marriageable age, twenty-three was ripe for marriage, but Betty was the baby of the family, there were older unmarried sisters who must precede her. Betty was the most American, the most modern, the best educated; in the United States women were the equal of men, they could work as long as they chose. She was in no hurry to marry; she had learned a lot at the Henry Street Settlement.

Every night Blüme worried until she heard Betty's quick step in the hallway. It was foolish, she knew it was foolish, but Betty was such an innocent, so trusting, anyone could take advantage of her. "Ginger brought you to the door?" Blüme spoke only Roumanian. Betty answered in English, "Yes, Mammele. Ginger brought me." "A nice boy. Come, have a glass of milk before you sleep." Blüme came to the United States from Roumania with her daughters, but only part of her left the old country. If it were not for the pleading and weeping of her children she would not have made the terrible crossing, she would not have left the grave of her young husband in Jassy. Now she kept house for her fatherless daughters who had to go out into the rough streets of this city and work in shops for long hours. To live long enough to see them safely married, that was her devout wish. She herself never went out alone except to market. When she did, she wore her black silk with her fine cameo pin at the neckband, her head always covered with the prescribed wig. In the streets, where other women laughed loudly and hailed their friends and smacked their childrn, Blüme at the fish stall selected the carp and whitefish with care and then paid the asking price. The fish-monger might be disappointed: no haggling or cursing or flirting in that exchange; calm, friendly, Blüme did her marketing and re-turned home. She held herself apart, she knew she would never grow accustomed to the bewildering new world.

Betty slipped into bed beside her sister Clara. Someday, she thought, I'll have a bed to myself. And a toilet that's private, not down the hall, with three other families. Why did she think of the fellow who brushed against her and ran up the stairs without even excusing himself? He was a street ruffian. She could tell by the angle of his cap.

She saw him again the next day. There was a buzz, a small excitement running down the street, and as Betty approached she could see Belle Baker on the corner with two fellows. One of them was Joe. Belle was a famous singer now in music halls on Second Avenue. She wore rouge and lipstick and mascara, she wore the clothes of an actress with bugle beads and silk fringe. But she remembered Betty well. Weren't they always first to take each other's hands and form a circle when the hurdy-gurdy man came to their street? Didn't they both love his droll monkey, dressed in a little suit and a bright red hat, who rattled the two pennies in his cup to prime the collection? The girls who loved to dance ran out of the tenements or from behind their mother's skirts at the first sound of the irresistible music of the hurdy-gurdy, the little girls in their European clothes, with their ears pierced and their hair flying, holding hands, twirling and skipping in breathless abandon. Even then Belle played to the audience. "Show-off," the envious whis-pered.

"Introduce me to your friend."

"Betty, this is Joe," Belle said gaily. "Watch out for him. He's a devil."

He could be, Betty thought. Black brows, bold eyes, sensual mouth. He could be, dangerous.

This time Joe kept his eyes on Betty. Quiet Betty, in her white broadcloth blouse and her tailor-made skirt and the shining braids around her dark head. Betty with Victor Hugo's *Les Misérables* under her arm, on her way to the Henry Street Settlement.

Joe was leaning against the doorway of the tenement on Rivington Street when Betty came home that night. "Let's take a walk." "My mother is waiting. I have to get up early." "Only down the block." He didn't take her arm the way Ginger did, politely, protectively; he took her arm to touch her body to his, and she wanted him to. Down the street slowly, and around the corner and home again, hardly a word exchanged. He followed her into the dark hallway, she said goodnight, he stood close, he pressed her against the wall, touched her and whispered in her ear and moved against her and kissed her, and left abruptly.

Betty could not believe she allowed this to happen. She did allow it; she not only allowed it, she responded. Betty went upstairs slowly, she waited on the dim gas-lit landing before she could face her mother. She was sure her mother would see that she was not the same Betty who left that evening. How could Joe, a stranger, have recognized her passionate nature, awakened and aroused her, penetrated the armor of her high ideals? Betty was not provocative; she believed in the sacredness of love, she respected her body; it would be a gift overflowing to the man she married. Growing up on the lower East Side she had been protected not only by her stern and loving family but by her own timidity and fastidiousness. "Refinement." She dressed modestly, she carried books, she used the streets to go from home to somewhere: school, the Settlement House, to work; to a concert or a play. Not to stroll up and down with friends, to be noticed by boys who hung around the candy stand just waiting to whisper indecent proposals. She didn't think of herself as a prude, she was as capable of high spirits as anyone. Young men, like Ginger, could play, even be romantic, but they could control themselves. They didn't "take liberties"; they didn't go "too far"; they didn't attempt to "cross the line." The ravishing beast was kept within bounds.

That night Betty's life changed, she felt like another person. Joe was there waiting each day when she finished work. She had no time for her classes at the Settlement House. She had no time for Ginger. Ginger might be heartbroken; her mother might be wary: "Who is this Joe? Who are his people?" Joe introduced her to his New York. He took her to Second Avenue cabarets; she heard lewd songs and bawdy jokes. She sipped the strong cordials he ordered for her, she, who could be intoxicated by a phrase in a book, a "divine spark." She looked around for White Slavers, she imagined this was the kind of place they would frequent, looking for their prey. Joe took her to see his friend Benny Leonard fight. Joe told her Benny Leonard was the first Jewish lightweight champion. They had ringside seats. Betty tried not to show Joe how it sickened her to see the fighters savagely hurting each other, and how revolting were the cheers and curses of the red-faced men and women around them. She tried to think of it as an initiation: how to be a "good sport." Joe enjoyed the fight, proud to be the champion Benny Leonard's friend. This was Joe's world. He was a rough diamond, Betty decided; he had a good mind, it simply had never been cultivated. He could be transformed, he could go back to school: he could use his drive and his abilities to become a real leader. With missionary zeal she imagined how she would lead him out of Gehenna.

The greater mystery was Joe's pursuit. Ever since he was a boy he had easy success with girls, chasing them into alleys, ending up on rooftops: hot, eager, willing. What attracted him to the serious virgin who dressed like a schoolteacher? She didn't know anything about life, or having a good time. He had to watch his language around her, his table manners; Joe struggled with his desire to please Betty and his determination to shock her. "I don't have any use for schools," he told her. "I'd get there in the morning, hang my cap on the hook, say 'present' when the teacher took attendance. Then I'd leave. I came back for my cap when school was over." Betty *was* shocked. "But you didn't learn anything . . . " "I learned. One day the teacher said, 'Hold out your hand.' She cracked me over the knuckles with the ruler. Hard. I slapped her face, took my cap, and never went back."

Though Joe wanted Betty to hear his contempt for her world of books and ideas, he hoped she would recognize his pride, his independence, his courage to stand up to authority. What counted in this country was money, money and power; he would figure out how to get it. Yet he was really impressed by the way she talked, she used words he never heard before; her vocabulary, she called it. Betty was different from other girls; each day he could not wait to be with her. There was this confusion in Joe, these contradictions. But when they made love both idealistic Betty and cynical Joe were lost. She was more abandoned than any girl he had known, and he was as tender as a poet. One morning Joe awoke with the thought: Not for me. Not yet. He was not ready to settle down, with a steady job, a wife and kids: responsibilities. He couldn't find a way to tell Betty that this was going nowhere. He didn't want to hurt her. He was really doing her a favor; she was a beautiful girl, she would find a doctor, or a lawyer. She would remember him, he knew that. He stopped waiting for her after work, and he avoided the tenement on Rivington Street. He stayed away from Rivington Street altogether.

Betty grew pale, listless; she lost interest in food. She cried out in her sleep: Joe, Joe! Blüme could not bear to see her suffering, how she pined. Her daughter would make herself sick. Blüme appealed to Aunt Magda, the family matriarch, a businesswoman, a woman of the world. "Is he a good boy?" Aunt Magda asked Blüme. It was a many-layered question: has he scandalized the community, has he fathered children out of wedlock, has he broken the law, served time in a reformatory? Does he honor his parents? Does he observe the faith? Many layers. Blüme considered; she would not admit her doubts. "He has a good job. I think he comes from a respectable family. Russians. In the Temple they say his father is a scholar."

Aunt Magda made her own inquiries, she had an intricate network, and one Friday night, when Joe's family was sure to be gathered for Sabbath dinner, she visited. She climbed the three flights with measured tread and knocked on the door. Joe's sister Rose answered; impressed by the tall commanding Magda, she said, "Come in, come in." When Magda entered everyone could see she was a personage. Aunt Magda introduced herself in her grave voice, she was offered a seat, and speaking careful English she came at once to the point: "I would like to speak to Joe. I would like to meet the father, and the mother, for the reason that my kinswoman Blüme, who is not very well or she would have come herself, is worried about her daughter. It seems this daughter, who is my niece, Betty, thinks about your Joe all the time."

There were seven people around the table, it was easy to see which was Joe, all eyes turned to him. The father introduced himself and his wife, stubbornly using their Yiddish names: Moishe and Fagel, and reluctantly giving the Anglicized names of his sons, Joseph, Samuel, and Herman, and his daughters Rose and Sarah. A glass of tea was fetched for the visitor. Joe didn't expect an emissary from Betty's family. He ran his own life, no one called him to account, no one reined him in. He didn't tell his family what he did, or who he did it with. He had cut loose; he hardly ever went to the synagogue, only on the high holy days when he couldn't deny the fairness of his father's "While you are in my house . . . ," his father's voice made hard with deep disappointment. Moishe could not influence his sons, or his daughters. In this country the devil was strong.

Aunt Magda kept Joe in her eye while she spoke: Betty, her niece, she said, "is a beautiful healthy young woman. She is a skilled milliner. She is a loving daughter and a faithful sister, the flower of her family. A good heart and an educated head." Betty's father died when she was a child in Roumania, she told them; Betty's life would have been very different had he lived, he was a wealthy grain merchant. Aunt Magda gathered impressions as she spoke: she didn't think much of this family. Common; Russian peasants, muzhiks. She set the father apart; he had a distinctive head, a scholar's inwardness; quiet. She could tell he had lost his authority. She heard that Joe's mother Fagel had been a servant in the father's family in Stavisk. She was a sturdy, comely woman with Slavic cheekbones and high color; her blue eyes were cold. In fairness, Aunt Magda had no fault to find with her housekeeping. Given their modest circumstances, the family's Sabbath table was decently laid with linen, there was a cut-glass wine decanter and cruet on the table, silver candlesticks and samovar on the sideboard. As far as her eye could discreetly see, the apartment was orderly and clean.

At the heart of her investigation was Joe. She considered herself an infallible judge of men, and these were delicate matters. She knew he was uncomfortable, but she caught him listening intently. She was encouraged by his intelligent eyes and manly bearing, but Aunt Magda's first responsibility was to her niece. She would not knowingly betray her. She would deliver the young man to her, let Betty decide.

Aunt Magda knew when enough had been said.

"Now I want to know from Joe. Do you love her?"

Joe sighed. He didn't look at anyone.

His father said sternly, "Well? Speak!" The solemnity of the occasion allowed Moishe to once again assume the inquisitorial patriarch's role, and Joe to obey him.

"Yes," Joe was barely audible. "I love her."

"Tell her then," said Aunt Magda. "Tonight. She is waiting."

———

Aunt Magda arranged a meeting of the families at her house: Blüme and Betty, Moishe and Fagel and Joe. Tactful and adroit, Aunt

Magda sat in the background, advancing when just the right word was needed, retreating when there seemed to be agreement. With her copper-gold hair, her rich clothes, her ambassadorial bearing, she was easily the authority, the uncontested arbiter. Blüme said little, and she said it civilly; she tried to conceal her distrust of this union. She did not feel as sanguine as Aunt Magda about Joe. He had a trade, it was true, and, Aunt Magda said, he was ambitious. But Blüme thought he was a young man with dubious worldly appetites; he did not have a very good reputation, he ran around with poolroom bandits; her daughter Clara heard that. His people were cut from different cloth, and now they would be Betty's people. Blüme watched her daughter, so beautiful, so fine. Blüme could only pray that she was not making a terrible mistake in being a party to this marriage; she could only hope that the Russian young man would appreciate Betty.

Across the table from Blüme sat the Russian mother, Fagel, dressed for the occasion in her best, a toque hat on her head and her fat little hands quietly at rest in her lap. She appeared placid, even benign, but she too had her reservations. First, she calculated her loss of revenue: they would now have to manage without Joe's weekly contribution. It seemed the couple would be getting their own apartment. They, her Joe and this Betty, could save the great expense of setting up housekeeping if they moved in with her. Her family would make room; it would be a little crowded, but other people managed. Fagel could count on a share of Joe's wages, and Betty's wages, for their room and board, and, after a while, when they saved a good sum, *then* they could look for a place of their own. Looming large in her thoughts also, involuntarily causing her mouth to tighten with disapproval, was the lack of dowry. No dowry, but there was the rich aunt. Fagel acknowledged Aunt Magda's style, and her generosity. Aunt Magda would, she said, make the wedding in her house, to be followed by a dinner at one of the best restaurants on East Broadway. It was understood that only the immediate family would be invited. Fagel's further reservation was the girl herself, her daughter-in-law-to-be. It was mystifying how Joe could choose such a girl. Too thin, too tall, too dark, too quiet, and, contemptuously Fagel thought, observing her wrists, and her manner, too delicate.

———

Under the wedding canopy in Aunt Magda's house the Rabbi intoned the binding words. Joe stood stiffly beside Betty, wearing his yarmulke, repressing his feelings of humiliation, of bafflement. Joe glanced covertly at Betty; she listened to the Rabbi, rapt in her solemn joy, beautiful in her gown of ivory silk. Joe knew he wanted to take care of Betty for the rest of his life.

———

Blüme died. Betty's grief, her inconsolable grief for her mother now lost to her forever, shadowed the first year of her life with Joe. He consoled her; he diverted her. Indeed, she found herself sometimes forgetting she was in mourning. The day she felt the new life, the day she felt her baby stirring, was such a time. Betty had her bag packed for weeks; now the pains were unmistakable, her time had come, and she knew it as soon as she awoke. Joe was anxious, excited; he would not leave her. In the doorway of their apartment building she took shelter from the sharp December wind. He pulled the collar of her coat close around her throat, kissed her, and ran to the corner to hail a cab. Betty was solemn, fearful, and resolute, all at once. She would be the first woman in the family to have a baby in hospital, Beth-David Hospital; the name sounded reassuringly biblical. Still, it was an institution, cold, associated with pain and death. She was determined to be a groundbreaker, a twentieth-century woman, an American. Joe did not leave the hospital; he stayed with her through the night. His joy and relief after her safe delivery, the unexpected tenderness of his gaze when the nurse put me in his arms, well, Betty never thought Joe would be so crazy about being a father.

Chapter Two

GROWING UP IN NEW YORK CITY

EACH TIME I sharpen my focus, to get back there, in there, I think, why these scenes? Why are these scenes indelible, in amber, and not a thousand others. When did they become fixed? At the moment of their happening? Or did I select, edit, because they confirmed my view of how things were?

———

"Let's go to Child's," my father says. At the curb of a broad avenue in the city, I am between them: my mother holds my left hand, my father holds my right hand, they tower above me. "One, two, THREE!" they chorus, and swing me up and over the curb, and safely down. High spirits, they love each other; they love me, I can feel it; the current runs through our joined hands. I can't wait until we cross the avenue, I think we are going to a restaurant just for a child. What a disappointment: it's a big place with adult-size marble-top tables, bare and utilitarian, as Child's was in those days. I am not yet three.

———

It is winter 1921. We are on a subway platform, a dangerous place, but I am safe with my mother. A woman calls her name, "Betty!" They embrace, my mother and her friend from Settlement House days. I look up, I can't see their faces in the dim light, in the press of grownups in their heavy dark clothes; the three-year-old I am holds tight to my mother, the center of my world, and I listen. "Let me look at you! Pregnant again, Betty?" My mother's rueful laugh, her principles for planned parenthood, five years between babies, betrayed. Soon I would have a brother or a sister, I knew that, but I had just heard something else: a new word. Our train comes in, I press closer to my mother, the roar is so loud, the platform is so high above the tracks, the space between it and the train is so wide, so dark, so yawning, the clanging and banging so deafening as the train shudders to a stop. But once on the train I am safe. I take my position, kneeling beside my mother on the wicker-covered seat that runs the length of the car, my back to the subway passengers; I'm ready for the exciting hurtling race through the underground tunnel where the scary Plutonic darkness is punctuated by flashing signals. I'm safe beside her, my mother. Before the train starts I remember the new word and I say in a loud clear voice, "Pregnant again, pregnant again?" My mother is embarrassed; she thinks the whole subway car, every passenger, every man and woman, observes her rounded belly and smiles. She says, "Hush," but gives her surprising child a hug.

I have a baby brother, he is named Paul for Aunt Magda's dead husband Pincus. He was a very big baby, I hear them talking about how hard it was for my mother to be delivered of so large a child. I enter her lying-in room at the Beth-David Hospital, holding my father's hand. All whiteness: the bed, the nurse, the walls, and at the center of that intimidating whiteness, my mother, her dark hair spread against the pillow, her eyes only for me and mine for her. Radiant, effulgent, she stretches her arms for me, leans towards me; I am folded in her beloved presence. How I missed her. "Careful," my father says needlessly, she is infinitely precious. I am a sister now.

In a new six-story brick building we have our apartment; in the Bronx, near the Park, almost country. We can see trees from every window, my mother allows no spot to mar their shine. After her girlhood in the dark rooms of tenement flats where the view was air shaft or courtyard, she tells me she loves the light here. My mother is listening for my father's step; he is always home by seven; she is ready, the baby nursed, clean in his crib, sweet bubbling sounds come from the bedroom. I am in my nightclothes but I am allowed to stay up until my father comes home; he wants to see me, he's been gone all day. My mother wears a blue-and-white-striped dress, suitable for the kitchen, a housedress, but belted to accent her slim waist, her shape restored. The soup simmers on the spotless modern gas range, in the oven she has a surprise. She has set the table for two, everything is in order, she hears his step and lights the candles. They are not devotional candles, they are to imply gracious dining, although it is only a three-room apartment in the Bronx; she is educating my father in the finer things in life, carefully, covertly, so that he will not resist.

My father is at the door, a sound her whole day is keyed to; she is there as it opens, his arms around her, the cold March air in with him. "Here's your Daddy," he calls, and I run to him. "Daddy," not Papa, or Father; another move toward being American. Into the kitchen, he comes behind my mother who stands at the stove; his arms circle her waist, he breathes her dark hair, with its damp curling tendrils, the mingled baby smells and the good smells of the simmering pot. "Sit down, Joe," she says, and she serves the soup. He thinks that is dinner, a thick, nourishing barley and bean soup. She asks about his day at work, and then, after removing the soup bowls, she opens the oven door and triumphantly reveals her surprise; two golden squab. He's impressed; she takes her seat opposite, she can't wait for his first taste, she watches the fork carried to his mouth; I watch the fork carried to his mouth. Then: "You used garlic!" he accuses. "I can't eat it." She looks at him in disbelief, then speechless with disappointment, she leaves the table, leaves the room. He follows, apologizes, consoles. My baby brother doesn't wake, and after a while they return to the kitchen. My mother puts the birds out of sight and pours their coffee; my father lights a cigarette, Lucky Strike. I can't linger any longer over my bedtime warm milk, I must go to my bed, beside my baby brother's crib. My mother does the dishes; to restore the calm, to regain her ideal of domestic tranquility, she sings almost to herself, in her expressive, true voice:

> Just a song at twilight
> When the lights are low
> And the flick'ring shadows
> Softly come and go . . .

Does he compare her to the hot little blonde chanteuse who stopped at their table in the Second Avenue cabaret and kept her eyes on him as she sang,

Yes *Sir*, that's my Baby
No Sir, don't mean maybe
Yes, Sir, that's my Baby Now-ow.

———

My mother gives Elocution lessons to a neighbor's son after school.
He's a big boy, about ten years old; he wears brown corduroy
knickers, his socks are never wrinkled, he removes his cap; my
mother says he is well-mannered. His lessons are timed for my
brother's naps. If the baby is awake I am to amuse him, if he is not
awake I listen to my mother, I listen to her pupil; she is teaching him
an eight-stanza dramatic recitation called "Bijou," full of pathos and
peril. I watch the gestures the boy makes in imitation of my mother,
I listen to her corrections of phrasing and pitch. One morning, while
she nurses my brother, I recite "Bijou," all eight stanzas, with
gestures. I amaze her, I delight her; she asks me to repeat my
performance for my father.

———

My father wakes me in the middle of the night. Any time I wake in
the dark it's "the middle of the night." Wrapped in a blanket, I am
taken half-asleep in his arms to a taxi waiting at the door. My mother
is already there with my sleeping brother. The street is empty, dark
blue, and mysteriously different, lit by glowing lamps on tall posts.
We drive around in the sultry summer night, just drive around and
around the Park. The baby sleeps, I am quiet, now wide awake and
listening. My father is making amends for some marital violation.
My mother's voice is low. I am still safe.

———

We have moved again, near another Park, Prospect Park in Brooklyn. I am skipping rope, I pass our door, I round the corner, still
skipping, and I am on a street I've never seen before, not in our
neighborhood. An old man sits on a brownstone stoop, his hands
clasped on the head of his cane. His hair is silver white, his eyes are
blue, he smiles, I stop skipping, I stand before him, and I smile.
"What is your name, little girl?" I tell him, moving closer. "Pretty
child. Will you give me a kiss?" No question, no hesitation, I lean
over, I kiss his cheek. "Thank you," he says, and I skip rope back to

the corner and turn into our street. I wind up my jump rope, go upstairs to our apartment, and tell my mother about the old man who asked me to kiss him and I did. Her face changed, alarm and fear in her eyes, her voice insistent: "Where is he? What did he say? Did he touch you? Where is he? Come with me." She roused a neighbor, another neighbor, three women now directing me to lead them. I hear words, terrible words: Degenerate, Molester, Pervert. "Show us!" This is wrong; it's a mistake; don't make me. He was kind, he was quiet, his hair was so silver, his eyes so blue, he didn't hurt me, he didn't do anything. When we turned the corner he was not there, he was nowhere in sight; he was safe from the determined mothers. Not yet six, I am not safe, say my vigilantes.

———

When I was six years old, the third and last child in our family was born, a girl named Rita. Now I had a brother and a sister. The family was complete and falling apart. Voices in the night, my father curses, barks, growls; I hear my mother cry. I can't shut them out. The baby wails, my mother rocks, soothes, I pull the covers over my head, and finally sleep. In the morning, when I wake, my mother is gone. There is terrible confusion: my father has not gone to work, he is trying to deal with the baby, diaper her, feed her; he is made more helpless by his anger. "Hurry, hurry, get dressed, dress your brother, we're leaving." He bundles us into a taxi, and we set off to find my mother. Our first stop is Aunt Clara's, who instantly becomes hysterical, demands, "What have you done to my sister! You . . ." She can find no words, seizes a knife, and threatens him. He backs off, the baby awkwardly in his arms, herding us into the cab again, and we drive to Aunt Magda's house. My mother is not there either; Aunt Magda attempts to give my stricken, outraged father the consolation of her experience. "She'll be back, Joe. A mother's heart . . ." A rare woman, she asks for no explanation, offers no judgment, but there was the plain fact that whatever Joe's transgression, it overwhelmed Betty's concern for her children.

We are gathered up, down to the street again, into another taxi, to his family, where he is sure to find sympathy, where the children will be taken off his hands, and where Betty will be certain of censure. The telephone rings, my father's sister runs through the railroad flat to the front room and calls, "For you, Joe." It is my mother. She is at Pennsylvania Station, about to board a train for Philadelphia, where her sister Frieda lives. She is torn, in anguish, but she tries to sound collected: "How is the baby? Paul? Blanche, how is she?" My father, after all she's put him through, speaks quietly, but there is unmistakable urgency as he tells her, "They need you, they miss you . . ." *He* needs her, and he sweet-talks her out of Penn Station, into a cab, up to his family's flat in Harlem. She arrives, I am at the door and fling myself into her arms crying, "Don't leave me . . ." My father's family barely welcomes her— "What kind of a mother *is* she?"—but they agree to care for me, and the baby, and my brother, while my parents celebrate the happy ending of that terrible day with dinner at a restaurant.

I am no longer safe. If my mother could do the unthinkable, if a day like this could happen again . . .

———

My mother, convinced I was no ordinary child, was determined to open all doors, to give me every advantage the great city of New York offered, and as early as possible. When I was seven I attended Saturday morning classes at Vestoff-Serova's School of Ballet. Each week we took subway and bus, my mother carried a hatbox packed with my ballet slippers, my tights, and my tutu. We walked down Seventy-Second Street and turned into an imposing building, just the two of us, I had her to myself. In a vast high-ceilinged studio, its parquet floor fringed with other little girls in tutus and tights and slippers, there was a faint air of Czarist Russia. In the dressing room the other mothers eyed the competition, planned strategy, calculated returns on their investment. She was not like that. It was not for career or gain or reflected importance that my mother persuaded my father to part with eight dollars a month for ballet lessons. She had a legacy, a trust she must pass on, given her by the dedicated teachers at the Settlement House. The ballet school's rigorous training would imprint my young body with a sense of form and rhythm and grace that I would remember always.

———

A leap of fortune, and we move again, to a larger apartment, one that will house a new Steinway baby grand in a gleaming ebony case. Twice a week, after school, I am instructed by Dr. Durmashkin, a kind, abstracted emigré, who takes me as far as Beethoven's "Für Elise" before he disappears. There were children's art classes at the Brooklyn Museum, recitals at Aeolian Hall on Fifty-fourth and Fifth, and one exceptionally fine day, after shopping for my clothes at Best's, my mother and I walked up Fifth Avenue to Central Park South. I am wearing my leghorn straw with the streamers down the back, my mother has a hat with a little veil. When we get to the Park she says, "Now we will do something we've never done before." She negotiates with the driver of a hansom cab, we climb into the carriage, and set off up the Avenue. Up Fifth Avenue at a brisk but stately pace, the sound of hoofs and the snap of whip louder than the traffic around us, to a French restaurant for lunch, just the two of us.

———

Only a few years, really, that I was in my mother's hands, when she presented to me, the impressionable child, a selective New York, a New York of gracious men and women surrounded by art and beauty. A New York different from my father's of money and corruption and steamy excitement. I didn't know much about him, he was an undependable presence: affable, or glowering, we were never sure who would come in the door. He seemed in his comings and goings to be his own law, independent. Once in, he was uneasy or impatient with children; he poured a drink, took up a deck of cards, a racing form, or the stock market report. My cynical, my profane, my ambitious young father; the independence was an illusion. He wasn't free at all. One of the boys in the Gang who had joined the Company of Men, he was moving up so fast he never stopped to question his membership. In the Company of Men Joe knew the drill: when he had money, he spread it around—"Easy come, easy go." He "dropped a bundle" at the racetrack; he made "a killing" in the market. He had a wife who was faithful always, a mistress who was faithful for the moment, and he kept each in style. Mink, conspicuous elegance, for his wife; leopard, moderate flash for his mistress. The aura of male power made men like him irresistible to certain women. Joe was often surprised by their variety.

In the Company of Men he rewarded himself with royal treats: luxe hotels, the best restaurants, at ease in his world of affluent razzle-dazzle, holding doors for women, discussing menus with waiters. Almost suave. He traveled with assurance in chauffeur-driven limousines, he wore custom-tailored conservative clothes like his bankers and brokers and his friend, the czar of the underworld. These men, mostly Jews and Italians, contemptuous of secular law, paid careful tribute to tribal morality. Whatever inspired this obeisance—veneration of the Virgin, lingering fear of Jehovah—rituals were observed, daughters were sheltered, old age respected. Joe was irreligious, but he did not want to attract Jehovah's baleful eye; nothing would interfere with his attendance at our Friday night Sabbath dinners, the equinoctial festivals of the High Holy days in the autumn, or the Passover Seders in the spring. They thought well of themselves, these good sons and husbands and fathers. They were not so small or mean to consider expense when sweltering streets of melting hot tar could be exchanged for green meadows; as soon as school was out in June, wives and children were packed off to a hotel in the Catskills. For my mother, who did not play bridge or mah-jongg or flirt with the social director or even sunbathe, it was exile. Two months in the country for us, not for him; joining us on the occasional weekend was enough. Emptied of wives and children, Manhattan in the summer was a special irresponsible playground.

Betty was the faithful wife who provided the frame, the backdrop, the secure constant. She was the caretaker of the health and education of the children; she was responsible for our safety. She found the good address, the large apartment, the live-in maid; she was the hostess for dinner parties to entertain out-of-town buyers, she wore the jewels and clothes appropriate to the wife of a man of substance. Drowning in comfort, she silently submerged the eager innocent who once planned to artfully, lovingly polish the "rough diamond," Joe. She never had a chance. She lost the light in her eyes; her body thickened; she laughed rarely; she slept with him even when he came from the bed of his mistress, despising herself. I read my mother's face, I hear her cry; it is she against whom I must harden my heart. She won't leave him, I can't help her.

———

By the time I was fifteen, graduated from high school and able to make choices, I had a rough plan. I chose art school over college. I was sorry to separate from the tiny band of radical classmates who were going to city colleges, bound for the professions and years and years of formal schooling. Of course my mother was disappointed that I would not fulfill her dream for me, academia, the serious joys of a college campus, but Parsons' thin veneer of life class and art history made it acceptable. She didn't know my plan, I would never stop studying. After three years at Parsons I would be eighteen, legally free, and independent of my family. I would have a job, an apartment of my own; I would be able to move through my city, that cornucopia, that bazaar of sensation, without restriction, accountable only to myself.

Off Union Square, on Thirteenth Street, in a dingy four-story converted loft building, were the offices of the *Daily Worker*, the classrooms of the Workers School, and on the street level, the Workers Bookshop. Each week on Tuesday evenings I traveled downtown to my Marx/Engels class. Students, union members, a few teachers, we all listened with earnest attention to the gritty lectures delivered by a tired, sarcastic comrade. After class I stopped at the Workers Bookshop, where I could sometimes find a copy of *International Literature*. It was a periodical badly printed on thin paper, the reproductions smudged and off-register, but it was authentically international. There were revolutionary contributors from all over the world whose stories and poetry could never be published in the capitalist press.

On Thursday evenings, at the New School for Social Research, Waldo Frank talked about Joyce, and Lawrence, and an obscure, unforgivably neglected Czech artist, Franz Kafka. Waldo Frank told us that Knopf had published Kafka's novel *The Castle*, ninety-four copies had been sold. Only a few streets away from the righteous seediness of the Workers building, the New School was worlds apart. Although it housed the Rivera and Orozco murals, and Rivera and Orozco were Mexican revolutionaries, the severe modern facade of the New School on West 12th Street interrupted the stretch of nineteenth-century brownstones with rich impertinence. Into this building the faculty, chiefly European emigrés, brought a spirit of wide-ranging inquiry, a ferment of art and thought, avant-garde film and music, avant-garde everything.

That was my immediate plan: Parsons for vocational training, the Workers School for political theory, the New School for the humanities. Buying books, assembling my own library, I spent hours in the stacks and at the bins of the Fourth Avenue secondhand bookshops. In the dim and dusty disordered shelves, just waiting behind a tantalizing worn spine whose title could barely be read, I might find anything: another novel of Jane Austen, a back issue of *Hound and Horn*; I even found a remaindered copy of Kafka's *Castle*.

What a feast for the greedy, New York City. From dancing and rent parties in Harlem, to concerts at the Lewisohn Stadium, to museums and galleries and upper East Side chic of Madison Avenue; to Fifty-seventh Street and the Russian Tea Room and films at the Little Carnegie. The theatre district in the Forties and the Theatre Guild, the Group Theatre and the Civic Repertory on Fourteenth Street; the double-decker bus to Washington Square and still another world: the Village. What a feast for me, who thought I could know every burrow and byway, who felt fearless and almost free in my native city. Inexhaustible, intoxicating city. So here I was at the beginning, fifteen, sixteen, with this great heaping plate, and along came the perfect friend to share it, Dorothy. Dorothy, a small person with golden hair and extraordinary gray-green eyes, a second-year student at Parsons of ability and diligence, determined as I was to be free of family. Free of our middle-class Jewish families, we imagined ourselves adventurous explorers, filled with passion and purpose, perfecting our skills, expanding our minds, working for justice. My parents didn't trust her influence, her parents didn't trust mine, and they were right. Together we would try anything.

Chapter Three

AUNT MAGDA THE ALCHEMIST, AND
LEPKE, CZAR OF THE UNDERWORLD
– 1935 –

I DIDN'T have a chance to use my key to our apartment on the twelfth floor of the old building on Ninety-second Street, my brother heard the elevator and had the door open. "It's good you got here," Paul whispered. "Mother's all wound up. The Slug and the Thug are coming." He was excited, he tried to look serious but his eyes were shining: tonight he would be in touching distance of the underworld, yet safe in his own home. I slipped out of my coat, made a stern face, and said, "Then behave, little brother!" He was my loving follower, my co-conspirator, keeper of the selective secrets I confided. "Is that you, Blanche?" my mother called. I followed her voice to the kitchen. She was intently arranging canapés on a tray. She surveyed the effect, wiped her hands on a tea towel, and to the maid, Alice, she said, "Put the dinner plates in the warming oven, please." Her voice lowered. "I'm glad you're home at last. What kept you?" She didn't wait for an answer, she wouldn't believe me anyway. "Dad's bringing Lepke Buchalter. Aunt Magda is here, she's staying to dinner. Oh, and that man who's always with him . . ." "Jake Shapiro?" "Yes. So there will be eight. Will you check the table? Alice is new. I must light the candles"—all this in her Friday night voice of tight control. "I'll change," I said.

But first, Aunt Magda. She was in the living room, no womanly congress in kitchens for her. She sat in the big wing chair, smoking one of her Sobranie cigarettes, always held between thumb and forefinger; composed, erect, a large woman with gold gleaming hair and a Titan's face. She did not need distractions, she sat alone, thinking, smoking, probably reviewing her stories for a new audience. Aunt Magda had many talents, but the one I thought most impressive was her eloquence as a storyteller. And her tenacity. She could sense the receptive ear in an assembly of guests. She would then sit patiently, let the sounds of small talk go on about her while she imitated interest, listening for a phrase, an idea, that she could pull out of the air and attach to a tale she had ready. If she said, "Let me tell you a story," she didn't really mean "Will you allow me?" No one could stop her. She wove such a tangle of Hasidic tales, gnomic sayings, Talmudic parables, and shtetl folklore, slipped so imperceptibly from one to the next, that her innocent listener, at first hypnotically held, sat on helplessly, eyes glazing. I thought to tell Aunt Magda there would be no receptive ear tonight. She had never met Lepke.

"Blanche darling," she greeted me in her Eastern European accent, affection and approval in the timbre of her voice, in her ageless dark eyes. I kissed her cheek. Aunt Magda had a faint herbal aura, her embrace to the few she allowed the intimacy of closeness. One more way she held herself distinct from the aunts and great aunts who were given to easy touching and hugging. "I've missed you," I said. I loved her. "Oh, I have been here. Two or three times this week—but you were never home." If there was reproach, it was merely formal, an echo caught from my mother. Aunt Magda and I were in unspoken sympathy: for independence, against domesticity; for the life of the mind, for ranging the universe. Even when I was very young, she did not condescend. I sat by her side while she talked to me gravely; she seemed always to have time. "You are someone special," she said that once, and I never forgot it. She had such authority. Tonight she adorned the room, Aunt Magda did, and it complemented her, with its rich, subdued colors and silk upholstery and oriental rugs. She made her clothes, mysteriously simple coverings for her ample body, in fabrics that seemed to be woven for her alone, background for her gold and diamond antique jewels. My mother told me that not long ago, for a great occasion, Aunt Magda cut a length from a bolt of mosaically intricate brocade, wound it round her body, secured it with pins in strategic places, and sailed triumphantly out for the evening.

My mother needed her Aunt Magda, her calm detachment provided a net when my mother's balance was perilous, when she wanted to shriek, tear her hair, run away. They spoke Roumanian in these bad times, my mother's voice broken, weeping. Aunt Magda was stern, but she didn't know all my father's excesses. My mother had too much respect for Aunt Magda, she couldn't bring herself to talk of the bold women, oh, there was more than one; morality, fidelity, true love, had no meaning for them. They would destroy a woman's life, ruin a family. She was silent. She knew Aunt Magda's disapproval of women who aired private pain. "He's a successful business man, a good provider, a good father," she would remind my mother. "You lack for nothing, you have a beautiful home, a maid," and, irrefutably, she would say, "He's a *man*."

I heard the elevator door roll on its track. "Here they are, Aunt Magda. I promised to help . . ." My father and his friends were in the door, heavy, deliberate bodies shrugging out of heavy dark overcoats. My mother welcoming, quiet, smiling; tense, tense. My father brushed her cheek, presented the weekly ritual purple tin of Sherry's chocolates. He didn't look at her, and her graciousness was wasted on the visitors. Lepke said, "Glad I could come," but there was no gladness in that man. He was the Slug, colorless and concealing venom. Jake Shapiro simply followed his master.

I never saw my father during the week, though he came home every night—another anomaly, like his faithful appearance for this Sabbath dinner. He came home at all hours in the morning, and he was asleep when I left for school. Something between us had changed. I was no longer afraid of him. I thought he was waiting for me to surprise him, beyond his indulgence I imagined wariness. I kissed my father, I kept my distance in greeting the visitors: I would not shake those hands. I went on to my room and closed the door. My room, a haven in this oppressive place. It was bare and functional. There was a bay window across the east wall with a wide deep-silled window seat, a studio couch covered in black and white, a black lacquer chest. My books and prints, my drafting table. Everything in my room was an intentional statement: the bourgeois accretion in the rest of the apartment had nothing to do with me. I was seventeen; I couldn't wait to leave. I changed quickly. I replaced the framed charcoal portrait of Lenin my mother took off my wall each morning after I left for art school. Ridiculous routine.

My mother said her prayer over the Sabbath candles with only my brother, our younger sister, and myself sitting quietly by. On this night, while Aunt Magda and the men were engaged in their talk and their apéritifs, my mother brought the heavy silver candlesticks from the sideboard to the table. She stood above them, bowed her head, and covered her face with her hands. She seemed to gather all her hope for the transformation of her life in the silence. I caught her lips move, just a tremor, in her private address to the Lord. Did she recite only the Sabbath prayer, or did she add more, a cry for help? The candles shed their beneficent glow equally on the festive table, on the despair of her supplicating figure, and on the faces of her children watching her. When her prayer was over, she took her hands from her face and raised her eyes and looked at us as though she had been away. She whispered, "Gut Shabbas," and we answered in subdued chorus, "Gut Shabbas."

The guests were summoned and dinner was served. Aunt Magda took her place at my father's right. A sense of queenly ceremony attended even her ordinary movement, a wise queen, who suffered her subjects' foolishness with patience. She liked my father. She regretted his crudeness, but that, after all, was an essential part of his vitality. And he, he couldn't say why, sought her good opinion. In some hidden place, beneath his braggadocio, he may even have feared her. He softened his dark eyes for her, unfurrowed his brow; his voice sounded rare deference. He carved for her the first choice cut of roast beef. He filled her glass; he attentively passed her favorite dishes.

Opposite my father, the long table between them, my mother sat with a straight back and an amiable mask: a handsome matron in costly clothes. Who could see the poetic Romany beauty that was surely dying within her? She maintained a discreet vigilance over the table; it was a splendid table, the silver heavy, the glasses thin. She rang the bell for Alice between courses, encouraged her with a smile. She turned her attention to her guests. She did her best, but I could see that after friendly inquiry about his wife's health and his son's schooling, and no help from the laconic Lepke, she retreated. Jake was hopeless, restricted to monosyllables; he ate steadily and rarely raised his eyes from his plate. Uneasy with these men at her table, she avoided thinking about their connection with my father. She trusted him not to jeopardize the family. It must be all right. But why did Lepke travel with a bodyguard? A cousin who knew the

Buchalters twenty years ago on the lower East Side told her Lepke's mother was a decent widow, orthodox, and strict with her children. They were a credit to her: one son was a dentist, a daughter taught school.

Lepke was undoubtedly successful, a very rich man with a fortune in Swiss banks. He lived on Central Park West in the Majestic apartments, his office was on Fifth Avenue. He was always driven in a long black gleaming limousine. His suits and shoes and shirts were custom-made, and he was impeccably barbered. He took the waters in Carlsbad, the pure air in Sun Valley; a taste of Latin vice in Batista's Havana. He was even-tempered, soft-spoken, sober, and so imperturbable he was known as "The Judge." No one was sure if Lepke was a racketeer, a gambler, or a gangster. Once when I was alone with my father I thought I might surprise the truth. My father told me Lepke was a business executive, that the newspapers lied as usual when they named his enterprises "Murder, Incorporated." "Lepke never held a gun; he never killed anyone. All lies. It is not in his nature to be violent." "What *is* his business?" My father, who was usually direct, who prided himself on his bluntness, was evasive. "Manufacturers' Protective Association." Silence. I waited. When he spoke again his voice was low. "We go way back . . ." They were boys on the East Side, boys on the East Side, where, the newspapers said, Lepke twisted the arms of pushcart peddlers who would not pay him "protection" against the pilfering bands of boys who were also organized by Lepke.

Evil had greater horror in a domestic setting. Lepke, seated at our family table, bland, almost colorless, was more menacing than a fanged monster in a Gothic castle. Why was he in my father's life? My father wouldn't tell me. He defended Lepke against the "lies," but beneath his defense I heard: I'm sorry I got into this. I wish I could get out. When the syndicate Lepke organized had seized control of trucking and shipping and moved into the garment industry, it was useful for Lepke to have an old friend among the manufacturers, a legitimate business man. My father could persuade the other men in the industry to pay the protection tithe demanded by the syndicate. There were many marginal, first-generation, under-capitalized "bosses" engaged in the struggle to increase profits and keep down wages. They would gain protection from the unions and the threat of costly strikes. How did my father describe the penalty for noncompliance? Would he say "These guys play rough. Save yourself a lot of grief . . ." If a recalcitrant businessman said, "No! I won't pay those scum," would he remind him sadly of what happened to Schonberg? Two men with hard faces, walking fast, pushed through the crowds on Seventh Avenue and Thirty-eighth Street and reached Schonberg as he was about to step into the taxi waiting to take him home. One man held him, the other threw acid in his face. Schonberg screamed, convulsively covered his eyes, and pitched forward into the cab, blinded for a moment, and blinded for life. The men disappeared into the crowd and returned to Detroit that night.

The syndicate's monthly levy on a business was only the first part of the equation. If a man paid for protection, he needed to be made regularly aware of its value. A union official on the syndicate payroll would warn the manufacturer that the members of Local 12, the local his workers belonged to, were restless, dissatisfied, threatening to strike. The union officials might be able to dissuade them. Doubtful, but he would try. For fifty thousand dollars he would try. This, he pointed out, would be far cheaper than the loss his business would suffer in a walkout, just at the height of the season. The pressure was firm; the manufacturer capitulated. The syndicate's coffers swelled. But the unions were growing strong and aggressive, "upstarts" did not trust the leadership, "hotheads" agitated. They were "too smart for their own good" and then "too dumb to live." Reprisal was swift. The police were never able to find who left a bruised and broken body in a doorway near the union hall.

I could think my father's sin was venial, his role insignificant, a courier perhaps. And my father could say that Lepke's methods were only different in degree from the uses of power anywhere. But my father was cynical, and he was a "boss," the natural adversary of the working man. Lepke couldn't really corrupt him. The assault on the unions was different. We contributed, my friends and I, to strike funds. We marched in the May Day parade with the Artists Union. The support of labor unions was basic. A just society would honor its workers. It was hard to imagine the depravity of a man like Lepke who would use workers' organizations for criminal ends. Last year our elevator men went out on strike. In sympathy I used the stairs for the twelve-flight climb; I wouldn't ride with scabs. My father was impatient with my innocence. "Do you know who runs the Building

Services Union?" "No." "George Scalise." I knew he was one of Lepke's men. "And do you know who supplies the scab labor?" I was not too innocent to guess.

Radical journals, even the conventional press, ran exposés on organized crime. I pooled my findings with my bother, he contributed his clues gleaned from time he reluctantly spent with Lepke's son. Harold was a solitary, a pale boy with weak eyes. His idea of swank was to call the head barber in the shop at the Waldorf by name, seat himself with the assurance of a regular patron, and order shampoo, massage, hot towels, manicure. He did not yet need to be shaved, to his sorrow. My brother offered me a piece for our puzzle. "Harold says Muggsy's in town." Harold longed to interest us. "Muggsy?" Sounds like one of Snow White's dwarfs. It wasn't funny. Muggsy was probably a Kansas City "torpedo," here to fill a "contract" put out on a rival in the syndicate's territory. We watched the newspapers for reports of a body found in the river or in the trunk of an abandoned car. Lepke himself was never involved. He steered clear of narcotics. And Internal Revenue violations. If he was brought in for questioning, his tough resourceful lawyers and political connections allowed him to walk nonchalantly away from the District Attorney's office. "We don't run for office. We own the politicians." My brother overheard that after one failed attempt to link Lepke to a bloody vendetta. And "All investigations collapse when no witnesses are around."

———

Aunt Magda was uninterested in the conversation. What did she care about the relative merits of Twenty One and The Hickory House or the odds on the heavyweight fight at Madison Square Garden. She wanted to impose herself on this man of dark repute. Aunt Magda looked at Lepke with her calm, steady gaze; she fixed her eye on his receding hairline. She said, "You know, Mr. Buchalter, I think you are too young and too handsome a man to lose your hair." "Not so young. I won't see forty again." He was complacent. His vanity was elsewhere, but he awarded her a faint smile. He was certainly not handsome, but Aunt Magda was not above a casual lure to change the focus of the company. She persisted. She was genuinely distressed by the sight of a balding man. In her hotel apartment she had improvised a tiny laboratory. There she concocted—from unmentionable ingredients some said—fabulous hair lotions, face creams, eye unguents; she was on the verge of developing a cure for cancer. "I have a preparation I make, Mr. Buchalter," she told Lepke in her deep assured voice, "that will not only stop your hair from falling out, it will grow new hair." She had his attention, there was the barest flicker in his cold eyes. He glanced at my father. Was she to be taken seriously? "It's true, Louis." In this occult area of Aunt Magda's potions, my father, a reluctant believer, earnestly used Lepke's anglicized name. "We had a Polish maid—Helen. Not a hair on her head. Wore a wig." He evoked the departed Helen and her dreadful wig: auburn, coarse hair, stitched down the center, bun in back. "She worked in a watch factory over in Jersey. Got radium poisoning, lost all her hair. Her husband left her." He surprised me. I didn't know he was sorry for Helen. "She took a job with us. Then Magda gave her some of that hair lotion"—he rapped the table— "and the damn stuff worked!"

I knew my mother would not, could not, resist this opening. The guests at the table, and my father the genial host, made her brave, assured her "safe conduct." "Yes," she said, "and her husband came back to her." She was deaf to my silent "Mother! Stop." She addressed Lepke, averted her eyes from my father, ignored the warning glance from Aunt Magda. "He begged her to forgive him. She told me he is as attentive now as when he first courted her." My father sighed. He asked me to pass the salad. My mother heard the sigh. In that breath expelled he told her she had grown tiresome. Ineffective. Embarrassing. Where was her pride, I thought. Why did she collaborate in this charade of family life. "What can I do? I have three small children . . ." Ever since words had meaning for me, when I loved her without reservation, I heard that cry. When her eyes were still lustrous, and she could laugh, and they had fervent reconciliations. Now I could neither witness nor help. I would not be drawn in. I wanted to get far away from their struggle.

Some years later an ambitious New York district attorney indicted and secured the ultimate conviction for Lepke Buchalter. Sentenced to be electrocuted, he was held in a federal detention center before being sent to Sing Sing. The poet Robert Lowell, World War II conscientious objector, was also held there. "What are you in for?" Lepke asked Lowell. "I refused to kill. I refused to join the army," answered Lowell. Lepke shook his head, "I'm here for

killing, and you're here because you won't—hell of a thing . . ."
And Lowell wrote a poem, "Memories of West Street and Lepke."
There was a line that brought back the evening with Aunt Magda:
" . . . Flabby, bald . . . he drifted in a sheepish calm."

That was my last Sabbath dinner with the family, the night Aunt
Magda the Alchemist met Lepke, Czar of the Underworld.

Chapter Four

I Find Jimmy, I Lose Jimmy

— 1935 —

JIMMY was living with Anne when I met him but I didn't know that. It would not have made any difference. I was looking for a man like him, an older man, a stranger, a man of experience who would, in a comradely casual way, initiate me in my first affair. Dorothy and I had been sitting in the big Sheridan Square cafeteria for hours that night in February. Our sketch pads were forgotten, and with them our pose of observers; we were about to give this night up as lost. I was seventeen then, and Dorothy was a year older; we had just begun to come down after school, after dark, to this most accessible meeting place of Village radicals and artists. We wanted to get close to the sights and sounds of rich, free living, to walk carelessly, familiarly, down the crowded noisy aisles of the cafeteria, bestowing a greeting here, a wave there. We fed on phrases eavesdropped: ". . . use your *palette* knife . . . ," fierce instruction; ". . . she almost sold a story to *Esquire*," contempt and envy in that voice; or sounding someone's political doom, ". . . he's a fucking Lovestoneite." We thought we could distinguish the true Villager from the hanger-on.

The pale, dark-haired graduate student who hailed us as we were leaving was definitely a hanger-on; he had come to our table last week, introduced himself, looked at our sketches. Gentle, persistent, and dull. Tonight he had a companion who might be, could be, a real Villager. He asked us to join him, and his friend Lillian, and reminded us that he was David. Lillian was a small person dressed completely in black, a mass of carelessly arranged dark hair around her sallow tear-stained face. She looked at us mournfully, repeated our names, asked without interest where we went to school. As David explained that Lillian had just broken up with the man she loved, she gazed across the cafeteria as though she were already beyond sorrow. David's persistent attempt to distract her with our new faces, with bits of gossip, had no effect. But we listened intently, and when David finally said to Lillian, "Jimmy's back from Provincetown. Let's go over to his place and listen to records," Dorothy and I, without exchanging a glance, determined to hang fast to this couple who could lead us into the private Village. David turned to us, an afterthought, and asked if we would like to come along. We hesitated as if there were a choice, and agreed.

So we left, we went through the cafeteria's revolving door and headed downtown in the sweet frosty air. We soon turned off Seventh Avenue, leaving its traffic and glitter of lights for the dark narrow silence of Bedford Street. We passed poor little shops with tenements above. Between two of these grimy stores we halted; David checked the number. "I'm right, twenty-six. This is it," and we followed him into the unlit entrance. The hallway seemed totally dark at first but gradually there was enough faint light to see the stairway. "How far up?" I asked. "To the top," said David. He and Lillian led the way with familiar indifference. Dorothy and I following behind were excited: this evil-smelling stairway was promising. At the turn in the hallway on the third-floor landing there was an odd interruption of the interior murk: a decorated door, Jesus crucified, the paint thick and the color wild. "Fanny Zakin lives here. Very gifted painter, and neurotic as hell." David did not lower his voice. Up another flight, to the top. A man stood in the doorway. "I thought I heard voices. No, come in. You're not interrupting . . ." He looked at us; David said, "Jimmy. Blanche, Dorothy." He nodded, he was unsmiling. I moved away from his direct gaze, suddenly shy.

This flat, this room, was more than I ever expected to find when I hoped for the real Village. I felt I had invented it: the paradox, the deceptive street entrance, the dismal gaslit staircase, the smells of poverty, and now this enchantment at the top. Candle-lit, the room was shadow and pools of light, a fire blazed on a small hearth, unframed canvases hung on whitewashed walls. There was a rough wooden table, on it a bowl of apples, and in the corner by the fireplace a low wide couch. A garret in Paris, a writer's room in Odessa. The man who lived in this flat, the reason for my sudden shyness, belonged here. Shaggy hair, tawny mustache, old black corduroy jacket; Scandinavian? Slavic? Dorothy and I moved around the room, looked at the paintings: the stormy landscapes, the bright distorted interior. A nude, a life mask that resembled the model for the nude. I expected there were many such girls who were part of his life but there were no signs visible of another occupant. The books on the crude shelves were mostly the Russians, the Hardy novels; Gaugin's Journals. The Meier-Graefe biography of van Gogh. Lillian asked him about someone named Anne. "She's at her own place," he answered briefly and turned away to look through his record albums. David was beside him. "Anything new, Jimmy?" "I want you to hear this. A late Beethoven quartet, the 'Razumovsky.'" We pulled off our boots, slipped out of our coats, and found seats on the wide couch. He put the record on the turntable and another log on the fire; he sat at the table opposite me and rolled a cigarette. Music filled the dark room.

He watched me. When our eyes met I tried to understand what he was saying. There was no humor, no challenge to my burdensome innocence, no invitation, but I thought, If he asked, I would come back alone.

The quartet was over. David praised the fidelity of the recording. Our host seemed tense and preoccupied. David asked, "How's your novel going, Jimmy?" "Farrell took it yesterday. His publisher wants to see it." That was how I learned he was a writer. He said he would brew some coffee; could we stay? David and Lillian followed him to an alcove that held a sink and a two-burner gas stove. They told him about a protest meeting, and what happened to people they all knew while he was in Provincetown. No one made an effort to include us; we were spectators. It was not rudeness, I knew that; they simply dispensed with meaningless social convention. I wondered what Dorothy was thinking; I felt separated from her, my heart's friend. "I must get home," I whispered, and she nodded. My mother would be waiting up, waiting to hear an account of my evening.

I sat on an old trunk in a dark room used for storage; he helped me on with my boots. We were alone; I waited for him to speak. "When are you coming to visit me again?" His voice was low, pitched just for me, and there was an urgency I wanted to hear. When I said, "Maybe next Monday," he relaxed visibly and took my hand.

It started snowing as we walked up Bedford Street, a slowly

descending fall of feathery softness. The sweet fresh smell, the cloud of whiteness, transformed the mean street. I was relieved to be out of his flat, and away from his serious eyes, yet I was excited to have my secret. I would tell Dorothy, later, but for now I wanted to hold it alone. "What's your friend's last name?" I asked David before we parted at the Sheridan Square subway station. "Cooney." "What kind of name is that?" "Irish." "Irish? He looks so . . ." So unlike the Irish I'd met: union leaders, my father's political friends, full of drink and big talk and old charm.

Dorothy and I stood on opposite platforms in the deserted station. We waved goodnight as her Brooklyn train thundered down the track. Minutes later I was on the uptown train, checking the theater section of the evening newspaper. I had told my mother Dorothy and I were going to try to get tickets for a play; I found one I knew something about, decided that would be it, and put the paper aside. I wanted to think about tonight. Monday seemed a long way off; I had chosen it because it would be less likely to rouse my mother's suspicions than a weekend night. Monday, a proper working sort of day, might slip by.

I was taking charge of my life. The writer on Bedford Street couldn't know that I willed him to ask me back. He couldn't know how humiliating it was for me to see the importunate college sophomore trembling to compose himself when the key turned in the lock at home. Jumping up from the couch, we were practiced in arranging ourselves in a plausible tableau before a parent passed my room. The boys I knew, and as if forever, were intense, glibly lustful, familiar with erogenous zones, and virgin. I wouldn't abandon them—they were my loving friends and comrades—but they would have to grow up and I couldn't wait.

Only the lamp in the foyer was on, the rest of the apartment seemed to be in darkness, but as I hung up my coat I heard my mother's call. I made no sound on the thick rug as I walked through the hallway, passed my brother's room, my sister's room, to the light that came from her door. She lay in one of the twin beds in the elaborate big room she shared with my father, propped up against several pillows. She put her book aside, the dark-eyed woman, my once-beautiful mother whose face had lost its light. "Why so late?" It made no difference what time I came in; I was always greeted with this question. "It's only twelve, Mother. We went to the play and we stopped for coffee." Routine lies. "Are you sure you haven't been to one of those meetings?" No answer from me. "I know better than you do that they are only interested in one thing." She was wound up. "And you young girls are taken in by their humanitarian talk. You think it's smart to sit beside the negroes they have there and let them put their arms around . . ." I broke in, "Mother, I must go to sleep." I glanced at the other bed, still smooth under its heavy silk spread. My father would not disturb it until three or four in the morning, if he came home at all. I kissed her, "You don't need to wait up now." "Oh, I can't sleep," she answered, turning her head disconsolately from me. When she sat up like that, late into the night, recounting her grievances and trials, there was sure to be a scene when my father came home. I wanted to be in my room, my door closed, gone in sleep, before that happened. They were getting worse, those scenes. I would hear her angry accusing voice first, then his, low and contemptuous; she would escalate her attack; he returned foul abuse. She would say fiercely: "Be quiet! The children will hear!" and then break down in desperate weeping, reach for a slipper, fling it at him.

I was separated from sleep by only the thinnest membrane when I remembered my father's friend Frank Cosgrove, in a taxi with us one night, saying drunkenly, affectionately: "Do you know, Joe, that we Irish are the lost tribe of Israel? Descendants of Noah's son Magog. . . ."

I didn't hear my father come home but there he was in the morning when I stopped to say goodbye. He was choosing a tie from his collection, all ties from Sulka, rejecting one, considering another. He flipped through his handkerchiefs and found one with a fine border in a matching tone. My mother, sitting up in bed, sipping her coffee, followed him with her eyes: Who was he dressing for tonight? "Can you give me a ride to school?" I asked. He nodded. He was never expected to be civil, certainly not so early in the day. He stood before the full-length mirror knotting his tie, sleek and satisfied as he approved his reflection. My mother tried to sound cold and indifferent when she asked, "Will you be home to dinner?" She couldn't fool him. He shot a look at her, a look we all knew well: "Don't start anything with me," it said. "You will regret it." But he answered neutrally. "I'll call you." Down in the elevator, out on the street, he moved toward the taxi he engaged to meet him each morning with the hunched swagger of a New York man-about-town. We rode in silence until we reached my school. I brushed his cheek and caught the faint barbered scent.

In 1935 Parsons School of Design was in an old red brick building on the corner of Eighty-first Street and Broadway. It was a serious place: buff-colored walls and dark, stained woodwork, black iron railings and worn slate treads on the stairway, and in the classrooms, chairs and worktables and easels in institutional oak. It was a serious place for some of us—not for the out-of-town debutantes who lived in residence clubs, or had their own apartments and didn't appreciate their freedom. Parsons was for them a kind of finishing school, a pause before marriage; it added cosmopolitan lustre to the steady glow of their youth and money. Dorothy and I, on our track to jobs in the world, had no time for these bourgeois darlings. Ignoring the babble and the visiting back and forth, Dorothy was at her desk, checking her notes, ready for the instructor's arrival. Before I could reach her I was pulled into a laughing group. "Our Texas child," Frances, a cool confident senior said of Leila, who smiled and blushed and looked beautiful, "says 'Good *morning*' to everyone she meets from Eighty-seventh on down. Can you imagine it? The Big Smile? And she doesn't know why men stare at her so 'peculiarly.'" I looked over at Dorothy. Idiots, our eyes agreed. "What's on the schedule this morning?" I asked when I reached her desk. "The Met. Medieval tapestries . . ." I gathered my materials for the crosstown trip before I asked, "What did you think of last night?" "Interesting," she was not going to say. Overnight was long enough to hold a secret from Dorothy. "I'm going to see him again. Next week." Now it was interesting. "You are? When did he ask you?" I told her. I answered her silence with my thought: It's only a detour, nothing to do with us. How could it? We were inseparable.

Out of the subway on Monday after school, walking rapidly down Bedford Street, I thought no one could guess by my nonchalance that in a few minutes I would be alone with a man in his Greenwich Village flat. I lost that bravado before I found Number Twenty-six. The purposeful stride, the eye quick to assess danger, the eye refusing contact, staying neutral, the armor I wore growing up in the city, was no protection. The nonchalance was a sham. Any minute a cab would pull to the curb, the door would swing open, and I would hear my father's voice, deadly and even: "Get in." No, that couldn't happen; he would never be in this part of the city. But suppose, I thought, as I started up the stairs, the man forgot he had invited me. Suppose he had forgotten *me*, an when I knocked and he opened the door he looked at me blankly?

The door opened; we faced each other. "So you have come." How blue his eyes were. "Didn't you think I would?" "I wasn't sure." We were alone together, and I astonished myself by wishing the others here again. We met in this intimate privacy, yet we still had not said each other's names. We sat at the table, he poured wine into ordinary tumblers from a straw-covered bottle; I lit a cigarette and offered him one of mine. "Ah," he said gratefully, "a tailor-made."

By his serious questions and the serious attention he gave my answers, he led me slowly out of my constraint. David and Lillian? They were chance cafeteria acquaintances. He'd guessed that. Dorothy? We're students at Parsons. I didn't tell him she was the friend I had longed for, the friend I never believed I would find. "What are you reading?" he indicated the book beside my bag. "*Point Counter Point*. I read it when I was twelve and missed a lot." He didn't smile. "How long ago was that?" "Oh, a long time. Five years." I could see he thought I was older; people always did. Could it make a difference? And he asked me about my family. The impediment, the shadow, the stone I must roll away. My mother, her aspirations blasted, cornered and trapped in marriage to my cruel and selfish father. My mother grown bitter and suspicious. Warped. I described my parents in words I had used before, words that signified the detachment I had won. But because of the way he listened, I was again inside my mother's pain. Why did he lead me in this direction? It was a poor prelude to making love.

In the melancholy silence that fell, the sounds of an accordion were a grace unexpected and he said, "A street musician. Come." He took my hand, we knelt on the couch; we looked out the window at the street below where a small man stood in the twilight. He stood near the lamppost, his glance roving up to the surrounding tenements as the old songs of Italy's lost green fields and streams and mountains flowed through his accordion into the narrow city street. Across the way a window opened, a twist of paper spiraled down, and the old man removed his hat and acknowledged the copper manna with a deep bow. Another twist of paper, another bow. He left my side, returned quickly, raised the window, and tossed his offering to the musician. "Do you know the story of Baucis and Philemon? The disguised divinity of beggars? I read that tale when I was a child. I believed it; I still believe it. To drop a few pennies into a blind beggar's cup, or a street musician's hat, was a secret way of sowing future blessings."

We turned from the window. The words "secret" and "blessing" mingled with the stranger's mouth, the stranger's hands, with our rising desire. He had the key, the surge and pause, the passion and control, that would open the door.

Not this night; I wasn't ready and he knew it as soon as I did. Regretfully he brushed my closed eyes with his lips; I looked at him, I had failed. "Sorry," I said. "I'm sorry." "Don't be sorry," he whispered. "There's time for everything."

We slowly returned to the sounds of life on Bedford Street, but there was a difference. I was so aware of my body and his knowledge of it, I was an echo chamber of our lovemaking, it went on and on. We left together. He would see me to the Christopher Street subway. I wondered, walking in silence beside him, if I seemed capricious; how could I confess it involved more than the consent of my will? I didn't understand it myself. It was a wild and remarkable landscape I had glimpsed; he was part of it, Nordic, Aryan, Celt, someone out of a myth. At the subway entrance he took my hand, we said goodnight. He asked, "When will you visit me again?" "Write me a note. I'll let you know." It was absurd; I wanted something tangible. It would be a memento, I thought. We would never become familiars; there could only be a few more meetings and our paths would diverge. I prudently gave him my Parsons address. I could receive mail there; he was my secret.

I checked my box in the office every day that week after mail was delivered but without much hope. Why would he write an impostor like me: a virgin—I knew men found virgins trying; a minor whose visits must be clandestine; a student living at home with a watchful family. But on Friday there was an envelope in my box. I walked off with it slowly, reading the school address, his return address, reading the postmark, until in a deserted part of the corridor, I tore it open. There were three lines: "Aruin, can you come again next Monday? And will you be able to stay and have supper with me?" Yes, yes. I would say yes to everything.

Not only was it always twilight when I arrived at his place, not only was the room dimly lit by the candles and the fire's glow, but our talk was, I can't say dark, but grave. I knew the scarlet anemones on the table and the Chopin nocturnes were for me, but his silences and his persistently somber manner were disheartening. I reviewed every thought before speaking, hearing it as he might: trivial, callow, or falsely knowing. I wished these preludes over; then I could know him in the exciting dark where his mystery was a leaven that dilated sensation.

As week followed week through February into March we had our hours together on Mondays. Only Dorothy knew, and all she knew was that I was seeing Jimmy, that we made love. It was so meager a description of what was happening to me, I could not have defined it even if I wanted to. It's true, he was an older man, certainly experienced, and a stranger with his own flat. But he was not casual, not gay; no fun at all.

"What is it about Sunday?" he asked. "Do you feel it too? So desolate." "Oh yes." I thought "desolate" too strong. "Suspended," a day suspended   but I was alert for any opening and agreed. "Why do you think of Sunday?" "I visited my family yesterday." It surprised me to hear he had a family, that they lived in so familiar and prosaic a place as Long Island. I had not imagined any life for him other than this, in Greenwich Village. "Tell me about them." "You'd find it dull, dull and dreary." He turned from the table, his legs extended before him, his hands clasped behind his head. He stared into the fire. "My mother—she's a schoolteacher. Gentle, patient, sentimental." His voice was low; I heard love, the old tug. He shifted in his chair, reached for a cigarette, dragged deeply, released a sigh in a plume of smoke before he said, "And my father— well, I don't know. He's a cheerless man to talk about or be with. Yesterday when I said goodbye and told him I'd probably see him next Sunday, he answered, 'Ye might be dead by then, James. Or so might I.' He seems to look forward to death." "Why?" How could anyone? "I don't know. Liberation from what he calls the World, the Flesh, and the Devil. Now that he's retired, he spends half his waking hours in church or prayer. And he has all the worst reactionary Catholic attitudes. Even anti-Semitism." A wave of fear and revulsion, and I was in the elementary school playground again, attacked by an Italian girl, a girl I didn't even know, who screamed, "You killed Christ!" "It was the Romans, darling. The Roman soldiers," my mother tried to comfort me. I could see she, too, was dismayed that here, in the country she idealized, such barbarism could exist.

On another day he told me about dory fishing off the coast of Provincetown with Portuguese fishermen. Jimmy the Red, they called him. "Are you a member of the Party?" I didn't know many bona fide Party members; my friends were fellow travelers and loyal to the Party line, but too young to be actual card-carriers. "I left a couple of years ago," he said. "Asked to leave, really. Disciplined for insubordination." He told me about Party bureaucracy, how the workers were betrayed by the hierarchy. He described direct action and the Unemployed Councils and his work with them. "I'm a renegade," he said wryly. That was family; that was politics. There was no grimness, no withholding, when he shared with me the writers he loved, the composers, or the painters. There he was the teacher, the mentor, who wanted to lead me to the men and women in the arts who were dedicated to "affirming humanity." We never talked, I never asked, about the women in his life, or sex, or love. That door remained firmly closed.

I did meet Fanny, the painter who lived on the floor below. She knocked, three taps; he opened the door and stood there. I heard them: "Got something for you, Jimmy." "Thanks, Fanny." "Some cookies just out of the oven. A little burnt around the edges, but it gives them a nice charcoal taste." He thanked her again, sounding patient, and starting to close the door. "Aren't you going to ask me in?" Resigned, he said, "Come in, Fanny. We're just leaving." She was the oddest person I had ever seen. She had a wide, friendly grin for me when he introduced us and beamed through the magnifying lens of her steel-rimmed glasses. She was like a bird, a small, sharp-beaked, inquisitive bird. Dressed strangely in moth-eaten, paint-spattered velvets, she was of indeterminate age and shape—a period piece in costume. But what was the play? She told him excitedly of her triumph at the John Reed Club, and what she told Bodenheim about his rotten poetry. She used forbidden words with gusto. She laughed wildly at not much. Jimmy said, "Thank you for the cakes. Maybe I'll see you later," and walked her to the door. In the hallway she lingered. I heard snatches: "Where'd you meet her? Very lovely. Italian?" "No." "Hmm. Pretty close-mouthed. You must be interested." "Good night Fanny," he said firmly. He shut the door. "You know that painting on Fanny's door? I bet there's a hole in Jesus' eye, so she can check on visitors. She's our concierge."

On our way down Bedford Street he said he would be moving in a few days, to West Fourth Street. He tried to sound matter of fact: "I signed a contract with Vanguard," but he couldn't keep the elation out of his voice. When he gave me his new address he said, "Do you think you could arrange to stay over some night?" I considered how I should manage it. Another big step. I would speak to Dorothy. "Don't call me at home, Dorothy, on, well"—I picked a day— "Thursday. I'm going to tell my mother I'm staying at your house." Dorothy set her cup down. "And?" "And, I'll sleep at Jimmy Cooney's." "Is that a good idea?" "It will be all right. You've been at our house, my turn to visit you." She looked worried. I said, "Do you mind?" "No. No, it's not that. What if your mother calls? I don't want to deal with her hysteria." I swept past her reluctance. "Don't worry. Thursday then." The announcement to my mother was casual, overnight at Dorothy's. "Why travel all the way out there?" asked my mother. I said, "She's here so often—it's only Brooklyn."

The new place on West Fourth Street was more a Village apartment, the smells less clamorous: lighter, cleaner, brighter. Instead of the dark cavern, there was a door, three stone steps up; instead of turning into the cave of the alien, I must stand up there, in full view of the street, press a button in a row of names, and wait for the answering buzzer. I thought he had sacrificed something in this move, but he seemed pleased with his new flat. I said, "I can sleep here tonight." "Tonight?" Why the question? Why not "Wonderful!" "Isn't it all right?" "Yes," he answered almost absently. "Yes, of course. How did you manage it?" "I'm at Dorothy's," I said, but he didn't seem to be listening. He walked to the window and stood there looking out. Then he turned and crossed the room to his desk. "Why don't you find something to read. If you're going to stay, I have some work to do now." And he sat down to his typewriter. "*If* you're going to stay." I should leave. He wanted to work; he planned to go out; he expected someone else. But he had asked me if I could arrange it, and I did. It would be hard to repeat: Dorothy was reluctant; my mother was wary. I found a book of Edvard Münch prints and lay across the couch, turning pages slowly, blindly. I was confused, and humiliated.

Excluded by the hard chatter of his typewriter and the oblivion of his back, I said, "I'm going to sleep," as if I had come there to sleep. There were longer pauses, silence, a few keys struck. Silence. He sat back, the chair creaked, he sighed and gathered his papers slowly together. He switched off the desk lamp, leaving the room in darkness diffused by the street light below. He lit a cigarette. And then the doorbell sounded: sudden, unexpected, imperative. He moved to the window and stood in its shadow; he remained there after the sound faded. He did not move when the bell rang sharply again. Then he turned away from the window. He turned to me, where I lay wide awake and waiting.

In the morning we walked up Eighth Street, my hand in his, past Joe Kling's bookstore, past the Jumble Shop, past the Whitney. I thought we were conspicuous, our first time together in daylight, he in his rough black clothes and striking fairness, and I, strayed from another world. When I boarded my bus on Fifth Avenue he said, "Next week, then." He had not explained the strange night, nor did I ask. But the next week and the next, there were other people on my Monday night, the night I thought he reserved for us. I sat by, listening to their parochial talk, all art and politics, hearing their partisan passions, watching their faces. His friends, true Villagers. I willed myself into a neutral detachment I was far from feeling; why had his ardor become kindness? He was attentive: he took my coat; he offered wine. But his eyes refused any intimacy. I had deliberately sought this affair. Now it was over, time to let it go, time to move on. But there was a possibility: if I put myself quietly before him he would one day rediscover me. He was a serious person, he would not trifle, he would not play at seduction. I would sit there, waiting; one day he would look up and see me again.

Dorothy and I walked in the park one afternoon late in April, loving the new warmth of the sun, the sweet and powerful and disturbing smells of hidden and teeming plant life, insect life. We found our spot on the rocks, a sheltered private place, and stretched out. Dorothy groaned. "What?" I said. "My period." The words I had not allowed myself to think were out: "I'm late." "Blanche." Dorothy was instantly alert. "How long?" "About two weeks." "My God! Didn't he . . . What are you going to do?" She sat up, urging me to show concern as she abandoned her own ease. "I'm going to wait. I'm sure it will be all right." "Don't be a fool! The longer you put it off . . . Did you speak to him?" "No." I turned aside, ashamed of feeling she intruded, afraid she would see it. "I will." I didn't want to reach into the dark place that linked us and bring to light a clinical fact. I didn't want to tell him, ask him, but I would.

It was not until the third time I pressed the bell that I heard the answering buzzer. As I came up the stairs I saw him on the landing in front of the open door. His feet were bare, and he was buttoning his shirt. "Hello, how are you?" "Sleepy," he covered a yawn. Sleepy? He stood aside as I walked in. On the couch lay a woman, a fair-haired woman. She looked at me expressionlessly through half-closed eyes. Jimmy said, "Anne, this is Blanche." I smiled in mechanical politeness, she made a minimal sound, raised her eyes in acknowledgement: appraising and wary. There were the covers on his side of the bed, turned back when he had to leave her to deal with my unexpected, my inopportune, my stupid visit. "Come in here," he said. "Anne was napping." I crossed the room, a vast distance under her scrutiny, willing myself numb. I followed him into the room where the floor tilted drunkenly and I sat on a stool beside the record player flinging phrases at myself. I named the tide rising: primitive, destructive, instinctive, possessive, irrational. Suppress it; transcend it. They are adults, not bound by bourgeois morality. I wanted a life like theirs, didn't I? He put the first movement of a Schubert trio on the turntable, lit a cigarette for me, and left the room. I could hear their voices, his voice mainly, explaining. "Just a kid." Naturally he would be offhand. I knew he implied uptown, middle-class, not one of us. He came back to turn the record over. I could hear her moving around, and then she called, "I'll be back later, Jimmy," and he, "So long, Anne." He wanted me to see her. He need never have opened the door.

Conversation, that's all it was, when, after she left, I asked: "Do you think it can mean anything? My period is late." His stranger's eyes, very blue, very calm, looked directly into mine. "Is it? I think it's common, in the beginning, to be irregular. Don't worry." It was not reassurance I wanted. Pregnancy, fear of pregnancy, had no reality for me. I wanted to hold our connection before him. It was slipping away. The real question, the immediate, consuming question was: Who is Anne? I had to keep the sound in my head until I could trust my voice to deliver it as a friendly neutral. "Who is Anne?" "That's her life mask." I looked at it. It was alive now, the shell that had been a decoration. "She's a painter. We've been living together for almost two years." His voice was level. And when I wondered where she'd been all those other times, he said they had an arrangement. Separate places, total freedom.

That should have been enough. There was no other accounting. The clues to my big questions were meager: How deep was their love? Was there love? Were they merely carnal comrades? Would it ever end? Still, when he said, "Let me know how you come along," I accepted that as a reprieve. It was not over; I could report: I had a reason, an important reason, to return. We passed her on our way down the narrow stair; she carried a large bag of groceries. "Will you be back soon, Jimmy? I'm going to start supper." "Just going to the station." Politeness for me. Lovers' plans for them. I nodded good-bye, staying close to the wall as we passed, suffering her fair beauty.

The doctor's office was on Washington Square in a brownstone. The doctor was a gynecologist, a Party member, particularly sympathetic to those who in one way or another had been betrayed in their pursuit of freedom. We knew that from the humane advice he dispensed in his column in the *Daily Worker*. The waiting room was shabby, filmed with accumulated anxiety. Ominous. Dorothy pressed my hand encouragingly as my name was called. The doctor was middle-aged, kindly; he met my eyes with warm attention. I began to feel my situation real only after he concluded his examination, as I watched the seriousness of his face, and listened to his measured words: "The probability, I say probability, is that you have conceived. Of course, I cannot be absolutely certain without a test." I asked him the nature of the test, and I asked, "What then? What if it is positive?" He said, even more kindly, "Why then we will have to see what we can do to help you." He never used the ugly word. Then he went on, an interested, helpful new friend: "Let me see, what color are your eyes? And the father's? What color are his?" And how the baby's eyes are determined genetically, he told me that.

"You are going to tell him, aren't you?" "Let's walk down West Fourth Street now and I'll see if he's there." Dorothy waited while I went up the three stone steps and pressed the bell. Instead of the answering buzzer, his window was flung open. He looked down at us for a moment and then he said, "I'll be right out." Dorothy did not comment on his failing to ask us up. She sat on the lowest step. My friend. The visit to the doctor was unpleasant, but still I felt no

alarm. I felt suspended; gravity was centered in Dorothy; she held it
for me. The door opened. He said hello and sat down beside me. He
rolled a cigarette as I told him about the doctor. "That man's a
fraud," he said contemptuously. "Why didn't you ask me before you
went to him? He's notoriously unscrupulous." "Is he? Really?" I
could see Dorothy assessing his unkind dismissal of our doctor. If he
suggested I was amateur and incompetent in these matters, so was
she. It was with her collaboration I had put myself in the hands of a
charlatan. We sat in strained silence until I said we had to go, I would
see him soon.

I was under the compulsion those days to pass his house, as though
it were the most direct way from Washington Square to the subway
station. Waiting for a break in traffic to cross Sixth Avenue, I could
see the building clearly, and as I watched, the door opened. First
Anne came down the steps, then he followed. I became absorbed in
the pottery displayed in the nearest shop window; I moved around to
the doorway where I could see them. He was reading a newspaper;
she walked contentedly beside him. The sun setting beyond the
Hudson River touched their hair. Their shadows merged; they
looked as if they belonged together. I would have watched them even
if they were strangers, I decided, they were so romantically, so
classically a Village couple. When they were safely out of sight, I
went on walking west, working on a fantasy. I had to accept that they
were joined. I had to accept being now, and before, completely
outside. But how different it would be, went my fantasy, if I were to
have this baby. I would be strong and resourceful and discreet. I
would carry and bear the child, and he would never hear of it. There
would be no communication. I would raise him—it would be a boy
who looked like him—with courage and pride. And then, years
later, today's scene would begin in the same way: the door opens,
they walk down the street, absorbed in each other. I approach them,
holding the child's hand lightly, and present the son to his father
with cool dignity. At this crucial moment I found myself at the
subway entrance, and in the hunt for my nickel the tableau evapo-
rated. It spun itself out again as the train roared uptown but I could
not take it past that presentation. What he would say, what she
would say. It was frozen there, that scene on West Fourth Street. I
let it go. The next night the lunar rhythm was re-established; Jimmy
was right. In the morning I was chastened, freely relinquished the

burden of heroism, happy to be quit of the doctor on Washington Square.

The windows were open in the flat on West Fourth Street. It was a mild day in May, and the sounds of the street magnified the disorder. The place looked abandoned: the books off their shelves and in piles; the curtains, faded and stale, to be left behind; all canvases off the wall and tied together. I sat on a straight chair watching him, with Anne, as they planned their imminent removal from the city. Which of their belongings were necessary, which could be disposed of? The things that could be sent ahead and those that would travel more safely with them. I wanted to hear everything they said to each other, to hear any unguarded intimacy, to watch for the private gestures. It was an interest, I told myself, not morbid—I was no longer involved. It was pure, in a sense; it was for memory I coveted these final impressions. When they were distant enough and when I was in focus and strong, I could look at them, these memories, as history. The first episode, first adventure, or just a number. I felt less vulnerable already, making him an abstraction while he sat before me in reality, thinking of a time when it would be an effort for me to remember his name, her face, this room.

It did not appear that Anne would leave, so I followed him when he carried a carton to the door. "I must go now," I said. He stopped there, half-turned in the doorway. "I don't suppose I'll see you before we leave"—a statement, unmistakably. "No," I agreed. "Are you all right?" I hesitated. I could leave it, a fine thread of an irritant, a pale flaw to mar the finish. "Yes. I'm all right. Now." Now. Do not think it was nothing, all that, for me. Whatever my answer would have been, his plans were made; this perfunctory check was a bare nod in my direction. "I'll write to you." He was so unconvincing. He never would write. We shook hands. I said I hoped they would like their place in the country.

Chapter Five

GETTING AWAY WITH IT

– 1935-1936 –

DOROTHY and I recognized each other at once, in 1934, when we were students at Parsons School of Design. Not only were we the only radicals, serious about literature and music and painting, we couldn't wait to be free of our families. A contrast we were, a foil for each other: Dorothy small; golden-smooth, silky skin; gray-green eyes; and I with my dark curly hair, my tallness and slimness. Close, as close as could be without being lovers, we were inseparable friends. We agreed about men—oh, there would be men—but we would not be entangled. The artist's life.

In the spring of 1935, one year before graduation, Dorothy and I just dropped out of Parsons, we decided it had nothing more to teach us. We thought we had the techniques and skills to get jobs, leave home, get our own apartment, a studio, make it marvelous. We inflamed each other; we would neither of us have done it alone, but together we had the verve and the confidence. I was seventeen, Dorothy was nineteen; we had both had our first affairs, and we were not schoolgirls any longer. We'd look around.

Every morning I left my parents' apartment on Ninety-second Street—for school, they thought—Dorothy left her parents' apartment in Brooklyn, and we met at Ed's office on Fifty-seventh Street: our meeting place, our headquarters, our message center. Ed was Dr. Edward Kallman, my cousin by marriage. Tall, fair, a balding man with blue eyes and glasses, in his late forties, he was funny and kind. Dr. Kallman's medical skill was respected in the family; in an odd way they were even proud of his quirks: the incomprehensible sums he spent on rare books; his bartering medical treatment for first editions or canvases with poor artist patients; his minor atheistic deviltry, fixing bacon with matzohs for Passover breakfast. All through my high school years Ed always welcomed me affectionately when I stopped on my way to or from the galleries and museums, he and his nurse/receptionist Stella. Old enough to be my parents, yet in no way responsible for me, I felt accepted as an equal. They were happy to take me with them to lunch at the Russian Tea Room just down the street, to have me meet anyone in their waiting room who might expand my world. Heywood Broun: "This is Blanche"; Kenneth Burke: "My young cousin." From the moment I entered the turn-of-the-century building near Carnegie Hall, everything about my visits to Ed's office was a pleasure: rising in the small grilled lift, the sound of an aria would sometimes rise with me from the studio of the voice coach on a lower floor. And then into Ed's waiting room: vast, dark-paneled, faintly ecclesiastical, with leaded windows on Fifty-seventh Street, a deep window seat covered in green velvet, carved mahogany chests, Chinese vases. Paintings: Reginald Marsh, Charles Burchfield, Raphael Soyer; some bought; some bartered.

When I brought my new friend to meet Ed, he liked Dorothy as much as I knew he would. He loved women of all ages, but his gallantry was so routine not even the most jealous lover could be roused. Safe; cautious, you would say. Married to my cousin Harriet, he had a small son, unaccountably named Malcolm, and they lived in stylish comfort. Visible only as the genial Dr. Kallman, I think I alone knew he led a double life. Ed shared his secret other life with his nurse/receptionist Stella. They were lovers, members of the Communist Party, with a cold-water flat in Hell's Kitchen under false names. Hard, where Ed was amiable, handsome Stella ran his practice efficiently and drank a lot. A free woman.

Ed liked having us drop in, to use the phone, leave our books. "Look at them, Stella," he'd say of Dorothy and me, dressed for job interviews with an advertising agency's art director; he beamed, he appreciated our style, hats and heels and skillful makeup. Ed very much liked aiding and abetting my truancy. A minor pleasure. One in the eye for authority; for my tough father Joe whose envy and contempt for Ed, "The Intellectual," was plain.

Madison Avenue advertising agencies looked at our portfolios, gave us guarded encouragement, offered no jobs. We explored apartments for rent anyway. In brownstones of character and history where the ceilings were high and the mantels were marble, off Fifth Avenue below Fourteenth Street, around Washington Square. Gramercy Park. We roamed the city, our city, that spring, uptown along the great avenues, downtown in Village byways and cul-de-sacs; we spent hours in the Metropolitan, in the Museum of Modern Art; the Whitney on Eighth Street, the New School on Twelfth.

Floating free, we were adrift. Our city began to feel different, irrelevant. We weren't connected, that was it; of all the people on the street, on the buses, in the museums and galleries, we alone had no occupation, no responsibilities, no schedules. "Let's leave!" Who said it first? "Let's get away!" No matter; Dorothy and I were ready, ready to put it behind us: parents, comrades; the city we didn't think we could live without. Away, away, as far as we could go. California. We would hitchhike to California. Just saying the words was intoxicating. Really see the country, struggling out of the Great Depression; talk to the people, hear their accents, sit in diners, stop in general stores at country crossroads. Across the plains, over the mountains, midwest, southwest—the whole vast nation ours to explore.

What an expedition! We must invent a job, a destination; invent a safe married couple traveling to the West Coast who would take us as passengers for shared expenses. I would get money from my father, a stake until I was settled; it was only reasonable. He would be saving tuition, and I would soon be self-supporting.

And so we began to scheme and plot.

The first hurdle was my father. Tough, cynical, shrewd Joe: business man, gambler, intimate of underworld lords; he must be deceived, convinced so cleverly that he would appear to himself the careful and vigilant parent.

In the living room alone, in the wing chair, nursing his Haig & Haig scotch whiskey, my father was reading the *Morning Telegraph* racing results; he was waiting for dinner, Friday night dinner, the one night of the week he joined us. I greeted him with a kiss on his cheek and pulled up a chair; he put his paper aside and picked up his drink, lit a Camel. Bored, he welcomed any diversion. My campaign opened in a minor key, no great excitement. "Daddy, there were some people from studios in Los Angeles, MGM, I think, interviewing at Parsons. Looking for designers for their costume department.

I'm thinking of applying. My friend, Dorothy, too." He listened, setting his glass down; he seemed to take this unlikely story seriously.

"There's a chance I'd be going to California."

"When? Don't you have another year at that art school?" "Daddy, another year at Parsons would be just a waste of time. And money," my time, his money, "I'm ready . . ." He looked sober, unprepared for the responsibility I had suddenly given him. There was a long silence before he spoke. "You will not go out there unless you have a guaranteed job," each word distinct. Then his voice lowered. "Too many girls end up on the streets," hinting darkness and degradation, my foot on the slippery slope to hell. This was rare. He didn't usually show concern. I don't know now if he trusted me, saw me, at seventeen, as wise in the ways of the world as I saw myself, or if he was preoccupied with his own life. But this "You must have a job" ruling was not negotiable, I knew that. How to satisfy him?

Early the next morning, before Ed's patients arrived, Dorothy and I held council. What we needed was a document, something that looked official, confirming jobs with a studio. In Ed's waiting room we took over a quiet corner and worked out a businesslike exchange: our applications, our resumes; their offer, our acceptance, their confirmation. A starting date. We polished rough drafts until we were satisfied, and then we took a walk, to the Park, to the Plaza. Our phantom representative from the MGM studio was in a phantom suite at the Plaza. After tea in the Palm Court we wandered into a lounge, each found a desk, sat briefly, then rose with a supply of Plaza stationery. Back at Ed's office, the last patient gone, our obliging friend Stella expertly typed, inventing proper movie mogul language. None of us knew much about that world, but my father knew less.

My father examined these "documents" seriously. I think he was even impressed. I heard him on the phone with a friend, "My daughter has a job with a Hollywood studio. Only seventeen . . ."

Where was my mother? Why was she muted, in the background? Why was he taking charge? The division had always been clear, the spheres drawn, tribal assignments accepted without question: my mother was responsible for us, the children—our health, education, safety. "Safety" from street sex and bad companions. My mother was responsible for all things domestic: choosing neighborhoods, apartments, servants, major acquisitions—grand piano, oriental rugs, dinner service for twelve. My father's job was to pay for all these things, to go into the marketplace, outguess, outbid the other scrambling fathers, and bring home the money. My father would trust my mother to have ready for display his attractive, intelligent, and well-behaved children in a setting that grew in conspicuous prosperity. Through the years the unhappiness of her life with my father clouded her beauty, made her tongue sharp, her hysterics more frequent, and as I moved out of her control she began to see the city as a huge trap. Constructed for just such nubile, impressionable girls, there was at every turn a seductive play, a profane book, suggestive blues and jazz. And most despicable of all, the snare concealed to entangle the idealistic young in the Communist Party. It was out of her hands now; let him deal with it, this leaving home, leaving school, going to the other end of the country. My mother thought of herself at my age, her naive, trusting, loving nature, and she looked at me: only seventeen, so unreachable. Almost a stranger.

My father wanted to deal with it. He was interested, suddenly, in what was going on at home. He told me, helpfully, "Twentieth Century Limited is the best train to the West Coast" and gave me an opening for our next move. "Daddy, we have a chance to get a ride with a couple driving to California. Friends of Dorothy's family . . ." and she would tell her parents they were "friends of Blanche's family." By the end of the week the chance became a certainty: they would take us, weren't we lucky? "But we'll have to send our trunks ahead, just take what we'll need on the trip." I was plausible, not too many details. "They'll be leaving in two weeks." "Where do they live?" "New Jersey. They want us to meet them at the New Jersey end of the Holland Tunnel." We made their point of origin New Jersey, another country, inconveniently distant to check; we made the time of meeting at the Holland Tunnel an ungodly 5:00 A.M. My father accepted the travel plan, and I could not detect a question, not a trace of suspicion.

Then he said, "I called Los Angeles last night. I spoke to Uncle Herman. I want you to stay there. They can make room for you and your friend." Caught by surprise, here was another absolute ruling.

Flexible, we must be flexible; ready to change course, move around obstacles without missing a beat. New to serious conspiracy, we discovered a natural talent.

Dorothy saw the advantage in having a landing place: "We'll have an address, a place to send our trunks."

"It will only be temporary; we'll get out of there as soon as we can."

"What's he like, your Uncle Herman?"

"I don't really know, I was only ten when he went to the West Coast. Nothing like my father."

When I was growing up, Friday night Sabbath dinner with my grandparents was ritual. The unmarried daughters, the married sons and their wives and children, the old father and mother, all took their place around the table. Dinner was ready. Someone would say, "Where's the Bolshevik?" Uncle Herman was the Bolshevik; he was not called "The Bolshevik" for his dangerous beliefs, he was actually a mild young man, but for his shock of unruly black hair. Uncle Herman was never more than a few minutes late to table, but he slid into his seat with a sweet and guilty smile and apologies all around. No one expected him to be so impetuous, so daring, as to leave the comfort of his family, his city, his tribe, and follow his love to California. But the next year, despite his mother's wailing, "I'll never see you again," and his father's fears—"You will lose your Yiddishkeit"—and the disapproval of his brothers and sisters, that is what he did. My last memory of him before he left New York forever was a series of goodbye visits to our apartment; he was fond of my mother, she was his ally; she thought his cross-country flight romantic. There he would be when I came home from school, winding the arm of our victrola, playing over and over again "Bye bye Blackbird." He'd sing, he'd hum, whistle, dance around, wave his arms:

> Pack up all your care and woe
> Here we go
> Da da da
> Bye, bye, Blackbird.

That's all I had, really, to tell Dorothy about Uncle Herman. Bolshevik, Blackbird, and Romantic Ardor. I guessed Uncle Herman had calmed down, a conventional man with a wife and two children and a house, and I guessed he was in debt to my father. He couldn't *not* say yes when my father asked him to take us in; it was his duty to be my father's surrogate, my protector in a strange land so far from home. What a burden on the poor man. Well, we would deal with that later.

Now we must concentrate on the trip, pack our trunks, our portfolios, and send them off. We reviewed travel policy: actual logistics and potential danger. We would carry lightweight canvas duffel bags, necessities only, and keep traveler's checks on our person. Aiming for androgyny, we would dim our bodies: wear pants, boy's jackets, tuck our hair under our brimmed hats; no makeup, no provocation. In color and shape as neutral as we could be. Accept rides only from single drivers and never from drivers smelling of alcohol. At the first suggestion of risk, at the first sly "Aren't you girls afraid . . ." we would talk politics, the depression, unions; in all encounters we would be frank and friendly, yet keep our cool distance. The oblique defense.

We would avoid short hitches, hold out for long stretches; we had to do the trip in seven days, our progress matching the fictional couple's steady journey across the country, because at the end of every day I promised to send a telegram to my parents. No cities, we would avoid cities; we would be off the road before dark, stay in tourist cabins, and be on our way again by daylight. Even our day of departure was calculated: after the weekend family and pleasure traffic, early in the week when commercial travelers were on the road.

So Tuesday, let's say next Tuesday. We were ready; we had our traveler's checks; we'd sent off our trunks; our duffel bags were packed. Dorothy would spend Monday night at our house so there would be no delay in our dawn departure.

"I've made reservations for dinner on Sunday," my father said, "a farewell dinner at Ben Marden's Riviera," a supper club my father favored in the New Jersey Palisades. "Just the family." Unusual, my father's attempt to be the convivial host in a public place with only our family. He did his best, but my mother could not disguise her anxiety; my brother, fourteen years old and trusted with The Secret was bursting with excitement. My eleven-year-old sister didn't really know what was happening, and I imperfectly, distractedly, played the honored one, the eldest daughter launched on her career. I was toasted with champagne, and halfway through our dinner my father announced, "I will drive you to meet the couple in New

Jersey." I avoided my brother's eyes, grown large in alarm. "At five o'clock in the morning?" "Yes." "On Tuesday?" "On Tuesday."

I couldn't believe this. I remained calm, lowered my eyes to the scallops on my dinner plate, and after a minute excused myself and left the table. What this meant was—what did this mean? Threading my way through the tables blindly, I headed for the lounge and a phone booth. I couldn't get in touch with Dorothy; I must find a man, and a woman, willing to be at the Holland Tunnel New Jersey exit at 5:00 A.M. on Tuesday, two days from now!! and in a car with New Jersey license plates. New Jersey, New Jersey plates. A classmate at Parsons lived in New Jersey. Maybe she had a car, could find a man. Susan Aldrich, in West Orange; I found an Aldrich in the directory. I guessed her father's name. It was right, and we connected. The phone booth door was closed, my eye on the passage leading from the dining room, I told Susan my problem, made it brief, bare-bones, and fast. Incredulous, she said, "You've got to be crazy . . ." and laughed and wished me luck. I stood there, leaning against the stamped metal walls of the booth; there must be a way, we've come this far; I wish I could reach Dorothy; I must get back to our table. A man, a woman, a car. A man—there was a man at Hotel Evans last summer from Teaneck. Lawyer? Dentist? Osteopath? who wanted a date. Too dull, too nice. I avoided him. Now I was after him. I rang him in Teaneck. Of course, he remembered me. "Please listen carefully. I must hurry," and I quickly told him what we needed and would he meet me tomorrow at Ed's office, "it's a matter of life and death," I said without exaggeration. He was silent; he hesitated, "I have patients . . ." "Cancel them," I said ruthlessly, and gave him the Fifty-seventh Street address, fixed a time, thanked him, and rang off. Back to our table. The rest of the evening was a blur of smiles from me, advice from them; I couldn't wait for it to be over. I couldn't wait for sleep, and morning. I couldn't wait to tell my conspirators.

As soon as Dorothy walked into Ed's office, as soon as she saw me, she knew something was wrong.

"My father is going to drive us to New Jersey tomorrow."

"Oh my God," Dorothy whispered.

"What could I say? And I couldn't reach you." I was back in the purgatory of that phone booth. "I had to think of someone with a car in New Jersey. I called Susan Aldrich. Remember her? Lives in West Orange? Not a chance. And then I thought of Norman Adler. He'll do it!"

"Who is he? Do I know him?"

"Doctor of something, or a dentist, he lives in Teaneck and he has a car. I think I overwhelmed him last night, I must have, he said he would cancel his patients and be here this morning, at ten."

Ed murmured his sympathy, Stella cursed our bad luck; I caught a worried look from Ed to Stella. Was he beginning to have doubts about his part in the conspiracy, he, a grown man? This had gone beyond truancy.

Dorothy wandered from office to waiting room. "Do you think he'll really come?" She looked out the window. "What time is it?"

"Don't worry. He'll be here." Why should he be?

I willed it. I pulled him from Teaneck across the Hudson to Ed's office on Fifty-seventh Street, and at ten o'clock he was there, on time, in Ed's waiting room. I beckoned him into the office, introduced him to Dorothy, to Stella, to Ed. I vaguely remember his nice hazel eyes, his neat ginger mustache, his whole neat person.

I knew we must in no way alarm him; I told him the plan, and how we got from there to here, how little time before we left, how crucial his help. "Everything is arranged, Norman. It's just this last part. We need you."

He didn't really have a chance. Once he crossed the river from Teaneck he was in our hands; his life was dull, uneventful. Here was intrigue; he was snared, I could see. He agreed.

Norman didn't think he could get a wife by tomorrow morning. We instantly took care of that: "Your wife has gone ahead to say farewell to her parents—we'll pick her up en route." Norman couldn't think of anything wrong with that, but he said, "If your father kicks my tires, he'll know I'm not crossing the country." We couldn't consider that now; we say thank you Norman, goodbye Norman, we'll see you tomorrow, 5:00 A.M., Holland Tunnel, and I walk him to the elevator.

Back in Ed's office we said our goodbyes; Stella was brisk, demanded that we write, hugged us both tightly; Ed hid his misgivings, said, "I have every confidence in you two. You could overthrow a Balkan republic," and kisses us both with fervor.

Everything was ready, clothes laid out, bags packed; I looked around my room, my books, the prints on the wall, my functional black and white and red contrast to the rest of the house; maybe I'd never sleep here again. Just before I got into bed, my brother, the only one in the family who knew we were hitching to California, that our job was a fraud, that there was no New Jersey couple, my brother Paul tapped on my door. He whispered, "I have my friend Dmitri's address," and in the spirit of conspiracy he gave me a slip of paper. "Just write P.R. after Dmitri's name on the envelope, and he'll know it's for me. Write as soon as you can" and then, a real sacrifice, he put his lucky penknife in my hand, "Take this with you." I knew he was saying "Take me with you." I was a deserter.

Paul begged a seat beside my father on the trip to New Jersey in the pre-dawn darkness that Tuesday morning, and my father was glad of his company. Riding through the passage under the river I knew my brother was worried. Maybe my father had sudden doubts; a tunnel can do that; there's something ominous about a tunnel. Dorothy and I, silent in the back seat, held one thought: the man from Teaneck must be waiting. Look for a blue Dodge, he said, and there he was, sitting behind the wheel, road maps spread before him, wearing a fedora hat, a trench coat, dark glasses. Empty suitcases in the back seat. Hasty introduction. "Goodbye, goodbye." "Be sure to wire tonight!" my father called, and our New Jersey savior took off at a sedate speed, then drove a circuitous route through Newark's deserted downtown streets, Dorothy and I checking the rear windows to see if we were being followed. What a surprise—not only was our rescuer resourceful in props and costume, he had also borrowed the key to a friend's office. We could wait there until daylight and only then would Norman put us on the highway. He stopped in front of a shabby building: liquor store below, offices above. We followed him up a dark stairway into a dentist's office: dreary, a little spooky, just right for our secret way station. We paced; we glanced at the framed diplomas; we made the smallest of talk. We watched the light come into the sky. Let's go!

On a strategic stretch of highway headed west, just before an Esso gas station, Norman Adler stopped. Pulled out of his orbit, swept up by our determination, he had now delivered us to the big dangerous world; he began to feel responsible. What was he doing? I was a minor. The Mann Act, contributing to the delinquency of . . . ; serious complicity. He came out from behind the wheel, fetched our bags from the trunk of his car, put them on the pavement. Moving slowly, he shook his head in mournful quandary; we were so young, so vulnerable; we couldn't possibly know the risk. Smiling, grateful, we assured him, "We'll be fine. Wonderful; it was wonderful. Thank you. Without you we couldn't have done it"; we would let him know as soon as we reach California. We shook his hand, kissed his cheek, now *go!* And he went, never to be seen again.

There we were by the side of the road on U.S. 40 early one morning in September 1935. Our small canvas bags at our feet, in pants and jackets and brimmed hats against sun and rain. Determined thumbs in the air. How could a salesman alone in his car, no radio, nothing but Burma Shave signs along the endless highway, how could he resist stopping for such cheerful and sensible-looking girls. Of course he couldn't, the first car on the deserted highway stopped and we were on our way.

All the way to Pittsburgh the first night, almost four hundred miles, never waiting between rides. Though it was after dark, and we were not going to travel after dark, and Pittsburgh was a city and we were going to bypass cities, we felt lucky for the great start. We found a Western Union office and I sent my first wire home. Across the street, in an official municipal kind of building was a YWCA; we headed for the desk in the lobby. Out of the night, off the street, two girls in pants, carrying bags, looking tired; appealing to the two Young Christian Men in charge on a dull Tuesday night. They were all attention. How could he help us? asked the fair one, eyes bright, clean shirt, bow tie. "Is there a YWCA?" No, he was sorry. But there was a Salvation Army hostel for women, right down the street. That sounded grim, but it had been a very long day. He would take us, no trouble; he found his jacket, asked the sandy-haired man to take over, and out we went.

On our walk to the Salvation Army we told our samaritan we were traveling across the country, New York to California. He was impressed. In that short walk we gave him to understand we were serious observers, not heedless adventurers. Independent we might be, but he wouldn't leave us, waiting to see if there was a room, lingering even after we had signed in. Can he come by in the morning and take us to breakfast? Thank you, we must get a very early start, sorry, goodnight, goodbye. In the odd building: convent, dormitory, women's correctional institution, we found our room, clean and minimal. Our first night on the road, under unexpected evangelical auspices, the YMCA and the Salvation Army, was so alien it made our distance from home immeasurably more than four hundred miles.

Heading west across Ohio, we found our hitchhikers' voice; we asked our drivers about their work, their families, their world; let it come easy, naturally. Answered their questions: Where did we come from? Where were we going? Curiosity and loneliness and kindness prompted them to stop for us; it was only fair exchange. Not to set ourselves apart, Dorothy and I saved exclamations of amazement—a Breughel! a Millet!—for when we were alone. Children of the city, the natural world was a revelation. Soon we had to edit ourselves even when we were alone, abandon Wonderful! for Marvelous! and both when we realized words were poor things.

Off the road before dark, outside Dayton, Ohio, our last ride dropped us at a tourist cabin office. We registered, had coffee at the lunch counter, and found our home for the night, Cabin Four. It was clean, no particular smell, and as soon as we can it's lights out and ready for sleep. A knock on the door. A mistake? The knock was repeated; now it was a sharp rap. Dorothy sat straight up in bed: "Who is it?" A man's furry voice answered, "I'm the owner—party in the next cabin wants a girl and he's willing to pay five dollars." He didn't sound drunk; it was a routine transaction. Dorothy said fiercely, "We're *not* interested. Go *away!*" and he did, he went away. Dorothy was cross with me because I put my head under the covers, it was so ludicrous; it was so unreal; we were in a movie, a Feydeau farce; she was so serious, so indignant. "I'm sorry, sorry I laughed. You did just right." She forgave me.

The heartland: Missouri, Kansas, the vast skies above us, the flat fields around us, and the lonely isolation of the homesteads we passed. At a diner near a railroad junction in Kansas all eyes turned to us when we came in. We were used to that; we smiled a greeting, ordered a bowl of soup, and paid attention to the main speaker we had interrupted. A boy, sixteen maybe, ". . . no work around here. I think I'll just ride that freight out of town, go west, get lucky. Find a ranch that needs a hand." He looked at us; I thought he might be

Norwegian, the special way his voice rose and fell. "Why don't you come?" He means us. "Easy to jump a freight. I've done it lots of times." Dorothy and I looked at each other. "Shall we?" I could hear us, far away and years later: "And then we hopped a freight in Kansas." "Come on. I'll help you, seventy miles to the next stop." He led us down to the track. We walked along quietly behind him, we're looking for an empty boxcar. "Stop," he whispered. On the other side of the track a railroad detective, inspector, or whatever he was, came along slowly, checking cars, swinging his lantern, checking couplings, alert for trespassers. We ran back to the diner with our guide, safe, free of our dare-devil-girl-hobo role, and headed for the highway.

Nothing on the horizon going west. One irritating car sped past in the wrong direction; we had a long wait. We sat by the side of the road, and I wrote in my journal, while Dorothy studied our map. Something was coming. The speck grew, became a big truck, a semi with about eighteen wheels. A monster. It slowed down, stopped; there were two men in the cab. They offered us a ride with matter-of-fact decency. Daunted by the deserted highway and the time we had lost, we decided to risk it and climbed in. They were older men, in their thirties, and they had come a long distance. They were tired; I could see that in their red-rimmed eyes, and they still had a long haul before they could rest. Too tired for much talk, we drove in silence; after about twenty, twenty-five miles, the driver shifted down, slowed, pulled to the side of the highway, and stopped. "You girls had better get out here." "Here" was nowhere, an expanse of emptiness. "Here?" "It might not be safe . . ." We got out, obedient, confused, and the truck pulled away, picked up speed, and was soon out of sight. We stood there, our bags at our feet, and looked at each other, amazed. They were protecting us, they didn't trust themselves, acting on what gallant impulse, what knights-of-the-road code, we couldn't imagine, but there we were, intact, handed our safety. Dorothy and I couldn't stop marveling at their decency, our good luck, the chance we took. It was sobering.

We didn't take another chance until Denver; I'd sent my telegram, it was late afternoon, we wanted to get out of the city before dark and find a tourist cabin on the highway to Colorado Springs. We weren't having much luck, the traffic was thin and mostly local, when a shabby pickup stopped. A lean weathered older man driving and two young men beside him. Yes, they were going our way. We could hop on the back, where there were a couple of old tires we could sit on. Off we went. The boys—maybe they were our age, but they were only boys—told us they lived in Denver, that they were working a gold mine on their summer vacation on Lookout Mountain. "Gold mine," I repeated. Dorothy and I nudged each other; we were so ignorant we thought gold-mining had ended with the forty-niners. The twilight deepened, the truck turned off onto a narrow, wooded dirt road, one lane wide, and we started to climb. "Is this the way to Colorado Springs?" I wondered. "Shortcut," said one of the boys. "Not on our map," Dorothy whispered. The sky darkened, the road grew steeper, soon there was no road at all; we were riding on top of a mountain and this was no shortcut to anywhere.

We went on for miles it seemed, alone in the western wild with these strangers. Dorothy and I sat close through the bumping and jouncing, kept our voices normal, normal and calm. And made no sound of alarm, not even surprise, when we saw a light ahead, a doorway, a man framed in it waiting our arrival. *Another* man. The pickup came to a stop, and the driver got out and went into the cabin. Someone called to us cheerfully, "Come on in—need any help?"

Before we climbed down, while we were still out of earshot, Dorothy and I hastily took stock: "Now there are *four* men." "Total isolation." "We don't know where we are and no one knows we are here." We whispered, "Treat it as a lark." "Oh sure." "Don't panic." But our hearts were beating fast. "Let's go," and we went in. The cabin was a rough camp lit by the one oil lamp. I could see bunk beds along the wall, a plank table, and benches. The fourth man said, "Sit down." He was old, around fifty, gray and grizzled. His voice was quiet, reassuring. "Have something to eat," and he stretched the pancakes to include us.

The two older men, the driver and the cook, were Wobblies, IWW, International Workers of the World, miners who moved around a lot, mostly in the West. The Denver boys were the sons of an old friend, they were getting an idea of the miner's life this summer. And here we were, where *were* we? Two city girls sitting around a table with these four strangers in a miner's cabin in the wilderness, talking about the labor movement, the Soviet Union, intelligent young radical talk, when we wanted to scream, "How do we get *out* of here?" At last I said, "We must find an overnight tourist cabin before it gets too late. Can someone take us down to the highway?" "Well, we're headed for bed. We'll take you in the morning."

We looked at the narrow bunk beds, two up, two down; four men, two girls. "There's a cabin, not far. It's empty. You could sleep there." Unbelievable. "Really? Do you mean it?" "Sure, get your bags, we'll show you . . ." The Denver boys were out the door, into the pickup; the taller one who almost has a mustache was driving, and off we went into the pitch dark. A quarter of a mile, half a mile, we were above the timberline, and we stopped. There *was* a cabin. We followed them inside. They had brought a light, a carbide miner's lamp, and by its fitful light we looked around. Deserted by a miner a month ago, he left some blankets on a rough platform bed; the windows were barred, against mountain lions and pack rats, they told us. Were they serious? And then . . . then they showed us how to lock the door with chain and padlock. They said goodnight. They would get us in the morning. And they left. They left! We heard the sound of the motor growing faint. Gone. Speechless, we shook the blankets, checked the bed for pack rats, snakes, lizards, or who knows what; we decided to sleep in our clothes, when the carbide lamp began to sputter and hiss. Panic denied had a focus now: What would the lamp do? Leave us in the dark, emit a poisonous gas, or *explode?* Get rid of it! I fumbled with the lock, the chain, the padlock. Dorothy put her jacket over her head, held the carbide lamp at arm's length while I got the door open. We rushed out with the grenade, the bomb, and Dorothy heaved it as far as she could. No explosion. We stood there in the night, how far from our abductors we had no idea, and shouted into the vast dark, "Come back! Come back!" Silence. Nothing but moutain lions and pack rats out there, circling, ready to leap. We ran back to our shelter—it was our fortress now— found the bed in the black jumble, and went right to sleep, deeply asleep.

The tapping on the window beside the bed woke us—the Denver boys, waiting outside, come to fetch us as promised; we saw only the hand that knocked, they stood with heads averted, respecting our privacy. Were we dreaming?

Morning changed everything. The menace and confusion of the night, our plans of desperate defense, a fight for our lives against impossible odds, vanished. The gang rape, torture, humiliation, degradation—all vanished. We were in a primordial world, a Garden of Eden. The Denver boys, our brotherly guides, led us to a spring, pure and icy, where we splashed our faces awake; fixed forever in my mind the trembling aspen. They walked us into the gold mine, explained the workings, found a souvenir nugget.

Why, then, did they take us from the highway to this mountain, these parfait knights; and I asked, "Why? Why did you?" They looked embarrassed. The tall one lowered his eyes, scuffed his shoe around in the dirt, and without looking up said, "Oh, we just thought we'd have some fun." "Fun? What kind of fun?" Was he as good and simple as he seemed? "Well, we thought you'd scream and cry, but all you could do was laugh."

After strong black camp coffee and biscuits with the Wobblies, who are now benign tribal elders, we gathered our things, thanked them, and said goodbye. The Denver boys were in the pickup, ready to take us down the mountain to the highway. They left us on the road to Colorado Springs, we exchanged addresses and promised to keep in touch. So enthralled with the remote beauty of the gold miners' camp on the mountain, Dorothy declared she would come back, live there, paint, marry one of the Denver boys. We did hear from them, a letter signed "Your Colorado Desperados." Our ingenuous, unbelievable, Colorado Desperados. To account for time lost, my next wire home was "Detoured to see the Grand Canyon."

On the eighth day, almost on schedule, we were on Uncle Herman's doorstep in Los Angeles. Practiced deceivers, we disposed of the New Jersey couple: "They couldn't stop," I said after we were in Uncle Herman's door. "They were late; they had to be in San Francisco." Soon we disposed of MGM: the head of the design department was an impossible lecher. We found work as illustrators for J.W. Robinson and rented a house right on the ocean in Long Beach. Our one trip to the Communist Party meeting hall in downtown Los Angeles was so disheartening we never went back. We missed New York, we missed New York. When my father called in December and said, "Mother isn't well. Could you come home?" we started packing. One last deception: I exchanged the Pullman ticket my father bought me for two coach seats, so that Dorothy and I would be inseparable still.

Chapter Six

JIMMY AND I MEET AGAIN

– 1936 –

I WAS NOT the unready virgin he met a year ago, nor the student he dismissed when he with his manuscript and she with her canvases went off to live in sylvan creativity, somewhere in the country. I had had many adventures. Dorothy and I had dropped out of art school; we had hitchhiked across the whole United States. Intrepid, we plotted and deceived to get away from our families; invincible, we came to no harm. So when I turned down Horatio Street and saw his friend Fanny in her colorful rags, I was not so— vulnerable. She was a reminder of a ghost, the first lover, safely in the past. I was prepared to walk by with a nod, but she stopped. She recognized me, she remembered my name. "Do you know Jimmy Cooney is in the city? Came in to see his publisher. . . . ," and she measured my reaction with open curiosity. I dissembled. I smiled as though it were of passing interest. I would not ask, "Is Anne with him? Where are they staying? For how long?" If we met, I decided, it would be by chance.

It didn't feel like chance when he came toward my table in the Sheridan Square cafeteria. He looked different, happy, recklessly focused on me. We might have been expecting each other. I stood up and gathered my things; I said, "I heard you were in the city." He said "I hoped I'd find you." He didn't say, "Come with me;" I didn't say, "I'm ready." We just walked out, heedless of the familiar din and familiar faces, into the night streets.

In that year's separation the ferment underground, silent, secret, unknown to us, dissolved impediments. "Anne?" I asked. "She knows it's over," he said sadly. "I love her. She's been my best friend." But he had never been "in love" with her; she was so familiar, he said, they were like brother and sister. "Your parents?" he asked. I brushed that question away. I was eighteen now. They were powerless.

He had the use of Fanny's flat in a tenement on Cannon Street, on the lower East Side, in the shadow of the bridge. In those rooms, the windows hung with India-print bedspreads, the walls covered with Fanny's wild paintings, we began the entanglement of our lives.

All through April he went back and forth to Woodstock; as soon as we parted we wrote. We wrote every day, sometimes twice a day. He never used the telephone; he never called me at home. No one there had heard of him. In the mornings I was awake and out of bed to be the first to pick up the mail at the door, to intercept the curious, the suspicious. But there was nothing I could do about hiding the heavy package, mysterious and sent special delivery; my mother watched as I unwrapped the box, a ten-inch square of Woodstock, bloodroot blooming. An unusual admirer (Who is he? and What's wrong with florists?), yet I could see the moist and fragrant surprise touched the romantic in my mother.

Quixotic, his letter: "You don't know me. You would turn away if you know how stubborn, how moody . . . how impatient, rude, short-tempered . . ." How could he imagine I would care about such imps of temperament? Nothing could discourage me. We must be together. It might be for the summer only; I knew these affairs could not last. I would leave the city. I could see it now as he did: a jungle, sucking youth and health, corrupting as it seduced. I would live with him in Woodstock. Anne was not mentioned. The taboo around her name was for the pain and loss she suffered and he suffered for their parting. A delicate matter, and private. I would leave my family. I would without hesitation put myself in his hands. His novel was published; Journal of a Young Man, under the pseudonym, Martin Delaney; he had a contract for the next book. There was the Writers' Project; he was resourceful. No one worried about money.

The idea of marrying was born of the jokes, hilarious fantasies about my rescue and my father's revenge when he enlisted his underworld fixers to raid the helpless art colony in search of his daughter. Steve was the man Fanny lived with that spring, a funny, laconic Midwesterner who embroidered these dire predictions with ridiculous menace. Ridiculous it might be, but the dramatic possibility seized Jimmy and sobered him. We would get married, I who did not believe in married bondage, he who despised the state's presumption to license love. It went without saying that the piece of paper, the recorded transaction, had nothing to do with us. It was a formal transfer of responsibility for me from one man to another, archaic, beneath contempt.

One more step. I took that on a Sunday morning late in April when only my mother and father were at breakfast. They were in their dressing gowns, reading the Sunday *Times*; I was fully dressed. I had that advantage. I judged the climate: suspended hostility. I poured a cup of coffee and sat at the table and said, "I'm going to be married." My mother's hand went to her heart; my father put aside the newspaper. There was a moment of stunned silence. My mother looked at me, her eyes wide and anxious; my father stared his disbelief. Who would speak first? I sat there between them, pale but composed, braced for her pain and his anger. My father, head of the family, immediately the stern prosecutor, demanded: "Who is he? What does he do? How will he support you?" My mother touched her napkin to her lips. I could barely hear her. "Where did you meet him? How long have you known him?" Her eyes implored: "You don't mean it. Tell me you don't mean it." There were no shouts, but the air was so charged I heard my brother and sister come out of their rooms and down the hallway and quietly station themselves outside the dining room.

In the days that followed, my father and my mother tried in their different ways to tell me of my shame, my betrayal, my ingratitude for the privileged life they provided. They accused each other: Where was *she*, he wanted to know, when I ran around Greenwich Village? What kind of example did *he* give, she cried, with his fast women and his freedom? Her voice was low and tragic as she told Aunt Magda, "She is ruining her young life for a penniless Irish writer. She'll live in a shack in the woods." In this family emergency my father was home every night. He paced the floor. In his confused wrath he would say, "I wouldn't care if he was a nigger, as long as he had a business" or "I wouldn't care if he didn't have a cent as long as he was a Jew." My mother warned: "You will be dead to us; we will sit shivah . . ." "Nothing," my father said. "You'll get nothing from me!" Putting out his cigarette in the ashtray with emphatic disgust he left the house, turned his back. He was finished with me.

Of course he was not finished with me; his toughness had limits. He urged his old friend, Bert Schaefer, to take me to lunch. Over lunch our old family friend told me how disastrous intermarriage was, how he knew from bitter experience that marriage between a Christian and a Jew was doomed. And if, God forbid, there were children . . . I looked at the kind man, his face creased in earnest persuasion, doing this not only for his old friend, my father, but for me, to save me. They didn't know I was so far away no threat or cry could reach me.

———

There would be a wait, we were told, when we filled out the forms for a marriage license in the office of the City Clerk. In the corridor of the City Hall building my mother stood apart from us, wearing nothing special, just an ordinary street costume chosen blindly from her spring wardrobe, nothing to suggest she was the mother of the bride. Under her arm was a French grammar she picked up as she left the house, as though this was merely a stop on the way to her French class. My father was out of town. "If she leaves my house," he said, "I want to know she is married . . . ," and he ordered my mother to witness the ceremony. Dorothy was our other witness. We wore hats, Dorothy and I—mine was a Breton sailor's felt—and everyday suits, and we covered our nervousness by pretending this was a routine occasion, like being vaccinated. We walked around, mocking the framed documents and the honorary plaques and their sonorous prose. My mother stood apart, staring blindly into the distance; the cold gloom of the Municipal Building, the polish and weightiness of walnut and marble, were a fitting scene for this black event. Jimmy leaned against a doorway, reading a worn paperback he pulled from his pocket; he glanced at my mother and moved to stand beside her. Speaking for the first time directly to her, he said, "Let me read you a poem." He could see, he could understand, her suffering; he wanted her to know that. He wanted her to know that it was a serious love he had for her daughter, that his desire to share his life with me, to care for me, went far beyond, had nothing to do with, the marriage legalized here. It was hard for my mother, he knew, coming from her bourgeois life, meeting him only that morning; maybe it was impossible for her to accept him, impossible for her to hear him, but he would try. Not embarrassed by my mother's silence, taking her silence for assent, he read Robert Herrick's "To the Virgins, to make much of Time": "Gather ye rosebuds while ye may, Old Time is still aflying . . ." When he lowered his eyes to the page, she was able to look at him. She could not believe her daughter would soon go off with this man, dressed in someone's ill-fitting clothes (No bullet holes, please Jimmy, Steve said. It's my best suit), trousers turned up at the cuff, wearing sneakers, a blue denim shirt open at the collar, no tie. A Christian, an alien. She couldn't hear him; she wasn't listening. He went on, asking her through Herrick to remember her girlhood, her bloom, "That Age is best, which is the first, / when Youth and Blood are warmer; . . ." he raised his eyes, blue, earnest, intense with the effort to turn her hostility. He met her dark gaze; she controlled her thoughts, wild, distraught. Maybe he was a hypnotist, or even a White Slave trader. He read Herrick's warning "And while ye may, goe marry: / For having lost but once your prime, / You may for ever tarry." I could see my mother's incredulity: what did he think he was doing, reading poetry when her heart was breaking? To come out of nowhere and take her daughter, full of promise, just beginning. . . . It couldn't last, but I would be tainted, marked forever.

The Clerk of Courts was ready, and we were ushered into his Chamber. Dorothy and my mother were seated, Jimmy and I stood before the functionary; the Clerk spoke, intoning with solemnity the binding words. Jimmy, fair, burnished, taut and grave and attentive, listened to the words as he kept his eyes on mine. When the Clerk said, "If there is any reason why these two should not be joined in the bonds of holy matrimony . . ." my mother half-rose. Dorothy put out a restraining hand, and my mother sat back, sighed deeply, and relinquished her chance to stop me. The Clerk asked for the ring, a narrow silver band Jimmy had found in a pawnshop, and said, "You may kiss the bride." Unreal, I thought, a charade. The ceremony was over; we were given our certificate of marriage.

My mother was expressionless when we parted on the street outside City Hall. I said, "I'll write." I said "Don't worry," and she allowed me to hold her, my arms around her stillness, her silence. The next morning we left the city, driving up to Woodstock, a place I'd never been; the sculptor John Flanagan gave us the ride. I sat close to Jimmy in the back seat, watching the city disappear. Goodbye, farewell—family, city, childhood. All ties broken.

———

Not with Dorothy; our tie held, she would follow in a week. Jimmy assured her she could live with us, find work as a model, and paint. The Salamander was not far from the road, Maverick Road, but surrounded by trees, no house visible, it seemed to be hidden in the woods. Painted green, the upper half of the Dutch door was decorated by a Maverick artist with a mythical coral orange salamander, significant for a structure that had survived fire. There was one room downstairs, dim and shadowy and green; there was a rough field-stone fireplace on the north wall. This was our room; my wardrobe trunk and boxes of my books and paints were in a corner. There was a spring and mattress on the floor near the hearth, a table and two chairs and a stool below the windows. The windows were two openings cut in the west wall, no glass, no screens, just crude shutters to close and latch against wind or rain or the curious. Above our room was a loft with a skylight and an outside stairway, really an inclined ladder, to reach it. A perfect arrangement for our privacy and Dorothy's. I didn't pay much attention to the housekeeping details; the privy was back of the house somewhere; the well was across the road. In the lean-to outside the Salamander there were two buckets: one for fetching water, the other for sponge baths and washing clothes. There was a rusty three-burner oil stove on legs, two shelves of odd crockery, an iron skillet, a derelict saucepan, a battered coffee pot.

What I did pay attention to, what occupied every waking and dreaming moment, was the love we made: at night in front of the fire, on our own bed in the Salamander; in the day, when we walked through the woods and lay under a profuse white lilac. Glimpsing the perfect blue of the sky through its branches, surrounded, enveloped, invaded, set free. Living on love.

Jimmy wanted to know everything about the year we were apart. "Tell me." He wanted every detail of our trip to California: how Dorothy and I outwitted my shrewd father, bypassed my anxious mother, to hitchhike across the country. Every danger we encountered, every disaster averted. He was less impressed with our triumphant intrigue in faking travel arrangements and design jobs in studios than with our foolhardiness. We were never afraid, I told him. We carefully planned it all: never travel at night, strict in our costume—pants and jacket, no makeup; no provocation; sexually neutral. If these signs were ignored, we talked politics, economics; we engaged our drivers in questions of local agriculture and industry and the ruinous Depression. The effect was dependably cooling. With these tactics, even when we were kidnapped by gold miners outside Denver, and spent the night on Lookout Mountain, we were unharmed. We made friends of our abductors, and we had letters signed "Your Colorado Desperados" to prove it. "Lucky, you were lucky," he said soberly.

———

Jimmy would disappear, to "see if there's any mail"; across the road and up the hill was the house he and Anne shared. He would return with a portable windup victrola, a Schubert quartet, and books I must read: *Sons and Lovers, The Rainbow.* Out of his pockets: candles, a tin of fish, corn chowder, saltines, something called "store cheese." What about Anne, up there on the hill, in the house with his clothes, his papers, his books? Why doesn't he say she's packing, she'll soon be gone?

When Dorothy arrived on the Maverick, she loved the Salamander, her loft, the good north light, the cooking arrangements, the washing arrangements: novel, ingenious, not a temporary encampment, but the way we would live. Jimmy brought Hervey, his landlord, patron of artists, to meet us. The use of the Salamander was his generosity to his young friend. Hervey said, "Let me know if you need anything." He did not intrude; he did not look around in a proprietary way. I thought I had never seen an old man so colorful.

Jimmy walked Hervey home. Dorothy and I were alone up in her loft; she set up her easel, hung clothes on nails, threw a cover over her bed, and we talked: "Dick Winston called you at home and your mother told him you were dead. Can you believe it?" "Poor Dick." "When he cried 'No!' she backed down. She gave him your address. You'll probably hear from him." She gave me a cigarette, we both lit up, and she told me more. "Ed is disgusted that you're throwing yourself away on "that Trotskyite"; he hopes you'll soon come to your senses. Gerry Noel says Jimmy thinks he's a *genius* . . ."

I didn't care about any of that. Although we were alone and Jimmy was nowhere around, she lowered her voice when she said, "None of his things are here. Didn't he move in? Isn't she leaving?"

"He says soon." It helped, in trying to understand Jimmy's dilemma, to explain it to Dorothy. "Anne"—I found it hard to use her name; it brought her into the room—"thinks it's a passing affair. She'll wait. It will blow over. Jimmy says he can't talk of leaving yet . . ." He described how frightening it was to witness her hysterical paroxysm when she cried, "Don't leave me! Don't leave me!"—so unlike the calm, balanced Anne he thought he knew. "He can't hurt her. He says he feels responsible. He thinks she'll understand she can't hold him; she'll accept it."

Dorothy listened, withheld judgment.

Dorothy got modeling jobs. She came and went; she brought some groceries; she brought a friend. We played house. We washed our clothes in a bucket, rinsed, wrung out, shook out, and flung them on a convenient bush; we sponge-bathed and dried in the sun. It took a week or two for us to realize these woods provided no privacy for walking naked: there was a studio nearby in every direction. We mastered the mysteries of the kerosene stove and figured out that when the flame flared yellow and smudged the pots, we too were marked on nose or forehead.

One morning I woke alone on our bed in the Salamander. From the loft above Dorothy called, "Jimmy? What time is it?" We had the only clock, and this call had become routine. "He's not here." "Where *is* he?" "He's with Anne." Her voice dropped, broke: "Oh, Blanche. How terrible . . ."

That's when I began to lose Dorothy.

I didn't think he meant it, the night before; he couldn't be serious when he said, "I must stay with Anne tonight. She's in a bad state." I turned away to hide my bewilderment. He did mean it. "It has nothing to do with us. It takes nothing from us." He sounded so troubled, so unhappy, I opened myself to his compassion for her; I managed to be calm, to still the demon jealousy, to find sleep. That night a pattern was set for the rest of the summer: alternate nights with Anne in the house on the hill.

I imagined that house across the road and up on the hill: a real household, where they were a couple and Anne cooked and people came to dinner or for the weekend and the talk was stimulating. I wouldn't, I couldn't, see them in bed together. On the nights he stayed up there I saw him working on his novel, typing far into the early hours of the morning, dropping in exhaustion beside the sleeping Anne: brotherly, chaste.

Fanny came down to the Salamander whenever she visited Anne and Jimmy and innocently provided me with tormenting glimpses of their life together. Maybe not so innocently, but I did nothing to stop her. Fanny was entertainment. Fanny was indiscreet. "Anne thinks Jimmy's infatuation can't last." She made it plain that these were not her views. "A spoiled kid like you could never put up with this life . . ." And she said, "Anyway, now that she's on the Project, I mean, it took her so long, she's not going to leave." We came in out of the sun, Fanny and Dorothy and I, and sat at the table under the windows, drinking coffee, nibbling the cakes Fanny brought from a New York bakery. Fanny gave me a drawing pad and two charcoal pencils. She loved giving things or services or other people's secrets; when I admired her little vest, red wool, the intricate design embroidered in brilliant colors, she took it right off her back. "It's yours," she said, and I knew I must be careful in my refusal.

"What kind of painter is Anne?" I asked Fanny. "She's all right. Academic. No guts." The ultimate negative. Fanny knew I wanted to hear such judgments, anything that diminished Anne. A wasp flew in the window, hovered over our table, then out the open half of the Dutch door. I pushed an ant off-course on its way to the bowl of sugar. Dorothy, glowing gold from the sun that tanned her smooth round limbs, leaned on her elbow, chin in hand, regarding Fanny, who was now on a tear of denouncing the fakes and the phonies and the pretenders in Woodstock, New York, and Paris. I busied myself in the corner of the room where my wardrobe trunk was closet and bureau, changed from shorts to my Woodstock skirt: full, cotton, midcalf.

Jimmy drove up the lane and stopped at the door. I was going on an outing, to Woodstock, in *her* car, their car, an air-cooled Franklin, antique and eccentric. I hated the car. When I walked on the Maverick it was unbearable to see Anne pass, sitting straight, and cool and fair, driving to the village, doing their errands. Jealousy was a constantly hungry companion, and I found fuel everywhere. I climbed into the hated car, and Jimmy drove to the Woodstock library. "How is Mrs. Cooney?" asked pleasant Mrs. Thompson, the librarian, and she didn't mean me. I went on out the door so that I would not hear his answer. We stopped at the Knife and Fork and sat in the sidewalk cafe, drinking iced tea and watching the tourists who watched us. An outing, a treat, but Jimmy could see it was clouded. "What was Fanny talking about?" He knew Fanny. "She said Anne is on the Art Project and won't leave . . ." "It's true, she is—it took us a long time to get on the Projects." Us. Only one member of a family—and Anne and Jimmy were considered a family—could be on the WPA Projects. It was her check that was the sustaining income for the two, now to be stretched to include me. What a tangle.

———

The summer waned; the evenings grew cool. Jimmy brought a few logs from somewhere and built a fire. The Salamander was an insubstantial shelter, and when the wind rose I wore a sweater and got under the covers to read. I read; I listened to music; I dissolved in tears at the slow movements, at a phrase, a passage. I wrote brief, deceptive letters to my mother, I avoided my friends; I kept a journal. Everyone kept a journal.

Dorothy started packing. She was going to live in Greenwich Village with a man she met in an art class in Woodstock. She had seen my unhappiness; she came upon me sobbing. "Don't, Blanche, don't," she said, stroking my head. "What is it? Did something happen?" I shook my head, "No," and subsided. I knew without her saying that she thought I should leave, that it hurt her to see my collaboration in ambiguity.

The summer theatre gave its last performance; the concerts were over; the season was over. City people got in their cars and drove away. Autumn in the country was overwhelming. I had never witnessed this passage, the transformation from living green to dying scarlet and gold, each tree, branch, and leaf distinct with glory. Jimmy praised a particular patch of woods, and I must see it, go with him, now. I was no longer a city summer visitor. I lived in the country. Lonely and trapped and in love, I wouldn't think of giving up. I made my choice: life with Jimmy, the artist's life. No comforts, no money, no decadent distractions, but I didn't expect to be in this limbo, immobilized, so dependent on Jimmy and Anne and their resolve. He loved me, I knew that, I never questioned that, but he could not, finally, tear the clinging Anne from him. While they worked out their parting, I must find a way to live without money from my father, or a taxi at the door. No meals prepared, or laundry done, or my room cleaned. No holding the eyes of a stranger for an instant's flirtation. No games. No friend to play them with. No Dorothy.

Hervey let us use the Canalboat for the winter: one long, narrow room, faced with stone and mortar, tight against weather. He made the offer in the morning; by afternoon we were out of the Sala-mander—I would never forget the Salamander—and settled in the Canalboat. There was a small fireplace, a steeple clock that worked, a reed organ; Jimmy hung his violin on the wall above it. There was a bed, a rough table, a couple of chairs. Three small windows high on the south wall added to the illusion of a barge on water. I had five dollars, sent secretly by my sweet fifteen-year-old brother, and I used some of it to buy large bandanna handkerchiefs; hemmed on one end, threaded with string, they were just right as curtains. The outhouse was in an attached shed, a real advantage in winter. The Canalboat was surely an improvement over the Salamander.

———

Jimmy had a letter from Fanny. Fanny, Jimmy told me, had a retarded younger brother who peddled shoelaces and pencils on the streets of the lower East Side and was often the victim of neigh-borhood bullies. A week earlier he had been beaten, his tray of wares kicked around, his coins stolen. Now he wouldn't leave the house. Fanny's mother wept over his bruises; Fanny couldn't think of a way to help. "Bring him up here," Jimmy wrote Fanny by return mail, "for a week or two." Fanny accepted gratefully.

Anne wouldn't have him in the house on the hill. Jimmy asked me: If we hung a sheet as a divider and put a mattress on the floor for Harry, how would I feel about his sleeping in the Canalboat? "Fanny has been so generous," he reminded me. When I agreed—and I thought it was hard for Jimmy to reveal Anne's coldness—it was clear I would not be expected to be alone with Fanny's brother. Jimmy's alternate nights with Anne ceased, and Harry was the catalyst, a strange instrument for the resolution of my pain. A dark, thin person, neither young nor old, a gnome; his nose beaked, his skin rough, his small brown eyes unfocused, he was carefully coop-erative. In his own way decorous, he put his pajamas over his clothes to get into bed; before going to the outhouse in the shed he asked

Jimmy to light the lantern: "I have to go to the T-O-L-L to take an S-U-T," spelling modestly his intention. He stomped around on the paths in the woods alone, carrying a staff, loudly declaiming: "The Lord is my shepherd, THOU SHALT NOT HAVE!" He too kept a journal. One sad entry: "The world is not flat. It's ROUND. If you want to commit suicide you have to jump off. One comma two comma three period." After those two weeks I never saw Harry again. Jimmy moved more of his books and his typewriter to the Canalboat, and he did not leave on alternate nights.

———

My first meeting with Emily was doomed. Jimmy and I had been married almost six months before he said, "Next trip to the city we'll go to see my mother." I was reluctant. She might also be a pious Catholic bigot, just as his father was. I was relieved that I would never know his father. Jimmy mourned his father's death the year before. He was filled with remorse for their last years of enmity, their bitter estrangement. He thought that in our marriage his father's hatred of Jews and my father's hatred of Christians would be reconciled, healed, transformed. No one I knew talked like that. "Your mother knows nothing about me. She doesn't know we're married . . ." "Don't worry, she'll be pleased. You'll see." Had she ever met Anne? Did she even know he'd been living with Anne for the past two years? Perhaps they hadn't been in touch at all. He was twenty-eight years old and independent of his family.

———

It was after Mass and before Sunday dinner in the Long Island suburb. The street was empty: no stickball games, no kids on bicycles, no raised voices, no music, not even a scrap of paper lofted by a sudden gust of November wind. The semi-detached brick houses lined the streets with aprons of tiny tended lawns and bushes clipped to lozenge shape. Jimmy pressed the buzzer. He stood in front of the door. I was beside him, one step down and a little to the right. He must have center stage for this meeting with his mother, who longed to see him and didn't know me. Standing there in our Woodstock art colony clothes—my full skirt and Basque jacket, beret, dancers' tights, flat shoes; his shaggy hair and rumpled black corduroy suit—we were as conspicuous as gypsy tinkers in a painted caravan drawn by rough-coated horses. Our freak car by the curb, the dusty 1928 air-cooled Franklin, was an affront to the neighborhood. It would be parked out there making its derisive statement after we were in the door.

The large, dark-haired matron with glasses embraced Jimmy with soft glad cries: "James! James! What a surprise!" His mother drew him in; we stood in the entry. I was still apart. "James. Let me look at you." I thought the wood smoke and tobacco smells around his jacket might be the cause of her faint air of distress, but she said, "Oh James, you do need a haircut." Jimmy turned to me. "Mother, this is Blanche." "How do you do, Blanche." Cordial and distant, she did not offer her hand. In the living room I chose a straight chair. Jimmy moved around, looking at the familiar Della Robia madonna on the wall, Saint Sebastian pierced, a crucifix. Family photographs on the piano. He paused at the bookcase, looking through the glass doors at the spines of the sets of Fenimore Cooper, Dickens, Scott. Not really looking, restlessly pacing the old cage, taking its measure. But I looked. I had never been in a house like this, so orderly and so lifeless; solid comfort, quiet prosperity, and not an object to quicken the eye. How could Jimmy, the adventurer, live as a child, grow as a youth, in this dun-colored box.

At the dinner table I thought I was being instructed by his mother: "You may see Jimmy as he is now, looking like a tramp, a vagabond, flouting convention, but this is the way he was raised." Proper Sunday dinner on Haviland china and all that went with it. I went through the motions of eating. I was not included in the conversation; I listened. Jimmy asked about family: his sister Mary Claire; his Aunt Nellie; his sick brother, John; his dutiful brother William. I noted names, relationships, and I waited for Jimmy to give me my place in the family. When he sent me a reassuring glance I had no response. Twilight deepened; lamps were turned on. Jimmy's mother said, "Will you stay the night, James?" "Yes, we'll stay." "Fine. Your friend can have the guest room," she paused, "and you could sleep in the den." He followed her into the kitchen. I heard him, a flat statement: "We'll sleep together." I heard her protest; in my ears her whisper was clamorous: "Not in my house, James." "If it will make you feel any better," he said, "we're married." I heard her long, helpless sigh. Jimmy's mother assembled the bed linen for the couch that opened to a double bed in the den, she put out towels and facecloths. She said good night to Jimmy. She ignored me.

In that bed in the den—our lair?—I lay beside Jimmy wide awake
and hot with shame. Of course his mother didn't believe him; to
announce our marriage, a solemn sacrament to her, in that casual,
irritable way, how could she believe him. Why did he make it so hard
for his mother, why was he so clumsy, so cruel, that his mother now
despised me? He slept, and I tried to explain him to myself. He was
embarrassed, that was it. Hadn't he told me how he challenged his
father on his views of marriage, how bitterly they clashed. Was that
what he meant, then, when he said his mother would "be pleased"
that we were married? Pleased that he had capitulated? Pleased that I
was not another of his casual Village girls, with transparent clothes
and bells on her ankles? We left early the next morning after breakfast served by his mother and no word spoken directly to me.
"James, would your friend care for another cup of coffee?" she said to
him. We drove back to Woodstock almost in silence. Maybe he was
thinking about how he might have done it differently.

———

In December we sent a Christmas package to Jimmy's mother.
Celebrating Christmas was not only new to me, it had the attraction
of the forbidden. Chanukah was our festival, Christmas was *Theirs*;
in hymn-singing assemblies at school no sound issued from Jewish
children. It was *Their* tree on the platform: aromatic spruce or
balsam, glinting and sparkling; it was not a good idea to look at it for
long. We sent his mother a jug of maple syrup, greens from the
Maverick woods, and my sketch on canvas of a Nativity scene.
Jimmy's mother wrote, in her schoolteacher's Spencerian handwriting, enclosing his usual Christmas check: "Oh, James, I know you
must find it tiresome to hear over and over again, but I hope and pray
that you will change the carnal life you lead. Thank you for the
Christmas package, though I don't understand how a person of your
friend's type could choose such a subject."

Early in 1937, when we knew I was going to have a baby, Jimmy
wanted to tell everyone, and of course, his mother. A declaration of
our serious bond, and our faith in the future. I proposed that we also
send her a copy of our marriage certificate, transforming his "carnal
life," altering my "type," and validating her first grandchild's legit-
imacy. He agreed. Essentially kind, and fair, Emily had not wanted
the censorious position; without denying her firm training, she

wrote, "Dear James, this is your first step in the right direction." Our next meeting was awkward, both of us shy, aware of injustice inflicted, injustice borne, but from that time on we were friends.

The news of my pregnancy was a different matter for my parents. Their hope for the collapse of my misalliance was shattered. "Just when Daddy was about to offer you a year in Europe," my mother wrote, on the condition that I have no contact with Jimmy. If, at the end of that year, I chose to return to him and go on with this marriage, my father would withdraw his objections and accept it. Too late, too bad; the trap was sprung, and I was caught. My mother persuaded my father to send me an allowance, ten dollars a week for food, so that "in your delicate condition your health is not ruined."

Chapter Seven

WOODSTOCK. *The Phoenix* ANNOUNCED;
NEW MEXICO; FIRST CHILD

– 1937 –

T HE LITERAL BELIEVER was a wonder to me: it was not enough for Jimmy to hold a belief—he must act on it—and not enough for him to act on it—he must teach, convince, convert. There I was, loving him, new to this life and ready to cast off the old: prime ground for seeding. Jimmy told me he lost his faith in the Catholic Church when he was nineteen. His youngest brother Thomas, the brother closest to him, most loved, lay dying in a Virginia hospital after a railroad accident. Not to taint his family in any way with his dark transaction, he went off to a wooded area near the family house on Long Island and there offered the devil his soul in exchange for his brother's life. Thomas died the next day. I couldn't imagine it; it wasn't credible: not in darkest Ruritania nor voodoo-practicing Haiti. Here, in New York, in the United States, in the twentieth century, to contract with the Devil, to believe in the, a, Devil. I listened, said nothing; I was getting to know him.

When he left home and taught school in New York City, at sea and rudderless and adrift, he lived in working-class neighborhoods on the edge of the Village. He was drawn to the speakers on street corners, thundering heat and fervor in their crusade for the downtrodden, for justice and equality: all the promises of the Catholic heaven, here on earth. And he joined the Communist Party. The Party I knew only from the fringe—the civilized polemics, the proletarian novels, the massing of symbols in protest—he knew as a Party member in action, in danger of arrest and jail.

I would never be ready to go to jail. But I could see that for him it would be worth risking, a chance to defy the system, and defend the poor. News of an eviction, an unemployed family out on the street, sitting on the curb, surrounded by all their worldly goods: a band of stalwart Party members would rush to the scene, remove the padlock on the tenement apartment door, break the seal on the gas meter and connect the fuel line, move the sad bits of furniture off the street, up the stairs, and back into place. Hands clasped; blessings and heartfelt gratitude.

It wasn't long before Jimmy's proposals for direct action exceeded the bounds of Party prudence: Let the homeless occupy the churches, the hungry occupy the cafeterias, and call the newspapers to witness and report. He was disciplined for his zeal and he left the Party, damning the bureaucrats.

That was before I met him.

Now, in Woodstock, in 1937, he fought wth everyone: Stalinists who defended the USSR after the revelations of the Moscow Trials, our friends who joined the Abraham Lincoln Brigade to fight Franco in Spain, his old anti-war comrades who enlisted in the U.S. Army to fight in a United Front against fascists in Europe. Insults traded, invective exploded: Trotskyite, Lovestoneite, Revisionist; Warmonger, Anarchist, Pacifist, every splinter a shard to sever friends and lovers. Jimmy's evangelical eloquence embarrassed me, and persuaded me; he was always ready to interrupt small talk, parochial gossip, and demand that burning questions be faced. Voices of ironic reason were overwhelmed by his urgency, pragmatic politics subjected to withering demolition. He had no doubts. He would not conciliate. "This is not like any other war in history," he said with bitter loathing. "There has never been such machinery for killing. You know the slaughter of innocents is inevitable. Do you think it is only the enemy who will burn, rape, starve civilians? I suppose all guns fired by our side hit the mark and deliver a clean swift death!" I watched our friends: uncomfortable, angry, then closed, not our friends any longer. "And who is the Enemy? Boys! Boys, drafted by evil old men in power. Filth! Filth and desecration." It always returned to the central question: Can immoral means serve moral ends. Ends and means.

Too late for debate. We must get out of the path of the storm, gather in small groups, in agrarian community, in remote places, in defiance and survival. D. H. Lawrence had just such a vision. How to get there? A little magazine to be called *The Phoenix* was announced in the Sunday Book Reviews of the *New York Times* and *Herald Tribune,* a literary quarterly. We would print it ourselves; it would be the rallying point, through it we would spread the word of a community of separate dwellings and shared land and stock and tools; through the magazine we would raise money, find kindred spirits. We would publish writers whose unpopular or seditious views would have no chance in the commercial press. Jimmy boldly announced contributors would be paid.

Frieda Lawrence wrote from New Mexico. She suggested we get in touch with a rich young couple who lived near her in San Cristobal. They might help launch the quarterly. "Let's talk it over," they wrote, and no sooner said than done. To finance our trip we sold books and records to sympathetic friends on the Maverick; privately they thought we were brave fools. Useless for the mothers, my Jewish mother, his Catholic mother, to express their concern for me. Not only was I, in my seventh month of pregnancy, going to a primitive village in the far Southwest where my baby might be born, I had not even been seen by a doctor in civilized New York.

We packed the racy little Whippet roadster we had just bought for forty-five dollars; ready to go, the motor running, Jimmy suddenly turned off the ignition and said, "I'll be right back." He gathered an armful of roadside daylilies and ran up the hill to Anne. I sat there waiting, taking my last look at the Maverick. I would not imagine their farewell, his guilt and remorse, her defeat. We might stay in New Mexico; maybe she'd never see him again.

———

In San Cristobal the rich young couple raised horses on a ranch high in the mountains. The country was awesome, primeval, sparsely settled—a few Anglos, mostly Indians. Dan and Jennifer Stevens were New England-bred, Harvard and Vassar educated, who on their honeymoon traveled on pilgrimage in Europe. They followed the track of the Lawrences in Italy and Germany and France and England, buying Lawrence memorabilia along the way. They bought the ranch, above Taos, not far from Frieda, in what they thought of as Lawrence country.

The Stevens were welcoming; they didn't show their surprise that I was so pregnant, or that we had all our belongings in the shabby little car. After all, they had only said, "Let's talk it over." They gave us a room, pleasantly large and light and smelling of sagebrush. The walls were rough white plaster, and so was the hive-shaped fireplace. Very Southwest. In the large kitchen, at our first evening meal around the trestle table, we met the ranch hand Pete, a local fellow from Santa Fe with the bandy legs and hard hands of a working horseman. And the other ranch hand, Enid Hilton. Sitting beside Enid was her four-year-old son Colin, very fair, very English. Our first meal was hearty and spartan: whole-grain bread baked by Jennifer, then sliced at table as thin as could be by Dan, and bowls of nourishing soup. After saying grace, and tasting his first spoonful of soup, Dan led the appreciation with "Jennifer, you outdid yourself!" and Jennifer smiled to the chorus of assenting mmm's. The soup and the bread and the ritual of praise was repeated every night.

Enid—what was she doing in this calculated earthiness, nodding off at the table in exhaustion, catching herself, catching my eye to smile her wry apology. Jimmy and I took to her at once. We knew Enid from the Lawrence letters; in the introduction to the collection he edited, Aldous Huxley acknowledged Enid's help: ". . . lacking her cooperation I should have been lost." Friend of Lawrence's youth in the Midlands, married to a cautious civil servant left behind in London. Enid was one of the people on the Stevens' pilgrimage. She sold them a Lawrence painting when they looked her up in London, and her Lawrence letters. This windfall made it possible for Enid to come to the United States with her child; she hoped to stay, to escape the impending conflagration in Europe. She was grateful to the Stevens for sponsoring them. Lawrence's influence was there to be seen in Enid's life: small, wiry, weathered, in her mid-forties, Enid confounded the doctors who said she couldn't carry a baby to term. Colin was delivered by a midwife in a village in the South of France; Enid would not be able to nurse, said the doctors, but she suckled Colin without any trouble through his first years. There she was now, with her healthy young son, doing hard ranch work her sedentary London intellectual's life in no way prepared her for, proof that the body's wisdom was to be trusted. As Lawrence said.

Kiowa Ranch, Frieda's ranch, was a few miles away. She lived there with Angelo Ravagli, a former officer in the Italian Army. They met in Venice, when Lawrence was dying of tuberculosis; after his death Frieda returned with Angelo to San Cristobal, to the ranch Lawrence loved. Frieda and Angelo built a substantial log house for themselves and used the original ranch house for guests.

We saw Frieda waiting on the porch, then coming down the steps to greet us as we drove up. She was grand, large and fair; her green eyes lit with humor, cooled with irony. She took us in, smiling slyly one of her first questions: "Are you getting enough to eat at the Stevens?" She laid a sumptuous tea, with beautiful tarts and lots of whipped cream. She wanted to know all about us and all about the magazine we planned and how the Stevens were working out as collaborators. Angelo joined us; stocky, swarthy, very much in possession of woman and place, and very soon bored with *Phoenix* talk. He invited me to see his studio. Frieda stopped listening to Jimmy to glance warily at Angelo.

The painting on the easel was almost finished, Angelo said. Dismaying. A swimming pool surrounded by Hollywood starlets, crude drawing, in primary colors. He gave me a chair at a proper distance for viewing, as though I were a patron contemplating a purchase, and like a patron I found a cautious comment. What did Frieda see in this oaf? Maybe it was his direct way into her life, into her body, the mindless thing Lawrence was always after and talked and wrote so much about. Maybe for Frieda Angelo was the natural spontaneous man Lawrence wished to be. Such was my nineteen-year-old's presumption.

Aldous and Maria Huxley were in the guest house that summer, the simple three-room structure where Lawrence and Frieda once lived. We went to tea with the Huxleys, and Frieda and Angelo joined us. We sat on the chairs Lawrence decorated, around the table he made, the Huxleys' European graciousness more notable for the primitive setting. The Huxleys were kind, though I could see he was dubious about a literary quarterly with such ambitious goals. He listened attentively, careful not to discourage. Huxley wore thick glasses; he was almost blind; very tall, very thin, with dark hair and a surprisingly soft, full mouth. His grandfather was Thomas Huxley, his great uncle Matthew Arnold; his friends were E. M. Forster, the Stracheys, Katherine Mansfield, the Woolfs. I didn't care what he said about quarterlies, I was prepared to sit there and listen to the accent of literary England forever. I marked the loving way he inclined his head to Maria when he spoke, his wife Maria, small, vivid, curly black hair—a Belgian beauty. Huxley asked practical questions about our intention to print and bind and distribute *The Phoenix* ourselves. Jimmy had ready answers. He had learned print-ing (he meant setting the Maverick concert programs once a week and running them off on Hervey's hand press) and I would set type. Angelo, hard-headed, asked, "How much will you charge?" Jimmy said confidently, "Fifty cents an issue. Two dollars for a year's sub-scription." "How many pages in each issue?" "Oh, a hundred . . ." Angelo shook his head in disapproval. "Two pages for one cent? Not enough . . ." Smiles all around at his fiscal severity.

Another day I was alone with Frieda and Maria. Although we were in New Mexico, eight thousand feet above the desert, high in the wild Rocky Mountains, Frieda's kitchen felt European. The tiles from Italy, the copper pots from Spain, the Aga stove from Sweden. The two women, Frieda moving around, easy in her large body, a German Venus, a von Richtofen, and Maria, very Gallic, animated, her dark eyes wise, both women showing me their friendship. I saw myself as they must see me: young, far from home, about to have a baby, following still another man with a purpose and no money. Maria worked on a wool coverlet for our baby; she planned a rainbow pattern, for Lawrence's novel *The Rainbow*.

I took walks with Enid's four-year-old son Colin. I liked being with him. He made real for me, for the first time, the new compan-ion waiting to be born. He told me about lizards and gophers and coyotes; I loved his English accent, his seriousness, and his treating me as an equal. There were no other children for miles.

Jimmy and I went down the mountain into Taos one day in our risky Whippet, taking the hairpin curves on the dirt road with no rails to guard against an abrupt drop into the canyon. We went to call on Mabel Dodge, the rich patron of artists who brought the Law-rences to this part of the world. Mabel Dodge gave Frieda the 160-acre ranch in 1924, when Frieda declared it the most beautiful place she had ever seen: the wildness, the clarity of the air, the trembling aspen, the raspberry canyon. "I want you to have it," said Mabel, and the Lawrences gave her the manuscript of *Sons and Lovers* in exchange.

"See Mabel," Frieda said, and the Huxleys agreed. "Jimmy might appeal to her." Jimmy would see Mabel, and I would see a doctor. It would be wise to see a doctor now, the women on the ranch in San Cristobal urged. First to Mabel Dodge's house, a fine adobe house with arches and iron grilles, where she lived with her Indian husband, Tony Luhan. We were uneasy, knocking on her door. We heard stories at the ranch of feuds and cabals, of the fierce fight over Lawrence's ashes, of Mabel setting herself against Frieda. It was a good thing we were not high in expectation. She was cold, "not interested in anything about Lawrence," and we took our leave as soon as we could.

At the other end of the town was the one-story adobe hospital Mabel Dodge had given Taos. The doctor took my medical history, hardly any history; he did not show surprise that I had not yet seen a doctor. He was matter-of-fact, jovial; after examining me he said I would probably deliver in six weeks, and "that's a nice little watermelon you're carrying." I didn't show I was offended, but I hoped he would not be my doctor. It didn't seem likely. The way things were going it didn't seem likely we would be there much longer. Jimmy and Dan Stevens saw things so differently: Dan was bland and measured, Jimmy was extreme and impetuous; Dan saw the proposed *Phoenix* as a literary quarterly, just that; for Jimmy it was the clarion that would call men and women to a new beginning, a guide to survival in a time of madness.

We soon said goodbye to the Stevens, to Enid and Frieda and the Huxleys, sorry all of us; but it was a gamble; we knew that. We sold the Whippet in San Cristobal, packed our belongings, got a ride to Taos, a bus for Santa Fe, and the Union Pacific as far as the proceeds of the sale of the Whippet would take us: to Chicago. In Chicago's Union Station we went directly to the Western Union desk; Jimmy wired his good brother William: "Blanche and I stranded. Please send train fare NYC immediately." And Bill rescued us. We sat up in the coach, making our plans, sometimes sleeping, facing our separation. I would go to my parents to wait for the birth of our child, he would go to Woodstock and find a place for us to live. I didn't need to ask, he didn't need to confess: we both knew he would be going to Anne. There had been letters, even a telegram from her when we were in San Cristobal; her unhappiness was on his mind. We parted at Grand Central: "Where can I reach you?" "I'll let you know. Just a few days, I'll be down . . ." He pressed two dollars in my hand for my taxi. "No, I can borrow it from the doorman . . ." But then I accept it, I can see it's important, he's taking care of me.

In the August heat, my oversize red cotton dirndl clinging to my swollen body, my thick curly hair grown long and wild, without makeup, laden with canvas bags and suitcases, I reappeared to my family. I had shamed them, angered them, dashed their high hopes, but they couldn't abandon me. They took me in. My old room: red, black, white, aggressively modern, was now a guest room. I was a guest.

"Where is he?" My mother couldn't bring herself to use his name.

"Jimmy went on to Woodstock. He's looking for a house for us . . ." And, I thought enviously, reading all the accumulated letters and manuscripts for *The Phoenix*. And consoling Anne.

"A job? Does he have a job?"

More positive than I felt, I said, "He has a column in the *Ulster County Press*—starts in September. . ." There was no point in telling her that a job, any job, would be part-time, freelance, and temporary. Editing and printing the magazine was our work.

"Tomorrow I'll call Dr. Lehmann for an appointment," my mother told me. It was the family doctor who would deliver the baby after all. "Daddy will take care of the doctor bills and the hospital bills," I could be sure of that, she said, but "what then?" Her "then" was distant, nebulous; I didn't give it a thought. My consuming preoccupation, separated from Jimmy, in seclusion from old city friends, in capitulation to my family, was deliverance and release, the birth of the child, and the end of Jimmy's entanglement with Anne.

I subdued the life in that apartment. The rancor between my parents went on behind closed doors; the quarrels of my brother and sister were muffled. I was both the center and the outcast. If there were just the two of us going down in the elevator, my father positioned himself as far away as he could and, from the twelfth floor to the street level, avoided looking at me. My thirteen-year-old sister kept her distance; I was a source of contagion and an awful example. She ushered her friends past my room quickly. Even my old confederate, my brother, was uneasy; he couldn't understand how I could mess up my life this way. Besides, he was too young to be an uncle. My mother and I were in truce, we were careful with each other; she tried not to hover anxiously, I tried not to rebuff her. But there were no dinner parties, no strangers, no one who would see me in my "condition," dressed in my outlandish peasant dirndls. Close relatives only came to visit, who already knew of my disgrace, who murmured in other rooms with my mother as though I were sick.

Letters from Jimmy. The envelopes addressed "Blanche Cooney" in his firm hand, inscribed with a broad-nibbed pen, c/o Rosenthal, much smaller below it, gave notice to the foreign power: she's your hostage, but only until our baby is born, and only because of the heartlessness of a system that does not provide humane medical care. A momentary defeat but galling nevertheless. In one letter he described the house on the Maverick that Hervey will let us have:

> There's one large square-shaped room that has a big skylight and a fascinating fireplace. Against the wall beneath the skylight there is a marvelously long, solid work bench made from old hand-hewn planks. Very enduring and pleasing, and conducive to much work with papers and notes sprawled all over. The floor in this room is wide-planked, the walls plastered. There's an immaculate, cheerful kitchen, small, but not too small, and a room that would serve excellently for a child. One wall outside is stoned, the others are partly stoned. I'm going to finish them. And there's a screened porch, good for eating, reading, sleeping, in spring and summer. The whole house has a subtle warmth and careless beauty. I like it very much. Hervey calls it the Quarry House.

Next morning, in my daily letter ". . . the Quarry House sounds wonderful. Could you get the dimensions of the windows? I'll make curtains; it will bring me close, I'm so impatient. I'll imagine as I stitch that I'm looking out on Maverick Road instead of high above Ninety-second Street. . . ."

To find relief from the late summer's heat and the oppressive family I would take a book, leave the apartment, walk along the river. Go up to the roof. Each time I went out my mother nervously asked, "Where are you going? How long will you be? Have you felt a pain?" And I would think: only three more weeks, only two more weeks.

Jimmy telephoned. That was unusual. He had found a ride for me to Woodstock with Lenny and Frances, "They're renting the Canalboat now. They want you to come; I want to see you. Come up for the weekend, darling, get out of the city . . ." When Leonard and Frances picked me up, my mother whispered her hope that the trip would not be too much for me; I knew she would have liked to beg them to drive with extraordinary care, avoiding bumps and steep grades.

Crossing the river, streaking up the Parkway in the Ford convertible, just being with our funny loving friends—I hadn't felt so free and happy in a long time. It was only months, but it seemed like years since I had been on the Maverick. Now it was in its dry late summer buzz and haze, tall dusty goldenrod, and Queen Anne's lace, sumac beginning to turn, wild aster blur of blue, vivid black-eyed susan. No lawns surrounding the studios hidden in the woods; oh, once in a while someone borrowed a scythe from Hervey and cut a rough path to an outhouse, but no suburban niceties disturbed the life in the tall grasses of toad, snake, squirrel.

Jimmy was there waiting; our discreet friends left us alone and went off on an errand. It was odd to be back in the Canalboat as a visitor, but Jimmy and I were together. Soon we would never be parted; no more cruel separations. We walked around outside the Canalboat, slowly, arms around each other; Jimmy encouraged, lent me courage, told his longing.

Leonard and Frances returned with a jug of red wine, mushrooms, tomatoes; Frances boiled water for rice. They wanted to hear all about San Cristobal. Jimmy showed us tentative plans for the *Phoenix* format. A Woodstock artist, Tom Penning, did a drawing of a phoenix; Jimmy had a cut made and pulled a proof that morning. "Fierce-looking bird" and should be, we all agreed. Frances and Leonard too were in love, recently pledged to each other: Leonard, small, graceful, with a poet's sensibility and a mockingly urbane Boston manner, and Frances, a sculptor, a dark beauty with a deep bosom and narrow hips who was raised in a Hebrew orphanage in Brooklyn. Jimmy, laughing or serious, read to us from *Phoenix* mail: some bizarre, some impressive; many letters from France and England. Leonard was never so witty, Frances was never so charming and sly; never did four people have such joy in each other as we did that day in September, in the Canalboat, in 1937.

The shadows deepened; twilight slipped into evening. It was almost dark. Jimmy took Leonard aside, spoke in an undertone; they left. Frances and I stretched out on the couch, their bed. Frances cosseted me, praised me. ". . . your skin, your hair . . . the way you carry yourself, and *it*. Blanchie, you're blooming. I'm so jealous . . ." I kissed my only, my necessary woman friend for that. I felt so clumsy and unlovely. Jimmy's private appreciations were biased. Sounds of voices outside, I saw Jimmy and Leonard coming through the woods, carrying a cot. They maneuvered it through the door, set it beside Leonard and Frances' bed. I was to sleep on the cot. Alone. Frances quickly spread bedclothes to cover its blatant singleness, the cruel arrangement. Leonard and Frances and Jimmy made an effort to return to banter and camaraderie, but it was no use. I was silent. Jimmy avoided my eyes; a pall was on our group. Someone yawned. It was catching, and we were all suddenly sleepy. Jimmy said, "Sleep well. I'll see you in the morning" and went back into the woods, up the path to Anne's house.

———

It would be this day. I knew it as soon as I awoke. I packed a bag, left a note, and walked down the street to the Hotel Windermere. Aunt Magda expected me. We had planned it: ". . . when your time comes, I'll go to the hospital with you."

Into the cave of the Sibyl, a dark apartment full of old family portraits and old family furniture. "Come in, darling." Slow, easy. "Sit down, put your bag there." I smelled the Turkish coffee she brewed every morning, the herbal aroma of her mysterious ointments. She was enveloped in a robe of some rich stuff, her gold hair was coiled and pinned and in order; she embraced me, calmly, with no special emphasis for the day of my first baby's birth. Aunt Magda set out the demitasse cups; she sipped her coffee, I sipped mine. She talked, unhurried musing about a sermon she heard Rabbi Wise deliver: it was not up to his usual standard. She ruminated about leaders, and prophets, and slowly, slowly, began to assemble a street costume, talking all the while. She set the tone: grave, and perfectly confident.

The doorbell sounded. Who could it be? It was my father; he had just stopped before going downtown to see if I was all right. He was uncomfortable to be showing concern; he sounded brusque. His taxi was waiting; did I need anything? He kissed me, met Aunt Magda's reassuring eye, and left.

At last, at last, we were ready; the doorman summoned a taxi. In the cab, after directing the driver to the hospital, Aunt Magda added with quiet authority, "Sir, please drive with care. This young girl is about to have her first baby," and the driver breezily over his shoulder assured her "Don't worry lady got five of my own."

In the small private hospital I am in a room alone, a labor room, the nurses tell me. Aunt Magda has disappeared. My mother is in the corridor. Nothing can have my attention but the great gathering effort, the task I must perform. I barely notice the kindness of nurses, their periodic checks. My father, his brother Sam, his sister Rose, appear at the foot of my bed; what are they doing here, they are interrupting my imperative work. I wish them away. "Let's go," I hear my father say, he can't witness my struggle. Hours later the tempo accelerates; on the fast ride on a gurney through the hospital corridors I catch a glimpse of my mother's anxious eyes, then into the delivery room.

An animals howls. And cries. The terrible sounds are mine, I can't believe it, I'm an animal, howling her pain. And then it's over, all over in a great sliding deliverance into our world. "It's a girl," the doctor says. "You have a daughter," and I hear her first cry. My last conscious thought before the merciful whiff of ether was my relief: it is not a boy and I won't have to face the issue of circumcision, Jimmy is adamantly against circumcision. Someone wires Jimmy, he takes a milk train from Kingston, and when I wake he is at my bedside to hold me and tell me his joy and relief. He leaves, he will be back in ten days to take us home.

The baby is put beside me, we look at each other: appraising strangers, just met; who is she, is she wondering about me, does she have anything to wonder with? I know now she was an exceptionally beautiful infant, but then I thought the exclamations of praise from doctor and nurses were routine, to make the mother feel good and stimulate her milk. I am in the heart of the marvelous, in it. The nurses are holy; the hospital is a temple, the doctor truly ministers. Each time the baby is brought to my bed for feeding I can't believe I will have her all to myself, with Jimmy, out of the city, away, in our chosen place.

We had months ago decided on "Deirdre" for a girl; names were important. "Deirdre" had the sound, the look on the page, the literary and Celtic resonance that pleased us. Deirdre? They had to practice saying it. They had never heard of it. My mother told the family that "D" was in memory of Great Aunt Deborah. "Christian," no doubt a Christian name, my mother said to me. "A Saint?" "No, mother. It's a pagan name," I reassured her. Nothing reassured her. Not even the doctor who pronounced me fit, certainly fit to travel after my stay in hospital. My mother could only think of how ignorant, how ill-equipped I was to care for a baby, and to take care of myself, after the ordeal of childbirth. "Stay with me," she pleaded, "at least until you get your strength . . ." No, no, I must go. Jimmy is waiting, he's coming for me. I'll be all right. A campaign is mounted. I receive calls to the phone at my bedside from aunts and cousins and my mother's friends, each one an experienced mother: "How can you go into the wilderness with an infant, Blanche. You don't know, you have no idea of the work. Your mother tells me you have no plumbing, no heat! You are not a peasant, you are too delicate. If you don't think of yourself, think of the baby, the responsibility . . . . Just a month or two." I said Yes, and No, and thanked them each one.

Aunt Magda stayed out of it; she knew nothing would induce me to return to the cold comfort of Ninety-second Street. My father did not see me again, but he ordered six of everything a baby needs.

Chapter Eight

BACK TO WOODSTOCK; *Phoenix*

LAUNCHED; SECOND CHILD

– 1940 –

O N A QUIET STREET in Manhattan, a big old sedan, a geta-
way car in a gangster movie, stood at the curb in front of the
private hospital. Ours? "Ours. A Marmon." Jimmy seemed pleased
with it. I didn't know anything about Marmons, but it was not the
car he shared with Anne; I took it as a sign. Jimmy led the way with
my bags and baby paraphernalia, I followed, then the nurse with the
baby. In the back seat, surprise, was Fanny. She beamed benevolence; Jimmy said, "Fanny is coming to Woodstock with us for a
while to help with the baby." Stretching her arms for the infant, she
wished to begin her help at once. "No, it's all right Fanny, I'll hold
her," and the nurse from Maternity put the baby in my lap. Considering my gypsy-witch helper, the dubious old car, the whole
scrappy entourage, the nurse earnestly wished me well. Taking his
eyes off the road only when it was perfectly safe to gaze at our baby,
Jimmy drove his precious cargo out of New York and up to Woodstock.

Fanny was more than helpful. Each morning she would spring
from her makeshift bed in the room with the skylight and the
fireplace and the red rug from my room on Ninety-second Street and
run to our room to answer the first cry, to scoop up, to rock, coo and
croon and diaper the rosy, delectable infant. I could see she thought
it was unfair: why couldn't *she* nurse the baby. I grew stronger. Oh,
go *away* Fanny, I thought. "She's starved, poor Fanny," Jimmy said
sympathetically. Nibbling at the crumbs that fell from Jimmy's

table, she wanted to be near him, and his baby. To observe me as mother. To go between the Quarry House and Anne's house on the hill with her fey mix of mischief and kindness.

The birth of the baby marked the end of Jimmy's struggle with Anne. Now, after so long a time, I want to ask Jimmy how exactly it happened. What did you say, what did she say. Did she silently accept, or was she inconsolable? Did you just stop touching her, just disconnect, ease away into neutral friendship? Was there a final, regretful lovemaking? I can't believe I never got the details. We let it heal over, a wound that became a scar, faint but permanent.

Anne continued to live on the hill, painting, on the WPA art project, driving her air-cooled Franklin. At the Maverick concerts she sat inside the hall, calm, smiling pleasantly, greeting friends, her thick gold hair cut in a bang and hanging straight to her shoulders. As Jimmy liked it. Jimmy and I sat on the benches outside the hall so that I could move away with the baby in my arms at the least cry that might disturb the musicians or the audience. Acutely aware of Anne, I would have made us invisible as well, so she could not be drawn to look at us together, at our beautiful child.

The Maverick was intended for men and women at serious work: musicians, sculptors, writers, painters—solitary, or coupled in temporary arrangements. Lovers, if legally married, didn't mention it; women kept their own names. There were no babies. So it was surprising, the sweet response from the Maverick community to the new arrival. "We just dropped in . . ." "We were driving by . . ." An antique cradle, a silver cup, a hand-knit sweater were bestowed with soft clucks and admiration. Hervey dandled her. Mousseau photographed her. How could they resist, she was baby incarnate: gold ringlets, blue eyes, round and fair and funny, loving and our darling. But we had work to do; the baby was not the center of our lives. I was not only "Mother." There would be no diapers hanging about; we would not lower our voices, or the volume of music, or the volume of smoke. With vigilance sensible and relaxed, mother's milk and country air, I would confound the anxious old wives back in New York City by the easy way I coped.

"Little magazines" are, for the most part, the mayflies of the literary world. Launched on implausibly idealistic manifestoes, briefly sustained by charity and overwork, and imperiled by an ever-worsening ratio of creditors to subscribers, they soon complete their scarcely noticed flights and sink away. . . . Ephemerality is the little magazine's generic fate; by promptly dying it gives proof that it remained loyal to its first program. From *Skeptical Engagements*, by Frederick Crews, Oxford University Press, 1986.

The Little Magazine

So much mail was generated from the announcement of *The Phoenix*, so many manuscripts. The drumbeat in the forest was heard in the provinces, in the towns, and in the cities, across the sea; so many ambitious unpublished souls behind every bush, bound to be heard. So many poets! There was enough encouragement, two dollar bills for subscriptions with notes of support, to let Jimmy know there was a readership out there to whom he had a responsibility. And of course he must deal with those manuscripts, writing as honestly as he could, telling the truth, in longhand and helpfully, to cushion rejection. Letters of acceptance were more than that: with praise came an invitation to visit "anytime; we can put you up." If we had had a telephone he would have called instantly.

He would have called Paris. In Paris, Henry Miller, scanning the heavens for signs useful to him, came upon the *Phoenix* announcement. "No doubt the first number is already set up," he wrote. "But if not, if in this first issue you would care to have something from me about Lawrence, I should be glad to contribute. As you have probably never heard of me, I enclose a few leaflets gotten out by my fool publisher in France. All my three books are banned in America and England. . . ."

So began the association with Miller. After a chapter from his Lawrence book was accepted for the first issue of *Phoenix*, the lead piece, we heard from Miller in every mail. Engaging, irreverent, a sophisticated and disarming hustler: "This morning I am full of oats. I have everything to give and I don't give a fuck about receiving money for it. I want you to have a good time with your magazine and start a little rumpus, set in motion a few air currents, cause an earthquake if possible. Only start something soon! We need you. The program of your magazine sounds good to me." Thus Miller casually saluted the *Phoenix* credo. "I have plenty of material along the lines suggested. That is precisely my forte. And I have at least four staunch and stalwart friends who will feed you incessantly."

Spread the word, anything to spread the word. Miller's correspondence was prodigious. He followed every lead to the rich, the influential: editors, publishers, critics, in the avant garde or the academy, in Europe or the United States. In his pursuit of patronage and publication even the unfledged *Phoenix* might further his career. To further his career, *The Phoenix* must fly, and so Miller, in Paris, acted not only as conduit for the writings of his "staunch and stalwart" friends, he also sent lists, "certified fertile," of possible subscribers. "And above all," he wrote, "keep in touch with the censor, Mr. Huntington Cairns. He has become a good friend of mine and will help you in many ways. It is not his fault that my books are banned. The law needs to be changed and it may be before long. This is confidential." Jimmy, not the overt opportunist Miller was, nevertheless realized the potential publicity for *The Phoenix* if banned Miller were banned again, and Miller became our European editor.

Who was the trickster, who was using whom; Miller, the wily confidence man in Paris, ready to go through any back door to U.S. publication, or Jimmy with his urgent vision of community, wanting a link with Miller's network in Europe before the world exploded? It was droll, their association. It pleased Miller to believe Jimmy was a cowboy, or roustabout, a Natural; God's fool. He couldn't figure out the drive behind Jimmy's passion, his assurance, his naivete; I knew he didn't really care. But I detected a note of relief when he wrote, in December 1937: "I want to congratulate you on the fine appearance of the prospectus—is that your press? Paper and type excellent. And the contents too. You are doing things in style—I could use a few hundred of these leaflets." No doubt he had braced himself for crude newsprint sprinkled with typos.

––––

Hervey liked the idea of a print shop on the Maverick, publishing a literary journal. He was reminded of the old days, other passionate beginnings, when he built the concert hall and the summer theatre. A studio with electricity to power the press was available; we could have that. He gave us his typestands, staked us to paper and ink. His undistinguished Century type would have to do until we could get the Garamond face we wanted, Garamond, with its graceful ligatures. We pored over Printers' Bibles, sought advice from master printers; this was our first shared work and we were aiming for graphic excellence. More craft than he cared about, Hervey said; he went in for happy accidents. He taught us all he knew and then stepped back, a friendly observer.

Only the Press was powered, and only Jimmy ran it. All the work in the print shop that led to the climax of the pressrun was manual, handmaidenly labor, each step important but without the tension and triumph of the crucial process. I learned to set type in the composing stick, one letter at a time, as fast and as accurately as I could, taking artful care in the spacing between words, even between letters, avoiding widows (an incomplete line at the top of a page) and rivers (a visible trail of white to mar the solid pattern of type). We read galley proofs meticulously—no "happy accidents" for us.

The print shop was a gathering place, a clubhouse, a forum. The press hummed in a golden hive, pollen gathered far away from the Maverick; the baby slept in her basket, lulled by the rhythm. Hervey brought visitors to look in, friends appeared for an afternoon, a weekend; poets, short-story writers: contributors eager to see the source of their first published work. It was so enticing, almost everyone asked, "Can I help?" There's the smell of ink, coffee's always on, soup simmers on a hot plate; we're camping in the shop now. Not just anyone can help, we're selective even though it's free and volunteer labor; we learn to weed the casual from the committed, and among the committed, the careless from the precise.

High on a stool by the window, in front of my typestand, I keep an eye on the baby in her pen outdoors. She is warm in her cap and sweater, she is content with her wooden peg toy. I tap the window, wave, she flips her mittened hand, dimples her incredibly rosy cheeks, assured I am close by. I am never not close by. Momentarily I lose my place in the manuscript, I find it, finish the sentence, the last in the type stick, secure it with a lead and remove a third of a page of precariously held type from the stick into the galley tray. Pied type is a hazard but I am a seasoned hand now, supervisor of novices. Take a break, the mail is due; brew another pot of coffee. The baby needs to be fed, and changed, and put to nap. Somewhere in the day or night I wash baby clothes with water fetched from the well. A bed must be found for a couple up from the city. A table must be cleared for the painter Joseph Pollet to examine the Jean Giono manuscript he may help translate from the French. *Refusal to Obey*, it was called, the title itself in the spirit of the *Phoenix*. Joe's daughter Elizabeth, an English major on holidayſfrom Bryn Mawr, set type at the other stand. A faithful and diligent worker who would later publish a novel and marry the poet Delmore Schwartz, she adorned the shop with her pale, quiet beauty.

Fanny was back. Proposing herself as a volunteer in the print shop she, now a Laurentian absolutist, wrote in unintentional parody:

> When I first laid with man, their use of myself as woman-need, disrobed from its past indefiniteness, became clear and sharp in pain as the freezing wind sting. My desire for communion, for oneness, for the intuitive flow between man and woman, subsided, while the waters of my physical need for man became turbulent, overwhelming in its physical thrust . . ."

She quit her project job in the city and rented her own place on the Maverick. Although she had not stopped loving the baby, she had given up her mad possessiveness. Helping with the magazine was her focus now, almost her mission; she was a dedicated worker, quick and dependable in folding, collating, sewing. Joe Pollet allowed her to interrupt him; he was tolerant of her fierce craziness. "Joe," she demanded, "do you know Lawrence's answer to Darwin's theory of evolution?" Joe was noncommittal, trying to get on with the Giono manuscript. "Unfolding! Humanity does not evolve. It unfolds!" She was suddenly distracted. "Mail's here. Shall I get it?" She knew she couldn't get the mail, but she kept trying. Jimmy jealously hugged this prerogative, and in he came, back from the mailbox down the road, laden.

Not just mail. Hermes, herald and messenger, was at work. Tidings from France, England, Babylon, the Orient: exciting, wondrous. There was a packet from Anaïs Nin addressed in her unmistakable elegant angular handwriting. The first among Miller's "staunch and stalwart" friends, we had accepted excerpts from her diary, *Mon Journal*—there were reported to be more than fifty volumes so far—and an essay in appreciation, "Un Etre Étoilique," by Miller. In this essay Miller did not mince words: "It is a mythological voyage toward the source and fountainhead of life—I might say an astrologic voyage of metamorphisis . . . a monumental confession which when given to the world will take its place beside the revelations of St. Augustine, Petronius, Abelard, Rousseau, Proust, and others."

Jimmy opened the large manila envelope: photographs, at last. One of Anaïs in Spanish dancer's costume, on a spiral stairway, when long ago she flashed a smiling eighteen-year-old's coquetry, lighting the dark sepia print. Another, a leaner, older Anaïs, her pale oval face framed in dark hair formally coiffed, serious eyes looking straight into the camera. Wearing a long draped gown she stood in the walled garden of her house in Louveciennes: the Banker's wife. On the deck of her houseboat, *Peniche la Belle Aurore* she was still another Anaïs, anchored off the Quai des Tuileries on the Seine in her serious artist's life. The photographs were passed around the shop; after Jimmy, I was next, then the others: friends, workers, visitors, no one was excluded from the daily event of the mail. At last a glimpse of the Spanish princess, Miller's lover and patron, whose career he promoted as she promoted his. Less aggressive than Miller in her pursuit of publication and fame, her writing was elaborately erotic, vaguely mystical, her professions of clairvoyance, intuition, all aspects of the extraordinary, grew finally too much. "I smell the incense," Jimmy said. But her letters to us were different: direct, warm, even practical. "How can I help?" and she too sent names of potential subscribers, donors, contributors, "check these names against Miller's lists; there may be duplicates." She was tender in her concern for our struggle to put out the magazine, and as our correspondence progressed, she found she loved us, dreamed of us.

On fête days we exchanged gifts, a copper candlestick, a string of amber beads. An embroidered sheet for the baby's crib. Borrowing handsome italic type, Jimmy printed letterheads on fine paper, a gift for Anaïs; Anaïs engaged Conrad Moricand to cast Jimmy's horoscope. Anaïs translated her gift to Jimmy from the French—ten pages of her perfectly formed script on her new stationery, faithfully conveying Moricand's findings. With only time and place of birth, he cast a chart of uncanny prescience, something to ponder, naming specific events and spiritual crises. Some past, some yet to come; astrology ceased for us to be entirely a joke for the gullible. Of Moricand himself, Anaïs wrote only that he was an incurable dandy, living the life of a beggar, who desperately needed her help.* Jimmy unwrapped the large package from the engravers: the score of a string

---

*In Miller's book *A Devil in Paradise* he gives an account of Moricand's visit to him in California in 1947. Moricand died penniless in Paris in 1954.

quartet by Frederick Hunt, a composer on the Maverick. Jimmy would print it all, almost twelve pages of musical notations incomprehensible to most readers, and an expensive symbol. I saw the engraver's bill. But Jimmy wanted music, the highest of the arts, to have a place in the *Phoenix*; I must admit when I saw the issue complete the score added an air to earth and water. Miller in Paris approved. "Music? Fine. I almost became a musician, you know."

There was a letter from Michael Fraenkel, now in New York City he told us. A Jew of Russian extraction, more nervously attuned to the sounds of war than his friends, he was the first of the staunch friends in Miller's Paris circle to return to the United States. Fraenkel was an essayist, the polemicist, the heavyweight in that group. He also had money, prudently invested. Taken with Miller's exuberance, with Miller's proclamations of himself as unregenerate outlaw, leaving wives and children in the tradition of the driven artist—Gauguin, Sherwood Anderson—Fraenkel had cautiously become Miller's patron. In Paris, in the Villa Seurat, a building Fraenkel owned, Miller lived rent-free; Miller, as European editor of *The Phoenix*, obligingly sponsored Fraenkel's philosophical essays. Now, Fraenkel wrote from the Hotel Albert in New York that he would like to see this little magazine get off the ground; he wanted to come to Woodstock and help. Oh, not the physical work, he was no good at that, but he offered his experience as a businessman, a pragmatic man. He was pleased with the first issue of *The Phoenix*, content as well as appearance. "I am sending copies to Jung, Keyserling, Brill, and others interested in my work, so you see the magazine will be going to important people in many countries. . . ." He was only waiting for his Greek wife Daphne to arrive in the United States; would we be good enough to scout a place near us in Woodstock they could rent for six months. His requirements sounded like luxury to us: at least one *real* bathroom; steam heat—he had lumbago and severe sinus problems; a good kitchen for Daphne—it didn't matter to him, he couldn't open a can of sardines; and an absolutely private study, a room apart. None of Hervey's houses would do. A stroke of luck: the Rondo Robinsons would be away for the winter, their house met Fraenkel's needs, and they agreed to lease it.

Fraenkel spent the winter of 1938 on the Maverick. A tiny man, about five feet tall, with paper-white skin, a badger-brush of silver and black hair, a little goatee, his gaze was keen and impersonally benign. Daphne attended her philosopher-husband devotedly; she was there before he beckoned, with dinner, a drink, an extra blanket for his bony frame when he napped. Healthy Daphne, pretty Daphne; housekeeper and nurse and audience; fetcher and carrier. Not exactly a friend for me, she was a comforting womanly presence, giving what attention she could spare Fraenkel to the baby Deirdre, concocting Greek treats in her well-equipped kitchen for all of us.

Fraenkel's mind, his intellectual adroitness, his analytic hair-splitting, was fascinating to me; he was cast off from Talmudic studies but remained somehow the Jewish scholar. His theme was Death—the Death of Western thought, the Death of bourgeois morality. Two of his books were printed in Belgium under Fraenkel's own imprimatur, distributed in Paris to avant-garde bookshops, sent for review to serious journals in England and the United States, but he remained obscure. While Miller could take Fraenkel's ideas, add bits of Dada, and the surreal, add scenes from his Brooklyn boyhood, sensations from the Paris streets, and toss them in the air, juggle, dance with them, and easily find readers to shock and please. Setting Miller's manuscripts in type was an acid test; I knew the entertaining, self-inflated nihilist would not need the pages of *The Phoenix* for long. Besides, Fraenkel, old Miller friend that he was, told us how Miller in the Villa Seurat laughed his head off at Jimmy's long letters from Woodstock. "He just doesn't understand you, Jim," said Fraenkel. Jimmy's letters to Miller, his European editor, were frequent and detailed; they recounted the woes and setbacks of the week: ". . . the electricity was turned off until we could find the money to pay the delinquent bill. Without power, I had to use the foot pedal on the press for each of the 750 impressions, and on the return, print the verso again 750 times. And that to achieve only one signature!" And after the printing, the endless collating, the folding, the sewing and binding. These were not complaints. Jimmy was merely sharing with Miller the problems of putting out a little magazine without funds; he really thought Miller wanted to know. Miller jollied him, man to man: "Don't work so hard, old cock." He'd like to help but he didn't have a bean.

"I need a laugh," wrote Durrell in Corfu to Miller in Paris. "Send me news of the body mystical, etc. in Woodstock. . . ." At the same time Lawrence Durrell wrote to Jimmy,

I wish I could express my admiration for the superhuman effort you have made on behalf of *The Phoenix*. It only goes to show that when a man has fire in his guts he cannot be pinned down by the world, however it tries. *Phoenix* is surely the most fertile effort in the direction of literature for some time now. I can see that you are the kind of man who does not need conventional good luck wishes. . . . If I am ever any good as a writer, or in a position to be of any service to you or your paper, I hereby assure you that you will not have to ask anything of me twice.

If I thought Fraenkel's duplicitous tattle would hurt Jimmy, I was wrong. Not at all. Any more than the reviews of the first issues of *The Phoenix* could discourage him. The more scathing the notices, the more excessive his response; he reprinted the reviews. He reviewed the reviews, with jeers and insults. Fraenkel applauded: "Good! If you had the approval of those desiccated academics you would know you were on the wrong track." Editorials written by Jimmy at night, when all activity ceased and the shop was quiet and he was alone, written in longhand, then typed, then set in the composing stick, letter by letter, grew, with each transfer, in hyperbole and out-rageousness. The messianic fervor that so embarrassed me attracted readers and writers, not only in the United States, but in Canada and England and Wales. We began to hear of other Arks building, to carry the adventurous to faraway places where land was cheap and the natives hospitable.

Fraenkel was promoting Mexico City. He had property there; he had useful contacts. "I don't see a colony, Jim. Just a few people." He didn't understand; it was not only writing and printing, sounding the death of the old world, celebrating the birth of the new; it was to make the new life actual, in self-sufficient communities, away from cities.

"I'm a city man myself, Jim," wrote Miller, telling us what we well knew. He wasn't ready to leave Europe yet, he didn't think things were critical. ". . . it always looks worse from the outside."

Anaïs didn't like to disappoint; it was with real regret that she wrote,

I don't believe in groups, Jimmy. Only two people can make a world together, and that only with deep creative force. It can only be an inner world we can create. . . . One has to keep on living in the outer world one hates. . . . Your horoscope reveals what I imagined, that in your dreams you live in a larger world—the myth—which alone can satisfy you. You will never be satisfied with the world no matter where you go.

In 1940, on her return from Europe, Anaïs came to Woodstock with her husband Hugh Guiler to stay with us for a few days. She wanted to meet her first American publisher, we wanted to meet the fabled Etre Étoilique. A great pleasure to look at, she moved like the dancer she was, a fluid supple line in a dress of purple wool. Or folded into our one armchair, she was still and attentive, composed in color and form, composed in spirit. Voicing in her Spanish-French-accented English her appreciation of the food I served, our family, the print shop, any bare comfort she could find to praise, she was as warm and loving as her letters. More real. Not a hint of incense. Hugo—Anaïs called him Hugo and he said we were also to call him Hugo—was the banker, an international banker. A tall lean Scotsman, gentle, handsome, he deferred to Anaïs, his adored one, his indulged one. No whim, no quirk, no passion or bizarre appetite would he deny her: Yes to a houseboat on the Seine, Yes to the Miller connection, to a fling with a woman, an English poet, a Peruvian Indian, Yes. But every now and then what started as a chuckle in the civilized Hugo would become a giggle and rise out of control. The banker was a paradox in another way he was too modest to mention. Hugo, Anaïs said, will be studying engraving with Stanley Hayter at the New School. Hugo had a definite talent; he will do the covers and illustrations for her books, she said; they will find a printer and publish privately. "My text and Hugo's decorations." Anaïs smiled into Hugo's eyes with intimate secret reference. The visit went well, no explosions, no denunciations, but Anaïs dismayed Jimmy by the quite definite way she answered, "No, Jimmy, I do not think we will get beyond war. I think there are waves, cycles, now a flowering, now a dark age."

The dark age was now, and now *The Phoenix* was militantly pacifist. Fraenkel and Daphne went on to live in Mexico, he conceded he could not influence *The Phoenix*, or the direction of the Press. Miller was dropped from the masthead, supplanted by Derek Savage, a poet and conscientious objector in England. Comradely connections were made with peace groups, notices posted in each issue, free printing offered. Although no one in the print shop was paid, neither workers nor contributors—and they were often the same—we barely made it from issue to issue. *Phoenix* work was put aside to do job printing: small editions of poetry, a book by a Woodstock herbalist, letterheads, billheads; Jimmy would tackle anything. The main thing was to get out the next issue, seize the attention of a benefactor with land to give away, and get the message to poets and artists who would join us on that land.

How did we live? We lived on loving friendships, and rousing fights and fervid correspondence: intensities. With none of the trappings of family life or domesticity, we were lovers who had a child, girding ourselves for pioneer adventure. Having no money for the superfluous, owning no encumbering possessions were badges of integrity, not hardship. A tank of gas for necessary errands in the old car, meals of basic sustenance punctuated by impromptu feasts: dry crusts and champagne.

So, in this dark age, it was a measure of Jimmy's power to persuade that I agreed to a second child, another companion on our desert island out there somewhere, a friend for our Deirdre growing among adults as an only child. I was almost asleep, but I woke when I heard Jimmy come in from his nightly ritual. A moment alone, out in the night; did he say the Lord's Prayer? "Are you awake?" he whispered. I turned to look at him. "If it is a boy, I invited the spirit of my father, or my brother Thomas. I would like us to name him Thomas . . ." It was so quiet, there was only the light of our bedside candle. His voice was low, filled with emotion past and present; he didn't touch me but I was held, he surrounded me, the stranger whose love was so entire that he chose me as the vessel for the solemn invocation. *You* invited? I repeated in silent outrage, what about *me*? At this moment he was not even aware of me as a separate person, I was a vessel, his vessel. Loved, yes, and adored, and why need a vessel give consent. I said nothing, I escaped into sleep, with Jimmy beside me mourning his dead, involving the new life I carried.

———

Michael was born on a blustery March afternoon in the Kingston Hospital. Named Michael for the Archangel, Defender in time of battle, Thomas was his middle name. As soon as my mother received the telegram from Jimmy, she packed a bag: "I must go to her . . ." "I don't care what you do," my father said, but before he went out the door he peeled off two big bills from the roll he always carried in his pocket, "Here. Give her this." She taxied to Grand Central, took the first train upstate, an iron monster breathing steam, wailing round the bend, each revolution of the wheels inexorable, reminding her that she was forty-five years old, her life was over, her marriage a torment, her children turned away. In Kingston, a city cold and strange, comfortless, she found a room at an inn near the hospital. Timing her visits to avoid Jimmy, civil if she encountered him, she resisted his careful overtures. For two days she came and sat by my bed; in a suit, and a brimmed hat she did not remove, she was formal and somber. There was a bleakness in her dark circled eyes she could not hide. She struggled; she managed to tell me she loved me, to tell me of her relief that I had come through, that the child was healthy, and comely. She must not cry: Will you be spawning baby after baby until you are spent? Your youth exhausted? Will you live in primitive places, far from me, where I can never see you? Never see the children?

But if she said nothing else it was her duty as a Jewish mother to raise the question of circumcision. She must talk about that, it must be done within a week of the baby's birth. "No, Mother. Jimmy feels very strongly. We will not do it." "It's routine now, Christians circumcise their boy babies, modern medicine approves, ask your doctor. For the baby's sake . . ." Trying every persuasion, she had failed again. She was not prepared to do battle on an issue so highly charged with emotion, tribalism, symbolism. Leave it, let my baby be; leave me out of it, Mother, Father, Jimmy. Released, unconfined, free to be myself again; the occupant for nine months was born, in the world now, waiting to be recognized. I had other things to think about. I can't wait to get out of the hospital. "Stay as long as you can, get a good rest," my anxious mother urged. I couldn't wait to get away from sanitary institutional kindness, back to Jimmy, my darling Deirdre, back to work in my real life.

———

Robert was in my real life. My androgynous friend. Jimmy and I both loved him but he was my pal, my constant companion. Hanging diapers on the clothesline, getting a meal for a crowd;

slipping into my place and continuing to set Kay Boyle's *Big Fiddle* when I stopped to nurse the baby, inviting the two-year-old Deirdre to a tea party when I needed a nap—he was there for me, dependably helpful, and dependably crazy. We were twenty-one, twenty-two years old, on the same wavelength, struck at the same time by the risible, the ridiculous. Dark, slim, his right eye off center did not detract from his beautiful faun look; it kept him surprising. Which Robert was looking at you, and was it you he was seeing.

He came to Woodstock, Robert Symmes he was then (he dropped Symmes for Duncan later), the adopted son of rich Californians. The allowance they made him, not munificent but adequate, saved him from jobs of drudgery or boredom or compromise. He was a poet, he knew he was a poet, and that would be the work of his life. He was never deflected. His poems were published in the early *Phoenix*, he stayed to work in the print shop, he learned to set type on his own poems. What greater incentive for excellence could a poet-typesetter have. For the last issue of the *Phoenix* to be printed in Woodstock, Robert set the type for his poem honoring the birth of our son. I quote the last lines because it is Robert at twenty-one, the world in 1940, and the poem is heartbreakingly foolish and brave.

A Song for Michael Cooney

Sing, because in the years before your birth no one
could sing. Dance, dance and make music
because in the years before your birth music was murdered.
You shall remember the death that we conquered
but pass none of it to your children, none of these things
we have known, our heritage of mechanical hell,
the years of killing and the diseases of steel,
the street of misery, the forbidden body
These things must be only as a myth to you,
so that you shall know that life springs at last
from the long ritual of such an age,
that peace shall survive.

Robert, at twenty-one, had the audacity to ask Hervey for the use of the Maverick Concert Hall on Sunday morning, before the chamber music recital. He wished to deliver a sermon. Not as a priest, minister, guru, but as a Shaman, in touch with the unseen world of gods, demons, and ancestral spirits. Hervey said yes. He couldn't resist audacity. Robert stood at the lectern, an Indian poncho over his clean shirt and jeans, and with perfect composure spoke to the assembled group.

This is a SERMON on the text: "Where there is veneration even a dog's tooth emits light." This is my first sermon here. It is the first time I have spoken to any group of people as I attempt to speak to you. It was suggested in a light spirit that some such meeting be held among us, and some among you are puzzled— you come here to laugh, to snicker, to continue to avoid contact. But what was said in jest passes into another meaning. And a time is made that I would have you keep for veneration. We are a community of people upon the Maverick. And we have times among us of buffoonery, we are silly, ridiculous—everything that human beings are, and then there are times when we are suddenly quite real, quite actual. When we are like tense points of electrical contact, cathode and anode to a stream of consciousness beyond us, when we are everything in the great sea of life. This afternoon, we will listen to Bartok, and such a time will come then for some of us, for he enters the heart of reality and his music runs the eternal movement of the spirit through us—the great sobbing of the cello at the heart, the many voices of that which is not said with words. And there are some things which we create, some prayers, which are not established through music, but through words. That is my art, and I have been practicing it here for several months now—and to whom among you have I brought what has been created? To whom have I opened the side wound and exhibited the machinery of the body revolving? I have avoided such pain, such a necessity, until now it can no longer be avoided. . . .

He stood up there, on the platform in the concert hall, speaking these words and many more with such quiet authority that none of the twenty or thirty people on the hard benches showed signs of restlessness or even smiled. Robert raised his hand gracefully for emphasis from time to time, his voice was inflected with care, not a trace of evangelical fervor; it was only the wild eye that escaped his control.

———

We sold the big press to Robert when we left Woodstock for Georgia. Robert, missing me in Woodstock, wrote to me, missing him in Saint Mary's: ". . . there are a million times when I've been startled again into realizing that you aren't just down the hill and I have to talk to myself . . . for all the momentous confidences and the crazy moods. I have become less efficient in my dreaming since you left. Everyone around the Maverick is only bored by the fact that I wander around with my mother in a caboose all night under threat of a shortage of water. . . ." Whenever Robert was in the city he saw Anaïs; she loved him, he was her monkey, her twin, she said, and she introduced him to her cousin Eduardo, to the temporary happiness of both. "Eduardo is a darling," wrote Robert to us, "he's a handsome Castilian knight with a grand childlike gentlemanly grace about him."

In a few years we would see that for ourselves when Eduardo came to live with us on our farm in New England.

Chapter Nine

Saint Mary's, Georgia, and the Loneliest Year

– 1940-1941 –

IT WAS ALMOST dark when we arrived in Saint Mary's, but there was a light within the General Store, a weathered frame building with a second-story balcony above the porch. The man leaning against a post came slowly down the steps. "Can you tell us how to get to Point Peter?" Jimmy asked. The man obliged, neither friendly nor hostile. He took in all he could, as he told us the way, without actually putting his head inside the car: the baby Michael in a laundry basket, our three-year-old Deirdre. He looked the car over, up and down: a long grey Packard roadster with New York plates. We started off, out of the village Main Street, only street, and down the road, following the man's directions. Jimmy found the turnoff, barely; we were on a sandy, deeply rutted track. Darkness fell; the road was so narrow, so densely wooded and winding, the car lights picked up only short distances ahead. I thought the forest opened reluctantly as we approached, closed behind us as we passed, and reached for us on both sides, brushing and scratching the flanks of the car. The children were asleep. I strained to see into the dark, we had passed the last habitation, a sorry shack, miles ago. As we wound and bumped our way through the night in our new country, I tried to deal with my phantoms. "It's an adventure," I encouraged myself, "we're almost there." Jimmy was concentrated, silent, maneuvering the vehicle loaded with our family and all our possessions. I knew he was aware of my faint heart. I knew he too must be daunted; he could say nothing of cheer, or comfort, something in his voice might betray him. He must keep his eyes fixed on the road, and by his firm grip on the wheel and his straight back give me an example of unwavering purpose. A lantern light ahead, the forest parted: there was a clearing. Hervey stepped out of the darkness to welcome us. At last, journey's end, we got out of the car, the sleepy babies blanket-wrapped; we gathered around the campfire. Hervey provided an old rug to set the children on, he passed around bowls of stew, and biscuits, and coffee. He looked wonderful to me in the flickering light: tall, lean, white-haired—a graceful old man.

I could see his log cabin off in the shadows. Clyde was in the shadows too. He came to the circle around the fire and mumbled a greeting, then he disappeared in the darkness to return with an armful of wood to replenish the fire. Clyde was a Woodstock native. Now in his thirties, small, sinewy, already gnarled somehow, he had been Hervey's loyal worker since he was a boy. He was driver, carpenter, companion on these winter trips to Hervey's Point Peter property. I took his hand. "I'm glad to be off the road, Clyde. Where's your cabin?" He was shy, he didn't meet my eyes. He smiled his crooked smile and nodded toward the river. "On the bank. Edge of the grove." Never a man to use an extra word.

"Come on up now and see the farmhouse. I want to show you what Clyde has accomplished." Hervey put the children in the car and picked up the lantern. "I'll walk up the lane; see, there it is. You follow." Jimmy and I had been waiting for Hervey's move. We left the comfort of the fire, waved goodnight to Clyde, and took our places in the front seat of the Packard. What a marvelous car: a wonderful rich playboy's car, with a golf club compartment, brown leather upholstery, and a twelve-cylinder engine that got about six miles to the gallon. Jimmy assured me it was in top condition, though vintage 1932, and a steal at seventy-five dollars. I knew nothing of its mechanical virtues; it was its appearance of extravagant folly that won me. In low gear we slowly, slowly followed Hervey's steadily moving lantern. We left the grove, we left the moss-hung trees, the mournful Spanish moss, and we were in an open field. We heard the river. Then Hervey stopped, there was our new home.

A real house, with a porch, and a gabled roof. Out of the car and in the door, all of us. Too dark to see anything, too tired to try. Hervey led us to a room with a small bed for Deirdre, Jimmy set up Michael's crib. We unpacked only what was necessary for the night and we put the children to bed. A partition divided their room from ours. Clyde had built a rough wooden frame for a bed and stuffed a mattress thick with moss; Hervey was proud of the result. "See how springy these boards are." He saw our exhaustion. "Good night. Sleep well. I'll see you in the morning. I expect you for breakfast. Count on us until you get settled."

We lay on our bed, I was near the wall, near the window, Jimmy on the outside. I was protected, the usual position for us in any bed. The moonlight streamed in. I began to sob, possessed by nameless loss. Jimmy consoled: I was tired. We had each other, we had our babies. In the morning it would be different, I would see. I would see how beautiful the place was, "Sleep, sleep. Go to sleep my darling." I subsided. Silence. Then the rustling, the scratching in the walls, the scurrying under the house: a nation of rats, with sharp teeth and blood in their eyes. "Listen!" whispered Jimmy. "No!" I turned my back to him. I covered my ears.

In the morning it *was* different. My panic, so overwhelming in the night, had dissolved in dreams, in sleep. When I woke, my arms were around Jimmy, our limbs tangled, he held my hand in his. I moved out of our bed before the sweet morning languor could seduce me, before Jimmy could sense my readiness. The house was more derelict than I imagined. The river ran deep and dark and swift, separated from the back door by only a narrow strip of neglected garden. There were no other dwellings beyond, the sandy track from Hervey's grove stopped at our house. Back down the lane, somewhere in its shadows, were his new log cabins. Twenty miles away was Saint Mary's, itself a dead-end fishing village.

Jimmy was busy unloading the Packard. Each time he came through the door he brought news of a fresh wonder. "The magnolia trees in the yard, magnificent!" "Did you see all the pecan trees? An endless supply—." "The fragrance—." "The birds—." "Marvelous," I said of the magnolia and the pecans and the exotic birds, and anything else so eagerly offered as a gift particularly for me. Deirdre, flushed with excitement, was at my heels. I ran out of answers to her questions and put her in charge of amusing her baby brother. I went out the door, to the well at the end of the porch. I fastened the bucket, lowered it, and, as I slowly pulled it up, I began to accept my new home. First, Deirdre must be taught that the riverbank was out of bounds. The house would have to be made habitable. It would mean dipping into the two hundred dollars we saved from our summer's work running the Maverick theatre concession in Woodstock.

We worked hard those first weeks at Point Peter. We bought a wood stove for cooking, and we bought white paint to obliterate the yellow-green walls. We put up shelves to store dishes, clothes, books; there were no bureaus or cupboards or closets. I decorated and shellacked the rough pine trestle table and benches Clyde had built for us. The kitchen was taking shape. It was large, light from the east window looking out on the river was glorious in the morning, the rising sun suffused the sky and glinted on the water. I spent hours of my day there, at the window, at the iron sink, scrubbing our clothes, bathing the children, cleaning fish, doing dishes. Dreaming. The bucket of water drawn from the well at the end of the porch was set on a board beside the sink, the sink's drain emptied under the house. In the kitchen also was our windup victrola, and a battery-operated radio. An oil lamp was the illumination, the wick trimmed by Jimmy, the chimney cleaned by me. And for color we put up unframed prints, flying the flags of our country: van Gogh, Bonnard, Redon, to confirm our taking possession.

Jimmy kept the basket, formerly Michael's bed, filled with wood—"Found" wood from the grove, the indispensable fat pine, pitch pine, hard Georgia pine for a quick hot fire; oak to hold a slow fire. Two doors opened out of our house. Through one I could go down three rickety steps to the overgrown garden and walk along the river bank, to see and feel the morning, to smell the narcissus, the orange blossoms, the swift water. There was no duty out that door, I could be out of reach for a moment. The other door led to the porch, the well, and the deserted road. I needed to use that door to fetch water. I went out that door to check on the children in the yard. Jimmy came in and out, sometimes Hervey. No one else. Between the kitchen and our bedrooms there was a central room, bare except for the printing press, a hand press, and a car seat against the wall. It was the only seat in the house with a back. There was a chamber pot for Deirdre; Michael was in diapers; we used the outhouse, a decent distance from the house in the day, a long walk with the lantern at night. It had three sides and a roof. One sat facing the river, a vista contemplative, or diverting. "Picturesque," said Hervey.

We shared the house with the rats. There was no barrier to their territory in the dark under the house, the house was raised on pilings. Each time we sealed their passages into our rooms, rat diligence found new openings. At night, when the stove was cold, we used the oven as a food safe; or we filled a bucket and lowered it into the well. It was surprisingly cold down there and it was a double triumph: the food was both refrigerated and safe from rats. Each morning we checked; a cry of disgust signaled defeat for our ingenuity. These were no ordinary rats.

Also in the house, to emerge when we painted the walls, were, to our horror, bedbugs. Bedbugs? Jimmy made positive identification of the blood-sucking insect he had experienced in his tenement flats on the Lower East Side. I could imagine his revulsion, "profound revulsion" he said. The young schoolteacher, escaped from his parents' sanitary suburb, to wake from sleep devoured by those devils and consumed by the primal command: kill! crush! Still, those tormented nights in no way spoiled his fascination for the life in the streets. He said he couldn't imagine a more wonderful, a more vivid place to live in New York City. Then. But now, what were bedbugs doing here, far from their proper feeding grounds, how had they survived in the abandoned house and what could we do about them? As soon as the children were put to nap I walked down to the grove, to Hervey's cabin. I was bursting with the dismaying news. Hervey set his book aside, and he gave me his serious attention. He admitted the "unpleasantness"; he offered a remedy: "a paste of egg white and bicarbonate and a dash of red pepper sometimes drives them away . . ." He was sympathetic, and so casual I was shamed by my alarm. I hoped he would not hear even a faint reproach: "Hervey you might have warned us." His generosity had no strings, and no guarantees.

Hervey was the first person I met when I joined Jimmy in Woodstock. I was eighteen then and we had just been married in New York's City Hall. I brought with me my books, my clothes, paints, and a few canvases. I left behind angry and grieving parents, and puzzled friends. I left my city and my middle-class life. I was in love, passionately, romantically, recklessly; everything was transformed. Hervey and the Maverick were part of my new world. In the early 1900s Hervey had separated from the recently formed artists' colony in the village of Woodstock. He bought a ninety-acre farm and called it the Maverick, to encourage the untamed. It reflected Hervey's vision of an artist's life as one of intentional poverty. Hervey's studios, called cottages or cabins if there were no skylights, were scattered through the woods, spaced for privacy, or its illusion. They were rough structures, really intended only for summer use. Such was their charm, so conducive was the Maverick to serious work, and careless play, there always remained a core of winter residents. They had family money, or borrowed money, or grant money; they bought wood stoves and axes and bucksaws and cut Hervey's wood. They weatherproofed their houses, bought chains for their tires, and made at least one trip to the city for good boots and a decent sheepskin coat.

Living in intentional poverty meant to us living without electricity, plumbing, or central heat; without telephones. It meant not having money in the bank, or a car that cost more than a hundred dollars. It was a life chosen, we felt privileged. We lived among kindred spirits. Hervey was a writer, a printer, a man of such civility that, without effort, in his company the bellicose subsided, the modest were encouraged. His friendships with both men and women were tender and faithful, but he was sexually aroused only by young men. On the hill, in the woods, Hervey had built the Maverick theater, rented each summer to struggling stock companies. Hervey had also built the Maverick concert hall, where every Sunday afternoon in the summer season there were chamber music concerts. The performers were stars in the concert world who lived on the Maverick, or were visiting. They played these concerts for Hervey, for the community, and for the great pleasure of making music in the rough simple building with remarkable acoustics, surrounded by the rustle of leaves and the sound of birds. There were tennis courts of capriciously maintained clay, where casual doubles or fierce single matches were played.

It all now seemed an impossible idyll. We could no longer live that way; nobody could. The world was being blown apart. Even in Woodstock, lines were drawn. A broadside against conscription that Jimmy had written and printed and passed around at a Woodstock fair had been ripped up and thrown in his face. He was marked in that community. The very way he walked and looked was a challenge: his blue eyes gleaming or hard or visionary attracted or disturbed, few were indifferent. We needed to take our children to a remote place, grow our food, build a haven for others, and support mutiny.

Hervey bought the Point Peter property when he went to Georgia with Clyde one winter. He returned the next year to put on a Passion Play in Saint Mary's, enlisting both negroes and whites for the cast. No one but Hervey could have so disarmed the citizens of backwoods Georgia. He came from the North and paid cash for his land. He was old, but he moved easily, like a young man. He wore shabby clothes that were not gentry but were not workingman's either. His cotton shirts were made for him by a Woodstock friend after a pattern for Russian peasants, Tolstoyan; they were usually faded to faint pink. Bleached blue denim pants and canvas shoes completed his costume. For gala occasions Hervey added a bright red cumberbund. His thick white hair, shaggy and covering his ears, and his trimmed short beard, were in the style of Edward Carpenter, or Thomas Carlyle: Hervey was rooted in the nineteenth century. It was not easy for people in Saint Mary's to know what to make of him. Coming out of the General Store/Post Office on his first day in town, Hervey stood on the porch, gazing up the one main street before going down the steps to his unprosperous looking pickup truck where Clyde sat waiting in the driver's seat. A man, yawning and scratching, looked back at his friends on the porch bench with a grin. He touched Hervey's sleeve. "Here, Gramp," he said. "Get yourself a haircut." And offered him a quarter. Hervey said "Thank you," pocketed the coin, and went on down to the waiting Clyde.

It must have been his mysterious assurance, his unthreatening quiet voice, his acceptance of things as he found them; whatever it was, both farmers and bankers, in New York and Georgia, trusted him. It was not surprising then, that he could convince his young friend, ripe for belief, to accept his offer of the farm on Point Peter. Our print shop in Woodstock would be blacklisted, Jimmy was sure of that. The small jobs, that barely bought paper and postage for the fugitive quarterly we printed and published, were already dwindling. Even money for groceries was tight. It was hopeless to think we could raise the down payment for a farm in New York State. The chain of persuasion began with Hervey to Jimmy, then from Jimmy to me. "Why don't you come to Georgia this fall, Jimmy? There was a farm on the Point; there could be again." Georgia? How could we

spend our lives in the Deep South? How could we deliberately move
to a country hostile to Jews and radicals, far from our friends. How
could we live with "Whites Only." "Not a stone," said Hervey.
"Level tillage. There's a good house." "Fish from the river at your
door; oranges in the yard," said Hervey. And he said, "Pecans, Plum
trees. Pomegranates." I think after Hervey said the magic words
"No winters," Jimmy was captive.

Then there was no withstanding his convert's zeal. Jimmy
brought a Jesuit's cunning to dispel my uneasiness. The Jesuit told
me not only of the narcissus and the flowering Judas, but of the
warm, open, helpful natives of unspoiled backwoods Point Peter. In
the great yea-saying, questions were dissolved before I could voice
them. Questions like: What will we do for Money? Schools? Doctors? People to talk to? Libraries? Music. Museums. And what about
Draft Boards in the South? How will they treat Conscientious
Objectors? I didn't ask the heretical questions. It wasn't easy. Worry
came more naturally to me. Anxiety, skepticism. But I was learning
to "consider the lilies," to live for the day.

Hervey was coming up the road. Not only did he carry a can of
milk, the first fresh milk the children would drink, but there was a
packet of mail in his hand. I was sure it was mail. I hurried out to the
yard, intent on getting the children in, and ready for lunch, so that I
could see the letters. I lifted Michael out of his wooden playpen and
carried him laughing and hugging; I called Deirdre to leave her sand
"porridge": "Let's see if Hervey brought any good mail . . ." Jimmy
was already sorting, the first fast scan for possible subscriptions. He
tossed a letter from my mother in my direction. "Two letters from
England . . ." "Mine!" I cried. "Mine," Deirdre echoed. Hervey had
long ago made himself independent of such distractions. He remembered though, he understood our hunger for links to the outside and
far away. Now he interrupted. "Take off their clothes, Blanche, and
look for ticks." "Ticks?" "Nasty little black insects. They carry
fevers." Jimmy and I avoided exchanging anxious looks. We stripped
Deirdre, grown solemn, carefully inspected her sweet rosy skin for
an invader. "Under the arms. Check the ears," Hervey urged. The
children were both clean. "What if we found one?" The treatment
sounded medieval. The tick head burrows under the skin, the body
protrudes. Apply heat; it will back out. "A match, or a burning
cigarette end will do the trick." Submit our babies' tender flesh so

close to searing heat? Monstrous insects. And so we did, Jimmy and I, alone or together, examine the children minutely after even a brief time outdoors. Every day, several times a day. Deirdre was the usual victim because she played in the sandy soil. "Watch for snakes," Hervey said. "Coiled in the shade under the house. Water moccasins. Some are venomous, some are not. You can't take a chance."

There were other disturbances. Deirdre and I walked in the woods, into the oak grove and "exploring" beyond. "Just like Hansel and Gretel," she told me. She sounded brave and frightened. I was older and taller and "Mother" but I could understand why she felt we were in a fairy tale. In this dark forest, the towering oaks and cypress formed so dense a ceiling of green that only a rare shaft of sunlight could penetrate. It was a celestial phenomenon, the finger of God, or a beam of light from His eye. The combination of the unknowable, and the ineffable, with the real menace of snake and vulture and scorpion, was daunting. "Let's look for a good place for our picnic," I held Deirdre's hand firmly. Then we heard a rustle ahead, Deirdre tightened her hold. A great crashing herd of boar and sow thundered through the underbrush. We stood very still. They were so near, I could see those brutally unfinished snouts, the tiny glinting eyes. Deirdre pressed close, hiding her face in my skirt, and I, willing myself calm, waited until the sound of the beast was distant. Wild swine had free range on the Point. We were fenced in. We turned back, Deirdre and I, out of the dark, moss-hung oak grove, through the open fields to our house. We had our pecan and raisin picnic on the porch. I added for consolation two carefully hoarded shortbread cookies.

Jimmy hung a swing for Deirdre on the magnolia tree. He marked off a garden piece. He built a shelter for our two hens, kindly birds that gave us two eggs a day. He fished, catfish and bass. We learned to use the good shrimp, sold cheaply for bait, in our meals, vying with each other in inventing new dishes to combine the shellfish with the rice and beans and canned tomatoes of our limited larder.

He sat at his desk in our room, at work on his second novel. Sometimes I would hear a burst of sustained typing. More often, silence; then he paced; he went out the back door and I could see him wandering along the river.

These lines were in his typewriter:

Turning back to his manuscript he resumed reading through the pages he had written. Before tonight they had seemed luminous and living to him, but now in his present downcast mood they appeared dull and stilted, cluttered with nonessential literary trivialities and a rhetorical wordiness that obscured his deepest feelings. He sighed inwardly and decided that the start he had made would never do.

As he struggled he became more withdrawn. The Georgia winter came upon us suddenly. One day it was cold. It was so cold in that house, colder for our balmy expectations, that we spent all our waking hours in the kitchen. It could be heated by the wood stove, and keeping the wood basket filled was welcome distraction for Jimmy. He brought his typewriter and papers to one end of the table. I entertained and fed and bathed the children. I washed our clothes, I washed our dishes. I turned the winding arm of the victrola, replaced Schubert with Mozart, then Chopin, then Haydn, then Schubert again; we kept their sounds around us. And I read. I read all my books, and Jimmy's: Lawrence, Joyce, Faulkner; Chekhov, Tolstoy, Turgenev, for the second time. I started on Hervey's: Willa Cather, Charles Kingsley, John Ruskin, William Morris, George Eliot. Herodotus. I read while stirring a sauce. I read while feeding Michael. I read in snatches; I read for hours, at night by the light of the oil lamp. I entered the worlds of these writers with special intensity; they were my dear companions in exile.

It was then, in that bare house, that I began to shape myself for a life without money, anchored in domesticity. I did not say "trapped." Dancing at the Savoy in Harlem, hanging around Village cafeterias, dressing up outrageously: all part of the past. If I could not see Cocteau's *Blood of a Poet* at the Little Carnegie, I could hear the exquisite song of the painted bunting. I could be arrested by the sight of the fair head of the baby boy, and the dark one of the little girl, bent over a chameleon in Jimmy's hand. I was in the "now" of essences. But oh how I hungered for the company of comrades. Serious, mad, funny; members of a secret society instantly recognizable. Jimmy was gone, entangled in a thicket of Celtic gloom. I could usually count on the children—he adored them—to pull him back to our center. But sometimes even that failed. I became a strategist. An innocent question: "Do you think Clyde could get the Packard battery charged in Saint Mary's?" masked my claustrophobic "How do we get out of here!" Or "Hervey said we could use his credit at the General Store. Do you think, this week . . . ?" covered the desperate state of our larder. Jimmy despised my transparent deviousness. "We'll see," was routine for my first try; if I persisted, the escalation was swift: "Get off my back!" Those were the burdens of the day. The nights were unchanged. We made love as intensely, we were transported as far, further. If, on our return, we silently, tenderly, told each other "sorry, sorry, sorry" for the bitter day past, I knew it would be the same in the morning.

Deirdre and I sat on the porch steps, I held her between my knees as I brushed her thick dark hair. We heard the sound of a motor, we watched a yellow van approach slowly. We both stood up, we asked each other, "Who could it be?" Then, "Deirdre, tell Jimmy. Someone is coming." The van came to a stop at the edge of the yard. They must be lost. "Can I help?" I asked. The driver called me "ma'am" and explained that he had heard the Point was a good place to hunt coon. He was just looking around before he came in at night. A woman and two little girls were in the front seat with him. He got out from behind the wheel, a slight man with sandy hair and an open country friendliness. "Would you like a cool drink? Bring your girls, your wife . . ." I tried to sound as though visitors were an everyday happening, and my offer a mere politeness. How could they know they were the ship sighted by the castaways, that they must disembark, and rescue us.

Jimmy and the coon hunter wandered toward the woods. The women and children were left behind. "Talk, talk to me," I silently urged the woman as I ushered her into the kitchen. "Tell me everything, from the minute you were born." I seated her at the table, covering my mad curiosity, my greed and hunger for human contact, with conventional questions. "Where do you live? How old are your little girls?" Feasting on the details of her meagerness, her freckled fair skin, her pale and guileless gaze. She was shy in her responses. I loved the sound of her soft Georgia accent, her odd archaic word. Her nondescript cotton dress, her scuffed low-heeled shoes: all indelibly catalogued, together with the way she combed her hair, and just what function the two barrettes served. If I had any excuse at all I would have put my arms around her to feel the yielding or rigid hang of her bones, to inhale her particular smell. I kept my fascinated investigation spinning as long as I could. I was reluctant to say goodbye, ever. Deirdre came out of her room, hand in hand with the little girls. She was radiantly, proudly proprietary: "Mommy, this is Bartha. And this is Thaelma." Bartha? Thaelma? Bertha and Thelma. I marveled at Deirdre's self-possession. She had no playmates except her baby brother, and that was so unequal it hardly counted. The men returned. The visitors climbed into their van. The event was over.

The sounds of dogs baying in the woods woke me that night. I could hear voices, the hunters urging their dogs. I slid out of bed and stood at the window; there was a lantern moving among the trees. Then another eerie call. I shivered, went back under the covers, moved against the sleeping Jimmy, and thought: this is seventeenth century, rural somewhere. More dramatically: this is primeval.

One of the fruits of my solitude was an intensified correspondence. I began to write of my loneliness to friends, casting off pride and risking disloyalty. It was hard to confirm their prophetic warnings before we left Woodstock, some discreet, others dire: "Hey, the rednecks will lynch you." I still dissembled in letters to my mother. If Woodstock was the "wilderness," a distressing habitat for her daughter and her grandchildren, then the move to Saint Mary's, the "jungle," was incomprehensible. So I sent her a weekly bulletin, a litany to lull her anxieties, of the blooming children, the industrious Jimmy, and the fertility and largesse of Point Peter's field and tree and river.

It was after the turn of the year into 1941 that I began to mark signs of deliverance. Answers to my letters came, bearing commiseration, sympathy, and suggestions chiefly outlandish. Jimmy—and this was the most telling sign—accepted my "breaking faith" in writing to our friends and he seriously considered their suggestions. We began a game: "What kind of house would you design if you could build anything you wanted," tacitly confessing to each other that we hated this house. We spent evenings making notes and sketches, pooling our very rudimentary knowledge of adobe brick or rammed earth, materials both free and organic. My fixed choice was a dwelling that haunted my imagination: built around a courtyard, with thick walls and arched doorways and long, shadowed galleries. There was an answering leap of memory and a welling sense of loss whenever I saw such a structure in a painting or a photograph.

One morning, the page in Jimmy's typewriter:

O! how he longed to flee from this desolate spot in Georgia. To get away! To be in the northern mountains again, or on the New England coast. In fields and forests where one could wander freely, without the coiled menace of poison-fanged snakes or swarms of blood-ravenous insects bearing fevers and sickness in their avid mouths. To get away! To escape from all the sinister shapes that writhed and flitted through the aura of nocturnal sorcery haunting this tropical region with its funereal forests and moss-shrouded trees where wild swine wandered and flocks of silently staring vultures perched, lurking like evil spirits incarnate. To find the way out again. To pass once and for all down that sandy road, leaving the derelict farmhouse with its mournful encircling grove of orange trees and the towering magnolia forever behind.

Early in the spring, Hervey began to break camp in preparation for his return to Woodstock. The night before departure Clyde and Hervey walked up to the farmhouse for a farewell meal with us. Hervey wore his red cummerbund; he presented us with a basket of perishable stores: onions and cornmeal, coffee and olive oil. We served our most successful shrimp and rice dish. Jimmy rolled about two dozen cigarettes; he put them in the Nürnberg Dürer House tin, on the table beside a bowl of wild flowers. We were sorry about wine. No wine had come our way in months. Clyde was his usual inscrutably silent self, but Hervey appreciated our festive effort. "Delicious," he pronounced the rice, fish, cornbread; he praised the strong black coffee as he smoked his rare cigarette. He asked about our garden's progress, and our expectations. He remarked the superior sweetness of the baby carrots in our dinner. "Did I ever tell you about Miss Little?" and he told us of the elderly maiden, a weaver and one of the early Woodstock colonists, whose gentility was shocked by the size of a carrot she pulled from her first garden. Hervey's tolerance for varieties of human expression, and his absence of malice were given a keen edge by his appetite for gossip and mockery. He was a famous storyteller. This night, his telling, and our listening, was a collaboration in pretense. Jimmy and Hervey and I knew the profound farewell we were making. We would not stay on Point Peter. We would not return to Woodstock. Hervey's resources in helping Jimmy were spent: the cottage on the Maverick, the press and printing equipment, the farm in Georgia. Father, friend, teacher. Confidant, benefactor. He was all of those. We did not know how, or where, but we were moving on.

In the morning we walked down to the grove with the children. Jimmy carried Michael; Deirdre trotted beside me. She was grave, this would be a major parting. She would miss her visits with Hervey. Clyde finished packing the truck. "Here, Jimmy," called Hervey from his cabin, "take these books." Jimmy put Michael in my arms and went to help. They came out together, in the doorway they stopped, Hervey kissed Jimmy on the mouth. They held each other close. Clyde was in the truck, behind the wheel, ready to go. He did not turn his head, but his eyes slid toward the scene in the doorway. I would never know what Clyde thought of his old friend's active pursuit of young men. Hervey hugged me, hugged the children; Deirdre wept. Then they were off, leaving the grove deserted, taking our last essential links.

"I never saw you kiss before. How do you feel about it?" I asked Jimmy later. His answer was long in coming, he looked off into space. "Unhappy." he said. "I wish I could respond. I can't." We never talked about it again.

Two months later we sold the stove, gave away the two hens, and loaded the Packard. We were going to Massachusetts to live in a tent offered by a sculptor friend. We raised money for the trip, gas, and lodging, by asking nine friends for five dollars each.

We stopped at the curb in front of my mother's apartment house in Manhattan. Jimmy turned off the motor and breathed his relief to be off the highway. Only then, still in the car and before I opened my door, did I reduce almost a year of dread and loneliness to "I never thought we would get out of there alive."

Betty in kimono, Catskills, NY, 1916

Betty, Joe, and Blanche
Rosenthal, NYC, 1920

Blanche and Deirdre, Maverick Concert, 1938, by Adrian Siegel

Jimmy with Chornya, Maverick Road, 1935

D.S. Savage, England, 1939

Hervey White, 1935, Konrad Kramer

Paul Rosenthal,
Woodstock, NY, 1936

Blanche Cooney, 1941

Michael Cooney on the hay rake, 1945, by Roger Coster

Jimmy in the tobacco field, 1945, by Roger Coster

Blanche Cooney, 1986, by Gabriel Cooney

Sunday in the kitchen after the vigil in Northampton, 1970, by Gabriel Cooney

Eliza Cooney and Deirdre Cooney Bonifaz, 1974, by Gabriel Cooney

Mary Randall Cooney and Michael Thomas Cooney at home in Plymouth, NH, 1976, by Gabriel Cooney

Isabel Harris Cooney and Gabriel Cooney, 1974, by Elizabeth Cooncy

Elizabeth Bzura Cooney, 1983, by Gabriel Cooney

Charles Sackrey digging potatoes in the farm garden, 1969, by Gabriel Cooney

Edwin Felien, 1969, by Gabriel Cooney

Jimmy Cooney at the kitchen table, 1981, by Gabriel Cooney

Chapter Ten

ASHFIELD, MASSACHUSETTS

- 1941-1943 -

IT WAS stretching it to call Randolph Johnston a friend. We had only met him for an hour or so when Hervey brought him to the print shop on the Maverick. A bearded man in his early forties, his dark hair streaked with gray, a burly man in good old country clothes. A sculptor, Hervey told us, who lived in Massachusetts, "a sterling fellow." He knew more than most visitors about printing presses and type fonts, I could tell by his questions, but he said nothing to suggest he had anything to teach us. Then and there he gave me his check for a year's subscription to *The Phoenix*; a dry, firm handshake, a warm smile, and off he went with the first two issues of the magazine. As soon as the sculptor and his artist wife finished reading *The Phoenix*, he wrote. He too was determined to find a way to escape the megamachine, "to live outside this materialist competitive society." He sent an essay he hoped Jimmy would publish, describing a bronze casting process lost since Cellini's time. It was too technical for *The Phoenix*, but he accepted both rejection and Jimmy's suggestions with good grace.

From then on he wrote frequently, in helpful camaraderie. "Do you know Pfeiffer's book on bio-dynamic farming? Sound techniques for growing without chemical fertilizers, with respect for the earth. . . ." He urged us to get Eric Gill's autobiography. If we couldn't, he'd send his copy. "An Englishmen," wrote Randolph, "an engraver, type designer, stone carver, and this is what he said: 'The work I have chiefly tried to do in my life is to make a cell of good living in the chaos of our world; to reintegrate bed and board, the small farm and the workshop, the home and the school, earth and heaven.'"

Randolph's letters followed us from Woodstock, New York, to Hervey's place on Point Peter in Georgia. In a gesture of imagination and faith, he sent six dollars for a three-year subscription to the now suspended *Phoenix*. A sterling fellow, as Hervey said. "For the first time, Margot and I can buy something we want, not something we need." From where we were, on Point Peter, without money, or the society of friends, the life he described in New England was enviable. They lived with their children in an eighteenth-century house that had water, electricity, and a furnace, with a barn he and Margot used as a studio. Only three acres, but enough to keep a cow. Teaching on the art faculties of Smith College, and the Rhode Island School of Design, giving classes at prep schools in the area, finding the odd private commission for memorial or portrait sculpture, he was gaining a small reputation, and a measure of security.

When we were casting about in Georgia for a way out, our next move, Randolph earnestly gave thought to each possibility. Not advice—he wouldn't presume—but his own view.

Mexico?

. . . for me Mexico would be no solution. One would go there, occupy the land that ought to belong to Indians, and be regarded by these Indians as interlopers. Then too, the Mexicans, white or red, have an entirely justified aversion to "Gringos," an aversion that might easily be fanned to hatred any time Mr. Hearst or the oil companies feel like pushing us into another imperialist war. I do not think it possible to live without neighbors, and I like to live with mine on terms of reasonable equality and cooperation, which I think would be extremely difficult if one formed a small island of white culture in a solid area of red.

Maine?

No, I don't know of any farms in Maine, or on the coast. I should envy you, being near the sea. I lived many years near the water, built and sailed small boats, and had a very good life altogether. It is the one thing I miss here. But most of the coast that I have seen is fairly low. I know that if I lived there after having lived among mountains I should miss them intolerably and be extremely unhappy, because I should be at the same time too poor, and too busy earning a living to be able to keep sailboats or have any fun in them. Besides, it is the tendency of rich idlers to crowd into all the desirable coastal areas, buying up the old farms and fishing wharves and forcing prices up far beyond the means of ordinary folks. These little towns and harbours then lose their integrity and become mere resorts, as bad or worse than art colonies. Another point is the poor soil in nearly all the farms. Agriculture is quite limited. I have not, however, explored northern Maine. It is quite possible that some good coast farms might be available. I thought that for me it would be out of the question because of its remoteness from the sources of supply for my work, and for potential markets, and for my lecturing. My work is so bulky, requiring the purchase of materials in ton lots, and the shipping to exhibitions of heavy crates, that it seemed impractical to go too far away.

I could not say anything to Jimmy as he leaned in one direction—California?—then another—Canada?—persuading me, persuading himself, but far away in the valley surrounded by the Berkshire hills coming into spring, Randolph Johnston must have heard me. When his next letter came I felt I had willed it. And a door swung open. "If you would like to come to New England," he wrote, "you might stay here while you look around. . . ." He offered the use of their tent, two beds; we were welcome to share their kitchen garden. It was April; we might even find a farm in time to put in a garden of our own.

Instantly Jimmy forgot Mexico and Maine, California and Canada; New England was our destination. Our destined nation.

———

South Deerfield was a market town for tobacco growers working the fertile river bottom land of Hatfield and Sunderland and Whately. Without really knowing it, in the isolation and loneliness of backwoods Georgia, this very conformation of mountain and valley and river was what I longed for. Rising from the valley, winding into the hills, there was, around every bend, a barn of just the right red and just the right shape, and a white dwelling with dark green shutters so perfectly rooted for at least a hundred years in that particular setting,

I wanted it to always have been mine. I might as soon covet Monticello.

Randolph was going to show us a place he had heard we could buy for four hundred dollars. Twelve acres, spring water, a house that probably needed work. Randolph drove his station wagon as far as he could on a road that dwindled to impassable. From that point, he carried the baby Michael, and I followed, bravely stepping from slippery stone to slippery stone across the stream fresh with foaming spring runoff. Jimmy was right behind me, carrying Deirdre. The one-room house we reached was a tumbledown wreck, the twelve acres mostly woods. Patches once cultivated were now gone to burdock and nettle. Bordering the state highway between Conway and Ashfield, it did not even have essential privacy. Randolph ruefully admitted the four hundred dollar place was impossible.

———

The Johnstons did every thoughtful thing for our tenure in the tent: they provided a two-burner oil stove, a chest of drawers whose top was a dressing table for the baby Michael; lanterns, extra blankets for the cold nights. We were to feel free to use their house for baths, for laundry. Margot and Randolph must have believed that good fortune loses its goodness unless it is shared, because at no time were we made to feel that our living in the tent behind their house was less than a treat for them, an expansion of their lives. But it was a tent; it leaked. The stove outside under a flap of canvas was cranky. The baby ran high teething fevers. It was churlish to even think it, but some days I would look at their colonial red house, so solid a shelter . . . surely there must be a room we could use. We were invited to occasional meals at their table, a trestle table, the top a polished plank of cherry wood, the ends two tire rims painted flat black and mounted on a wood base. It was, like most of the Johnston's furniture, designed for endurance and function and made right here in their studio. The food on their table, brought out of the orderly kitchen by Margot on earthenware fired in their kiln, was nourishing, moral, frugal, and even tasted good.

Each morning Jimmy said, "Wish me luck," kissed the babies, and left the lane beside the tent in our high-powered Packard roadster to find work, any kind of day labor, and to search for our farm. We had five hundred dollars from Jimmy's mother; she wished it could be more. We must keep that money intact for the down payment, and we must find a place before planting season was past. Randolph said, "Check the tax collectors in the hill towns, Jimmy . . . they usually know when property might move." A good idea.

The next day, after cleaning cabins at Ashfield Lake, Jimmy stopped at the Town Hall. He caught the tax collector on one of the two days a week he attended to town business. About to lock up, Clifford Howes wasn't sure why he agreed to return to his office. An outsider, this strong, muscular young man, but he didn't speak across a distance like the summer people. Clifford Howes was taken with his direct way. And so the tax collector opened his books. "There is a farm, a working farm, that might suit you—about three miles from the center."

"Can I see it?"

"Now?"

"If you will. . . ."

He was certainly in a hurry.

Clifford Howes sat beside Jimmy on the leather seat of our improbable Packard and directed him, "Down the Main Street to the end. Turn left on 112, then right on Bug Hill."

Bug Hill?

"Springfield paper mill owners bought a lot of acreage, around 1905, three or four farms. Summer places for their families." It was called "Big Bug Hill," in awe and derision. All but this one farm had now been sold by their heirs and the name had dwindled to Bug Hill.

———

Margot knelt by her flower beds; I sat beside her with our baby, she uncovered survivors of her fall bulb planting, she mourned casualties of the winter. "Mole, squirrel . . . some varmint," but never mind, here were the pale stars of daffodils, white clusters of narcissus, and the heavenly fragrance in the air above them. Margot snapped a stem of daffodil and tickling the baby's nose said, "Smell that, sweet Michael." I heard our car.

Jimmy wheeled into the driveway, slowed down. Stopped. He let the motor idle, then turned off the key, gathered some papers from the seat beside him. Something portentous about these deliberate movements; what was it? Out from behind the wheel, carrying his papers, he came around the car. "I found our place," he said quietly.

It would be wrong to shout his discovery—this was a serious turning point—but he had to smile; he just couldn't help it. He had to find my eyes and smile, promising—well, I would see. Our ship was in the harbor and he had just booked passage for the new country.

There was no time to lose, before the light left the sky I must see the farm. Randolph said he would like to come along. I ran up to the tent for our sweaters; Margot said we must have something to eat. Gathered at the Johnston's table for cheese and wheatmeal biscuits and elderberry juice, Jimmy, too excited to eat or even sit, reported: "The main house is a 1771 Cape." Main house? "There's another little house. I didn't see the inside. The main house has a center chimney, three fireplaces. The big one in the kitchen has a Dutch oven." Is the house liveable? I remembered the four-hundred-dollar wreck. "Very liveable; it's always been a farmhouse. Definitely a poor, working farmer's house . . ." He glanced at his notes, "Water . . . a never-failing spring, piped into the kitchen . . ." Electricity? "No, but the tax collector says he expects there will be a line run up that road before long." "How much land?" asked Randolph. "Seventy-five acres." We were all impressed. "It lays to the west, woodland and pasture; we can catch the last light of the setting sun . . ." Outbuildings? Oh yes, hay barn, dairy barn. Sound stone foundations. Sheds. Chicken house.

It didn't matter whose question Jimmy answered, or who he looked at, it was to me, to me, he gave the news. The others didn't know that descriptions, condition of this or that, were irrelevant. He could see the future, the ultimate form the farm would take. Other dwellings built, creatures in pasture, children on the lawn, gardens for beauty and sustenance. A print shop. A studio. A string quartet practicing by an open window. Still, I raised the question, "How much is it?" And Randolph, more experienced, "What is the asking price?" "Fourteen hundred dollars." Jimmy said the tax collector was sure Miss Phoebe Crane, heir of the Big Bugs, would accept a down payment of four hundred dollars and give us a thousand-dollar mortgage. Randolph said he was himself against mortgages, their place was free and clear, but it did sound a fair price for that amount of acreage and all those buildings.

In Randolph's station wagon we drove the fifteen miles of winding road up to Ashfield. When we turned onto a narrow dirt road we passed a pair of gateposts guarding a long drive to a distant imposing structure. The Big Bugs' main place, Jimmy said. Through a stretch of woods to a great open sweep to the west, and the barns, the house, came into view. Only then, before we came to a stop in the farmyard, did Jimmy mention the problem. A family lived in the house, that was the problem, tenant farmers for the Big Bugs for years. They didn't seem to be prepared for Miss Phoebe Crane to sell the farm, not now, not yet.

The front door was not the one to knock on; Jimmy led us around the house, through the shed, to the kitchen door. It was opened before we could knock, by the farmer, Fred Warren. "Yes," he said, we could see the house. "Yes," we could see the cellar. "Yes," they had finished their supper. Ay-yah. I would learn the different meanings of the New England "Ay-yah." Small, white-haired, pale eyes behind wire-rimmed glasses, a bushy mustache that muffled his bare replies; he was deferential and dim. He bobbed his head when Jimmy introduced me, and our friend, and our children. The woman at the sink slowly wiped her hands on the towel on the roller and only then did she turn. Daisy. Her sparse gray hair pulled back and up from her pale lined face, she surveyed us with a blank stare.

Fred pointed to the door leading "down cellar." Randolph had a flashlight and penknife; he checked the floor joists for termite damage, pronounced them sound. We followed him, watching our heads, stooping around the low-ceilinged dirt cellar, Randolph pointed to the ancient masonry of the chimney foundation. Cabbages stored for the winter hung head-down by their stems from the beams; seen in the fitful light of Randolph's torch, in the damp, earthy, mouldy smelling place, they looked like so many decapitated trophies.

"What's this?" Jimmy asked Randolph, startled. A gravestone, propped against the stone foundation, in a corner, barely visible. Randolph trained his flashlight on the stone, Jimmy read the inscribed words: "Ezekiel Miles d. 7 Feb. 1802." "Is he buried here? In the cellar?" "That's what the old settlers did when the earth was too frozen to dig a grave in the burying ground," Randolph said soberly. "The cellar below the frost line was the only place." A shiver of history, it added character to the house.

———

Miss Phoebe Crane agreed: four hundred dollars down and she would hold the mortgage. We met in her lawyer's office in Springfield. A maiden lady, glad to be relieved of the farm, she smiled amiably at our children, at us, whose current address was a tent. Sam Blassberg, a lawyer friend of the Johnstons, having searched the title to be sure it was clear, represented us at the closing for a compassionately small fee. A thousand-dollar-mortgage was an impressive debt, but we had no reverence for solvency; this was not just a real estate transaction. Soon there would be others who would join us; we would not be property owners but custodians of the land.

Miss Phoebe Crane's lawyer said we could take possession immediately. Not a thought for the tenant farmers, faithful all those years. So really poor they had no car, no truck, no tractor. All the farming done with horses, and one of the horses hitched to a buggy took them to the village once a week. An old couple, where could they go? Daisy's mute hostility was probably fear; Fred's subservience hid his bewilderment. Lock, stock, and barrel, all uprooted. It must be Fred's choked dread of the future that made him so inarticulate. We could not evict them. When we said we would like them to stay on, Fred didn't say much. He was so accustomed to bowing and bobbing and scraping to the Big Bugs, he and Daisy agreed to our proposal. We had not a stick of furniture, not a scrap of equipment, no stock; looking like tinkers, living in a tent, but we were the owners. "If you would clear one room for us now," Jimmy said, "and when you are ready, no rush, you could have the little house. And the barns, of course, you will continue using the barns . . ." And, it went without saying, the pastures and hayfields. In exchange, two quarts of milk a day and two dozen eggs a week, if Fred thought that was fair. Fred accepted the arrangement: "Ay-yah." He shuffled, kept his eyes lowered; he said, "Mrs. Brown won't like it." Who is Mrs. Brown and what won't she like? Fred looked unhappy. He mumbled, "Mrs. Brown's house is across the road."

Across the road and just in sight was the one house, our only immediate neighbor. Mrs. Maude Brown, the widow of a Shelburne Falls banker, did not actually live there. She drove up with a companion most fine afternoons, "to paint pictures," Fred said. They never stayed overnight. Due back from winter in the south, Mrs. Brown had not yet opened her house on Bug Hill. We looked in the windows that day; in the rooms with the forlorn air of a house unoccupied we spotted an engraving of Mozart. Mrs. Brown was a painter who loved Mozart. Promising. But what won't she "like?" Fred wouldn't say.

So began our life on the farm, in unlikely intimacy with Fred and Daisy Warren, who might easily have been the models for Grant Wood's *American Gothic*. At five each morning we woke to the crackling sounds of a fire being started in the kitchen range, stove lids lifted; smells of beef and potatoes frying in lard. Hardly a word spoken. Behind our closed door in the parlor, the room in the front of the house that has been cleared for us, we stir. We hold each other, reluctant to leave our one refuge of privacy under the covers of our bed. How long since we had a room of our own, the freedom of each other. The curbs sharpen desire. When Jimmy whispers "Don't blow out the candle yet . . . I want to look at you," it's all the prelude I need.

Jimmy went out to the barn as early as he could to help Fred with chores, to learn by watching. If Jimmy said, "Can I try milking?" who was Fred to refuse the owner, any owner. Jimmy's readiness to learn, his special courtesy for the less fortunate, and his natural ease around animals soon disarmed Fred.

There was no disarming Daisy, stony-faced, barely civil. I gave her wide berth. I kept out of her kitchen, I kept out of her pantry. It would be her kitchen while the bleak and homely pressed-oak chairs stood around the table covered with white oilcloth, while the feed store calendar was the only decoration on the wall. It would be her pantry while it reeked of sour milk. Milk set in pans, cream rising until it formed a thick yellow wrinkled skin: the first step in butter-making. After a week it was ripe and I watched Daisy lift the skin with the skimmer, her practiced hand holding the shallow perforated shell of tin between thumb and forefinger, and slip the cream into the churn. The Warrens didn't notice that their butter was terrible to smell or taste.

Daisy stood in the doorway of our room, watching me paint our second-hand wooden bed. I painted the body of the bed white, the simple carving of vine and flower on the headboard in primary colors. She stood there in silence, arms folded. When I finished she sniffed, in her nasal voice disgust and contempt mingled, "If I could do work like that you wouldn't catch me living way out here on a farm." She eyed our bags, our books piled in the corner, our laundry hanging on a wooden rack, our children. Not a word to or about our darlings from Daisy. "What's that good for?" She pointed to our new possession, our mill. "We're going to grind our own wheat and rye flour, Daisy . . ." I was not sure myself. The mill stood in our crowded room: about two feet high, a hopper at the top, a drawer at the bottom, and a big wheel at the side for the grinding. It was cast-iron, painted red, with gold and black scrolled borders, fire-engine style. The dealer in the junkyard where Jimmy made the lucky find said it had been used to grind coffee in an old general store. Randolph was sure it could be adapted for wheat and rye and soy. Well worth the two dollars. Daisy made no comment, I could see she was thinking "foolishness, all foolishness." White store-bought bread was the treat.

Country woman's pride had seeped away, petered out; in these descendants of crofters and yeomen there was hardly a trace of the pluck and determination that had settled New England. Driven up into the poorer farms in the hills they were, Randolph told us, by the Bloodless Revolution. By default, the fertile bottomland had been taken over by the Polish immigrants who came as hired hands and worked long hours in the tobacco and onion fields. Not only the men; the children and women, grandmothers and grandfathers were out in all weather, planting and cultivating and harvesting; living frugally on cabbage soup and black bread. They worked the farms in towns the early settlers named for memories of England: Sunderland, Hatfield, Northampton, Amherst. The Polish farmworkers saved and did without and gradually bought out their Yankee employers.

———

When will the Warrens leave? Weeks went by and there was no sign of movement out of our house to the little house. Weeks of waking to their alien sounds and smells, weeks of my practicing kitchen diplomacy under the critical scrutiny of the pursed-lipped Daisy. "We must say something, Jimmy." "Yes," he agreed. He had said "No rush," but it was time.

"When," I asked Daisy, and I knew I sounded too tentative, "when do you think . . . when are you planning to move out to the other house?" "It's too dirty," a flat statement. And I clean it; I borrow a broom and a mop and in one energetic afternoon sweep it to an approximation of clean. Jimmy helps Fred move. In a few days they are out. We claim our place, build a great fire in the kitchen fireplace, even in the Dutch oven; we celebrate.

Jimmy plants our first garden; in our dependable junkyard we find a kitchen range, useful pots; a churn, a breadmixer. Our own barn yields a hutch table, very old but usable; a chest of drawers. We're ready to summon our friends who are waiting impatiently to see the farm. To see us, to see the children and how they've grown. We can't wait to amaze them with the beauty of the hills, the ancient character of the house; to spook them with a trip to the cellar and Ezekiel Miles' tombstone. It's true the house is bare, clapboards unpainted, a little sad without a single flowering bush or tree to frame it; what could one expect, unloved and neglected as it had been. We would change that.

There is a telephone on the wall in the kitchen, our first phone; a brown box, black mouthpiece and receiver, and a handle to crank to signal the operator at the switchboard. An eight-party line. When it rings for us, one long and two short, it doesn't take us long to recognize by the giveaway clicks on the line that "listening in" was an accepted entertainment and information channel for the neighborhood. Jimmy picks up the receiver and says pleasantly, "Good evening, everyone," before speaking to our caller.

Early in May Mrs. Brown and her companion drove past our house, two gray-haired women with hats, sitting erect, looking straight ahead. The immaculate Buick turned into the driveway of the only house we could see. Fred and Daisy crossed the road to Mrs. Brown's house, after a while Fred and Daisy returned. Every afternoon that week Mrs. Brown and her companion drove up, every evening they drove away. Curious about our only neighbor, we hoped she would be curious about us. Surely Mrs. Brown would stop, introduce herself, welcome us to the hilltop; tell us how glad she was for the infusion of life; children so beautiful, plans for community so courageous. She would invite us to tea. We would ask to see her paintings.

After a week of her coming and going she made no move in our direction or acknowledged us in any way; maybe country protocol required the newcomer to call. So late one afternoon, near the time Mrs. Brown usually took her departure, Jimmy carrying Michael and I holding Deirdre's hand, walked down the road to Mrs.

Brown's house. Up the driveway, past the shiny Buick, three steps to the veranda and we were at the door: hair brushed, hands clean, and ready to smile. Jimmy lifted the brass knocker, the door opened at once, just wide enough for us to see the cold eyes of the companion.

"We're Mrs. Brown's new neighbors. I'm Jimmy Cooney; this is my wife . . ."

Before Jimmy could say my name, the woman said distinctly, "Mrs. Brown does not want to see you," and shut the door firmly in our face.

We stood there for a moment, looking at each other, as if we had been struck. We turned and walked slowly back across the road. What's wrong? We found Fred in the barn, starting chores. This time he could see we would not let him burrow in the safety of his shrug and averted eyes. He could see we were upset.

"What's wrong with Mrs. Brown? She didn't even come to the door!"

"Tell us, please tell us, Fred."

Fred looked at our feet. Reluctantly he said, "She had a mind t'buy the farm . . . She was in Florida when you folks . . ." Nobody told us, not Clifford Howes the tax collector, nor Miss Phoebe Crane the heir. ". . . going t'have me farm it for her. Stay on . . ."

All very strange. She owned the place she didn't live in, and she wanted this farm as well. We could expect no welcome from her, and that was too bad; but after all she wasn't there all the time, we could avoid her, ignore her. It was disagreeable, but, like Ezekiel Miles' tombstone in the cellar, she would just be a shadow, a tale to tell.

———

Everyone wanted to see the farm. They came hitchhiking, or by bus, hardly anyone had a car; stayed for a day, or a week. "Stay as long as you can . . . Sure, bring your friend, your lover." If the bed in the attic was occupied we could always find a corner for a sleeping bag; we could always find another place at the table. Always someone to pick up an axe and a two-man bucksaw and go off to the woods with Jimmy; and, sitting around the fire that night, while we talked until all hours, of the war, strategies of resistance, the draft, feel the elemental thrill of being warmed by the very wood you chopped. There was always someone to turn the S-rod in the breadmixer when the dough got stiff and my arm got tired, to help paint a room, pick berries, play with the children. Help in the garden. One literal friend took forever to weed a row of beets because in her reverence for life she carefully transplanted each weed. At milking time there were trips to the barn. Breathing deeply of ammonia and manure smells from some atavistic notion that these deep breaths were strengthening, invigorating, our city friends asked Fred incomprehensibly ignorant questions. Fred was getting used to these tours.

Robert found a straw hat, an English boater, in the barn, and a stick; he pranced, soft-shoe danced, pulled me in beside him and sang in a mean, sweet growl: "Gonna *come* to *get* you in a *taxi*, honey—" when Fred came in the door with the evening milk. One look at Robert, at me, and he looked away, embarrassed, as though he'd seen something indecent. Even after he was out the door Fred could hear Jimmy's laughter as he clapped the beat of the "Darktown Strutters Ball." Robert was leaving in the morning after a week of reunion, party every night. He made up for mistaking corn shoots for weeds, decimating six hills before he was discovered helping in the garden, by baking delicious pies and revealing to me the secret of foolproof, unbeatable, pie crust. Back in July, he promised he would be back for a month, and with Eduardo. He'd check our "bookings."

The comings and goings, the picnics in the grass, the fierce croquet matches. No plumbing, no electricity—who cared? In the poor farmhouse what mattered were the fireplaces, the wide floorboards, the handmade hinges and latches on the doors, the small-paned windows. In the house beside us, the inscrutable, inbred, up-country Yankee Warrens; in the cellar the gravestone of Ezekiel Miles; across the road, hostile Mrs. Maude Brown; all interesting instant legend adding spice to the bucolic.

———

A hot, dry summer, our first summer in New England, and by mid-August the stream from the spring into the barrel in the kitchen slowed to a trickle, then stopped. The never-failing spring had failed. Temporary, Fred says. "'I will come back." Meanwhile he stolidly carts forty-quart milk cans across the road to Mrs. Brown's dug well that never goes dry. It takes a lot of pumping to fill those big milk cans to water his cows and calves and horses; Jimmy picks up our two buckets and crosses the road to help Fred. "Do you think

Mrs. Brown would mind if we got our water here?" Fred shrugged, "Dunno." Not reassuring. We couldn't imagine that Mrs. Brown would deny us water, a natural element, an essential need, but we wouldn't risk testing her; Jimmy fetched water only after Mrs. Brown and her companion left in the afternoon. How to make one bucket of water serve many needs: first people and cooking, then reused ingeniously for floors and garden, not a drop wasted. It was a challenge, a game.

The drought was in its second week. Mrs. Brown and her companion had driven off. Dusk gathered, cows ambled out to pasture, the sound of their bells growing distant; the sun setting behind the forest that bordered the great flat expanse of meadow added an effulgent glow to the pastoral. "Like a Dutch painting," said Frances, "let's move up here, Lenny." She was only half-joking. We had just finished our first meal with Leonard and Frances, so happy that our separation was over, since Woodstock, and all through the long year in Georgia. We all agreed we had never tasted such sweet corn; grown in our first garden in New England, ten minutes from picking to husking to the boiling water in the pot. "What kind of person eats corn on the cob round and round, like a spool? And what kind of person goes across and back like a typewriter? Anal? Oral? Or greedy?" That's Leonard, I think he's in analysis. He raises his coffee cup, he's quit drinking, and offers a toast to the quick return of our spring, Jimmy's signal to pick up a bucket, take our Deirdre's hand, and cross the road through the tall summer grass to Mrs. Brown's pump.

A car rounded the bend at exceptional speed. We all heard it and ran to the window in time to see it turn into the driveway across the road. Mrs. Brown! She was out of her car, arm outstretched, holding a revolver aimed at Jimmy, calling "Get off my property!" Jimmy dropped the bucket, picked up our little girl, cried "You fool! Can't you see I have a child here—" and rushed back through the field and across the road.

We had seen it all from the window; Leonard kept saying "Jesus Christ." Jimmy was so agitated, I had never seen him so agitated. I held Deirdre: "It's all right; it's all right." Frances kept watch, reported "She's not leaving. They're sitting on the porch. Now there's a light in the house . . ."

"I'm going to call the State Police," Jimmy said. "She's dangerous."

"This is an emergency, operator," said Jimmy, and she gave him the closest State Police barracks, Shelburne Falls. "A woman with a gun threatened me and my little girl—yes, she's still here—across the road." Jimmy replaced the receiver. "They're sending an officer." He moved to the window. "She's still on the porch."

We sat around the table, lit by the oil lamp, anxious and excited, speculating on madness, the irrational, on misanthropy. I put the children to bed, quietly, quietly. The patrol car arrived. The state trooper came in and sat down and heard Jimmy's account, and our witness. He took notes, he took us seriously. He closed his notebook. "I'll talk to her," he said. We watched as he backed the cruiser out, drove down the road, parked in Mrs. Brown's driveway. All very slowly. Leaving his headlights on, he walked up to the porch where Mrs. Brown and her companion sat waiting, his arms extended to show he was not carrying a gun.

It wasn't long before he was back. He sat with us again, not formal exactly, but professionally skeptical. He looked at his notes: "She says she didn't have a gun. She pointed her umbrella at you." Jimmy was indignant. "An umbrella? In a drought? I think I know the difference between a revolver and an umbrella." I didn't expect her to admit it.

"It's really a civil case, you know," the state trooper said. "Neighbors' dispute over water. It's her land; she can order you off."

Ownership of land and water; boundaries and authority. We had signed into that world; we had called the cops.

"She's irrational; I think she's dangerous," Jimmy persisted.

"I wouldn't worry about her," said the trooper. "When her husband was alive he was a nuisance, always calling the barracks because some kid broke an ornament on the Christmas tree in front of his bank. In Shelburne Falls. Get your water somewhere else while the drought lasts. Keep off her property." He closed his book, "I don't think she'll bother you again."

We thanked him, he left; he meant to reassure us, but I thought: he's no protection against real evil, so ruddy and country and upstanding he couldn't even imagine it.

I was having trouble myself believing in the menacing Mrs.

Brown. We were not in vigilante or vendetta country, but here in New England where Randolph Johnston assured us he found neighborliness and civility everywhere. It was different for Jimmy. I knew there was something here that excited him. Raised the odds. Added drama. That night Mrs. Brown and her companion did not leave. They remained in the house across the road for a whole week, guarding the pump. During that week I imagined her training binoculars on us, following our work in the garden, recognizing our industry, finding our children irresistible. Hearing the music from our windup victrola, didn't she love Mozart? relenting, regretting, yielding: she would grant us water from her well.

One morning we woke to the triumphant sound of a full stream of water gushing into the barrel beside the sink. The drought was over. Mrs. Brown and her companion ended their vigil and returned to her house in Shelburne Falls.

The return of water was welcomed with such a revel of washing and laving and bathing; windows shone, floors were scrubbed; backed-up laundry flew on the clothesline The garden had suffered, but we carried watering cans to revive wilting tomato plants and pepper plants. No celebration from Fred and Daisy. He plodded on with his chores. Being relieved of filling the forty-quart milk cans for his stock seemed to make little difference. Droughts happened, he weathered them, they would happen again. "Isn't it wonderful, Daisy? The spring is back." "Ay-yah," she allowed. No smile.

———

In our mail was a legal envelope.

Jimmy tore it open, his face changed, "I don't believe it!" He read: "My client, Mrs. Maude L. Brown, has bought the mortgage on the property in your name located on Bug Hill Road in Ashfield, Massachusetts, said mortgage formerly held by Miss Phoebe Crane . . ."

"What! Jimmy, you're making it up!"

"You think so? Listen: 'From September 1, 1941, all payments are to be directed to Mrs. Maude L. Brown. Yours truly, etc."

Stunned disbelief. Mrs. Brown was brandishing a different kind of gun.

"Call the lawyer; call Blassberg . . . ."

Jimmy telephoned Blassberg. "Can this be done?"

"Yes, Jim. Perfectly legal."

"Our mortgage sold? Without informing us?"

"Yes," Blassberg repeated, "perfectly legal. Done all the time. It's a nicety to tell the mortgagee, but not required."

We called Randolph; he and Margot were appalled; they wished they had a thousand dollars free. We can't call Jimmy's mother, she's helped already. I certainly would not ask my father. How about John and Marion, they have independent means; we call Woodstock. "Listen," and we tell them, "Dracula is our landlord! How would you feel?" "Oh you Cooneys are so dramatic," they say affectionately. "She can't do anything . . . Just make your payments." I called Frances and Leonard in New York; Leonard had a job on *The New Yorker* now but he said regretfully, "We haven't got it sweetie, but don't worry, we'll be up soon and put a hex on the old bitch." Jimmy wrote Hervey—no telephones for Hervey— ". . . this woman, so filled with malice . . . we don't know her; she has not met us," and he reminded Hervey of the progression: from the slammed door to the threatening revolver, and now this, buying our mortgage. We needed Hervey's balanced view. "There are spiteful people," he wrote, "it's too bad you have one for your neighbor. You must make your payments *ahead* of the due date, and send them registered mail, return receipt requested. Keep records." Hervey would be coming soon, he said, for a weekend, with Joseph Pollet. He wanted to look at us, and our farm, before he went south to Point Peter for the winter. Only in his last line did he betray a note of worry, "Jimmy, I'm glad you have the man, Fred, on the place. Artists are not much as farmers; he should be a real help."

————

Hervey and Joe Pollet arrived one evening just as I took the bread out of the oven, four fragrant loaves. Perfect timing; Hervey could see how far I was from the city girl he had first met in Woodstock, it seemed years ago. He approved everything on our real farm: the old but sound house, the ample barns; what he could see of the woods on his walks. He listened to Jimmy's plan to sell cordwood, his only caution, "Try to work with a partner, Jimmy. Safer not to be alone, working in the woods." Hervey made a point of having a few words with Fred in the barn. Hervey could count on his early years as a farm boy in Kansas for the right language, but questions about feeding and breeding and raising dairy stock, coming from this old man in a foreign-looking kind of blouse, an old man as odd as the rest of our visitors, only served to bewilder Fred.

One thing Hervey did not approve. "Joe, let's take down that henhouse before we go . . ." Hervey wanted to leave a mark of his visit. We walked around the long, narrow, falling-down structure. A derelict. "An eyesore," said Hervey, "not safe for the children to wander around." Joe Pollet agreed. Jimmy and I agreed. It *was* an eyesore; we hadn't thought of the children's safety. So down it came in one afternoon of persistent whacking and chopping and tearing, triumphantly destroyed in a cloud of dust and rotted wood and old chicken shit and rat shit. "Nothing worth the salvage," said Hervey as he threw the window sash on the pile of debris left to cart away. An improvement, we all thought. Fred stopped on his way to the barn and looked at the remains. "Isn't it good to have the chicken house gone, Fred?" Ay-yah, he agreed without much enthusiasm. Fred had a neat coop for his hens in the barn. Daisy was indifferent, "Twarent bothering me none."

I have a portrait of Hervey with the baby Michael in his arms. Hervey is about to depart after this three-day visit. The tidy debris of the henhouse is evidence of his everlasting wish to help, some way, any way, in Jimmy's life. In the photograph that hangs, framed and matted, over the green velvet couch, Hervey is lean, tan, fit; the old Pan, looking thoroughly happy, his eyes alight, smiling into the camera on the late summer afternoon. The baby is looking off, serious, probably looking at me, his hand on Hervey's. It is the hands I find so beautiful; my eye always goes to that detail in the photograph. The baby hand, plump and smooth and new to the world, resting on the firm, brown, long-fingered, almond-nailed, well-kept hands of the old artist-worker, our old friend whom we would never after that day see in this life.

———

Money. Oh, Money. Talking about it. Thinking, worrying, scheming. No matter how frugally we lived, nor how ingenious the substitutes we devised, there were still the inexorable mortgage payments each month. Randolph found customers in the college community for our firewood; Jimmy swapped labor with a nearby farmer for the use of his truck to deliver it. Our friends found discreet ways to leave a five- or ten-dollar bill when we refused contributions for their visits. I couldn't see an end, ever, to the scramble, and I was suddenly flooded with intransigent rebellion. Far from freeing ourselves of the trappings of the bourgeois-meaningless-world-of-things, we were mired in the Thingness of finding money.

Anaïs knew a book dealer who had a mysterious market for erotica; the dealer would pay one dollar for every acceptable page. Anaïs was the go-between, the liaison; she wanted to help us, her neediest friends. She wrote erotica for the dealer, Robert tried, Eduardo couldn't, Miller did it briefly, Jimmy was good at it.* He spent hours at night typing away by the light of the oil lamp. Not to have the money to sit around some Paris café on the Left Bank drinking absinthe, but to buy a heifer calf, a hay rake, to make those mortgage payments to Mrs. Brown ahead of time, registered mail. That winter he even earned enough money to fix the leaking roof. During one spell of freezing and thawing we had six buckets in the attic catching the steady plunk-plunk-plunk of brownish drip.

In the spring Jimmy started to repair the roof. Randolph told him how to do it; not for the first time did I think how lucky we were to have Randolph as a guide, a man who knew so many useful country skills. Jimmy was up on the roof with a bundle of shingles early each morning, hammering away. I could never work up there; I didn't even like standing on a chair. Jimmy wasn't easy on heights either, but he would never admit it. When he came down for lunch he would report on the world from the rooftop, naming a bird in flight, a tree in bud. "I saw a wild azalea just coming into flower, swamp pink they call it. I bet we could transplant it to the doorway on the south side." It took him a week to do the shingling; on the last day he came down with a different kind of report from his lookout on the roof.

"Something funny just happened. A strange car stopped at the Warrens' door, two men got out . . ." I saw the car; I wondered too. "The Warrens stood in the doorway; the men stood on the doorstep," Jimmy said. They wore suits and vests and carried briefcases. They pointed west, they pointed north, and after about ten minutes they left. "It couldn't have anything to do with the Warrens' leaving, could it?" I asked. Jimmy didn't see how it could.

Fred and Daisy were moving to a tenant farm in Buckland, not far

---

*Anaïs saved hers. Her *Delta of Venus*, published posthumously, is a souvenir of this time.

away. "You'll be needing your barn afore long," Fred said. We felt only relief. At last the little house would be free, for the refugee writer from Karlsruhe, for the pacifist couple from Chicago, for the nucleus. We could begin.

It was not long after the congregation on the doorstep of the little house that the letter came. Another legal envelope. What could it be now? All mortgage payments had been made on time, ahead of time, and all receipts had been returned, signed. We saved every bit of paper.

"It's a foreclosure notice!"

Eduardo and I were waiting for Jimmy to say more.

"A threat?" asked Eduardo.

"No!" Jimmy was choking with outrage. "We have ten days to vacate the property."

Jimmy phoned Sam Blassberg. "Sam, this just came in the mail," and Jimmy read the letter. Silence from Sam, then, "Jim, you and Blanche had better come to my office." Eduardo would go with us. he must. And of course the children, who went with us everywhere. We made ourselves presentable for Greenfield, a mill town and conventional; Jimmy resisted; he *wanted* to look like a farmer pulled away from his chores.

We sat in front of Sam Blassberg's desk while he read the foreclosure notice. He made no comment; he read it again. He didn't look at us. He picked up his phone. "I'm calling Mrs. Brown's lawyer." He spoke a few words in opaque legalese, hung up, and said, "You're too late. The farm has been sold to Mrs. Brown." Sam looked solemn, and sad.

Why? Why? How?

"Wanton strip and waste of property is the reason given . . ."

The henhouse! And we told him about Hervey's visit, the three of us talking at once. "If you could only have seen it!" "Sam, I just spent a week on our roof replacing shingles . . ." "Sam, we've done nothing but improve . . ."

"Don't you see the local paper?"

"No."

"Notice of foreclosure sale must be posted in the County newspaper three times running, and then the sale must be conducted on the property."

"It wasn't!"

Yes. Now we remembered the gathering on the front step of the little house. The Warrens knew. Everyone in Ashfield knew. They must have thought we were crazy, fixing that roof.

"How can we fight this?"

Sam thought. "There is an instrument to halt eviction proceedings in a foreclosure. It's called a Bill in Equity. Gives us time. Stops everything until there can be a hearing."

A reprieve, a leap of hope.

"Tell us about the hearing, Sam."

"It's not before a judge. And there is no jury. It's not a trial. It's a hearing before a Master in Chancery, in a special room in the Superior Court. Charles Stoddard is the Master . . . very fair," said Sam, "a good man."

As soon as we got back to the farm Eduardo sent a telegram to Senator Henry Cabot Lodge: "Grave miscarriage of justice in Massachusetts . . ." It sounded excessive but Eduardo must send it: Jimmy had convinced him that it was our pacifism that made us Mrs. Brown's target. ". . . letter follows." Eduardo really believed his friendship with the Lodges could count, that the mighty senator would turn his attention to the foreclosure in Ashfield. Sam Blassberg said we must prove the henhouse valueless, that was the pivot of our case, we must keep that focus. Anything else was extraneous. Jimmy wanted to make a speech to the Master of Chancery, to describe the background for the foreclosure: the door slammed, the gun leveled, the mortgage bought. Sam wouldn't let him, and Jimmy reluctantly deferred to strategy.

———

In the Superior Court in Greenfield the Master in Chancery presides, facing a room divided. On the one side, we the foreclosed, with our lawyer and our witnesses; on the other, Mrs. Brown, her son in Navy uniform—the uniform is ideological witness—and her lawyer.

Sam Blassberg called Randolph Johnston to the stand. I had never seen him in his college-teaching, patron-persuading suit, with his beard and hair so kempt and trim. He was the very picture of authoritative witness. He set a bulky bundle on a table and took his seat.

"Will you tell the court your occupation, Mr. Johnston."

Clearly, and modestly, Randolph listed professor, architect, engineer, sculptor.

"What can you tell us," now Sam addressed him as Professor Johnston, "about the henhouse on the Cooney property in Ashfield?"

"I checked the buildings on the farm before my friends Blanche and Jimmy purchased it. The old chicken house was the one useless structure, simply waiting to be removed." Randolph stood, said, "With your permission," addressing the Master, unwrapped the large bundle and revealed a rotted timber he had retrieved from the pile of debris that was the henhouse. He pointed out its hopelessly deteriorated condition; he dug his penknife into its spongy rot and a shower of sawdust descended. Mrs. Brown's lawyer had no questions.

Equally impressive was the Yankee Clifford Howes, a town official, obviously not partisan.

"Will you tell us, Mr. Howes, what is the tax liability on the chicken house in question?"

"It has not been taxed for thirty years," he briefly, dryly, reported. "It has no value. Been taken off the books."

Sam didn't want to take the chance of giving Jimmy a forum so he called me to the stand. He asked me to attest to "all mortgage payments tendered and accepted and up to date," and I said yes, I kept all records.

Then Mrs. Brown's lawyer advanced toward me; in a badgering tone he demanded, "Did you notify Mrs. Brown of your intention to remove the farm building?"

A simple "No" implied guilt, or at least my failure to be a responsible mortgagee. "There was no reason to . . ."

"Answer the question please. Yes or no."

I regarded Mrs. Brown's lawyer with wonder, he was so perfectly typecast for hectoring the witness: portly, beady-eyed, pugnacious jaw. When he made his concluding remarks to Charles Stoddard, the Master in Chancery, he lowered his voice. Letting a note of infinite repugnance be heard, he said, "There are elements in this case I would rather not mention . . ." but a few words escaped: "Disloyalty." "Communist." "Impeding the war effort." Mrs. Brown sat even straighter; the braid on Mrs. Brown's son's naval uniform gleamed brighter.

Jimmy was bursting, his derisive laugh cut short by Sam Blassberg's warning look. Sam stuck to the facts: Mrs. Brown had not established "wanton strip and waste."

The hearing was over.

Before the Master in Chancery handed down his judgment, Jimmy and I decided we would find another place. No longer did we think of it as our farm; it was blighted, blasted. No one had planted a flowering bush, there was not a trace of herb or bloom. No woman of perennial hope had come out in the spring to dig in her garden and ease her heart. Ezekiel Miles was in the cellar, and the terrible Mrs. Brown was across the road.

The representation by the attorney Blassberg, the witness of our friend Randolph, and the good citizen tax collector Howes had brought us justice in the hearing in Chancery. We won.

But our business with Mrs. Brown was unfinished, I agreed with Jimmy. She had gone to such lengths to drive us out, we had to know why. What was the *point*?

———

So it was not perversity that prompted us to call Mrs. Brown but some indistinct longing for dramatic consolation. Let us offer her the farm, if she wanted it so badly. I sat very still, trying to imagine Mrs. Brown in her home in Shelburne Falls; Jimmy turned the handle on the telephone box, gave the operator Mrs. Brown's number, and waited. Would she be surprised, would she hang up? The exchange was civil and brief: Yes, she would like to talk about it. Would we come to her home the next day.

In the Victorian house we were ushered into her parlor by a woman servant; it was a dark afternoon, the room was shaded by the porch, the porch was shaded by a great elm tree on the lawn. Mrs. Brown received us in the dim gloom, asked us to be seated on a dark velvet sofa while she took a chair opposite. There was a corner cabinet with bits of Sèvres china, inlaid chair-side tables, and the smell of lemon oil pervaded. A tray was brought in by the servant through a doorway hung with beaded curtains. Mrs. Brown served tea. Lace around her throat, cool and spare and precise in her movements, she spoke to us in a low, cultivated voice. For the first time I looked into her eyes; they were black and fathomless, I fell into them, I pulled away.

In the years since her husband's death, Mrs. Brown told us, she had been trying to get in touch with him. She had reason to believe that the hilltop in Ashfield was conducive to sending and receiving messages. Interfering currents, she was not more specific, have made that impossible, and so, No, she no longer had any interest in owning our farm. Bound for occult reunion with Mr. Brown, whose spirit was reluctant to be made manifest, the widow had no personal animus toward us. We just got in the way.

Chapter Eleven

A Real Farm, West Whately

- 1943 -

Mrs. Brown, wielding her gun, brought my father back into my life. It piqued his interest, carried a whiff of lawlessness and mayhem, good guys and bad guys. Our struggle with Mrs. Brown brought him out of New York City to Bug Hill Road in Ashfield, Massachusetts; he drove his big Cadillac into the farmyard for his first neutral encounter with Jimmy. He paced back and forth in his city haberdashery, glanced in the barns; careful of his shoes he walked the edge of the pasture; he came into the kitchen, accepted a glass of cool spring water, and looked critically around the house. He saw enough to make his quick and firm assessment: a poor place, it had always been a poor place, it had never prospered and never would.

"Sell it," he said. "I'll give you $3,000. Get a farm you can make a living on."

He might think he was impressing me now with his largess and superior judgement, his all-around man-of-the-world view of our deplorable condition, but I knew he wanted something. Something had changed. It was not that he ceased to despise my choice of a primitive life; not only could he not fathom such a choice, but it was an insult, it made nothing of his hard scramble from immigrant poverty to American success. Yet he was trying, I could see, to still the wolf, the ruthless trader, and show us another face: He's not such a bastard; he has come forward to do this considerable thing. Although in the six years since my marriage to Jimmy I had been too proud to beg, and my father too proud to unbend, our bond was there, the mystery of blood and seed. Something had dissolved his cold disgust; he wanted, he needed, our connection.

Surprising Jimmy helped him. The Russian bull and the Irish bull, both capable of roaring, spoke in soft and civil tones. My father, in one stroke, could move us from the marginal Ashfield farm and instantly erase years of struggle, naturally Jimmy would be grateful for that. Joe—Jimmy called him Joe—offered Jimmy an Upmann cigar from his Dunhill case. Jimmy, who disliked cigars, accepted; before my father could flick his silver cigarette lighter Jimmy struck a wooden kitchen match. He held it for my father, they lit up, they drew and puffed. My father saw now not the lay-about-Bohemian-bum I had thrown my life away for but the strong, hard-working, fearless Jimmy who adored his children and loved me forever. That's what I thought. I thought also how reconciliation of outraged father and outcast daughter, stone of hostility displaced by balm of benevolence, dramatically pleased Jimmy. But apart from that, Jimmy and my father met in an incommunicable realm: in a field of tribal bullishness an understanding took place between the providers and protectors of women and children.

After two hours my father was ready to leave; he couldn't wait to leave. Jimmy and I thanked him for his visit, and his offer; Jimmy assured my father that with the $3,000 from him, and the proceeds of the sale of this Ashfield farm, we should be able to make a down payment on a really substantial place.

"We'll let you know as soon as we find the farm, Joe, I hope you'll come . . ."

My father cut him short. "I want the deed in Blanche's name." He tempered that peremptory order with "in case anything happens to you she'll be protected."

"Sure." Jimmy said he understood. He understood too that no mention of community, subsistence farm, reverence-for-the-land agrarian philosophy would be prudent.

Michael traced the line of chrome on the Cadillac's hood. Deirdre held Jimmy's hand, ready for the farewell. As he was about to open his car door, my father's eye lit on the children. He was awkward, clumsy, wary with children. But these children were set apart, his grandchildren; he was not sure what was expected. Jingling coins in his pocket, he drew out a handful.

"Here," he urged, "the biggest for the boy, and the shiniest for the girl." Michael and Deirdre, puzzled by this overture, looked at us. I called him their grandfather, I said "Go on. Choose one."

When my father put his arms around me and kissed me goodbye, it might appear to be his seal of relief, hostilities at an end, but there was something more. There was something more. I learned the sober, unhappy, real reason for my father's visit when my mother telephoned that night.

"Tell me," she said, her voice tense, "how was he?" She didn't wait for my answer. "Did he give you anything?"

"Yes." I told her he made the generous offer. "He was—friendly." Silence. Did she hear me?

Then she said, her voice flat, "Daddy's moving to California. He wants a divorce."

After all these years, twenty-five years, a divorce? "Why?"

"He wants to marry his . . ." she faltered, "his mistress."

"Oh Mother," I couldn't speak. Then I said, "Why? Why marriage?"

"He says he deserves his happiness," now she could not keep the bitterness out.

So that's what he was doing. Retiring from business, he only forty-eight years old, to a sybaritic life of perpetual holiday with his Christian blonde wife (cocktail lounge hostess? barmaid?), he was tidying his affairs, discharging his responsibility, closing accounts.

"He's giving me little enough, but he has a duty to you. Take it, whatever you can get. She"—the unnameable she—"can't have it all."

Because my mother must be silent about the crushing end of her womanly life, she talked about money. Money was the only tie that remained to pull him to attention, to attach him to her, to their children. She was soiled, shamed, reduced; the romantic girl he married was a hard woman now, determined he would not "get off scot-free."

———

Eduardo returned from the city in time for dinner. The children were asleep. The three of us, Jimmy, Eduardo, and I, sat up late, through the steeple clock's midnight striking and beyond, talking about my father's visit, and my mother's call. "Guilt," said Eduardo of my father's gift. "Remorse," said Jimmy. "I think Eduardo's right," I said. "It is guilt. He's not capable of remorse." Whatever the prompting, guilt or remorse, my father left a high charge in the air of the old Ashfield farmstead. We couldn't wait to get started, to comb the hill towns for our new place. Jimmy and Eduardo listed essential requirements: pasture, tillage, barns, a good house, accessible road, and privacy; a view. A setting both wild and cultivated. But really only the sky was the limit. "School," I said, "near a school bus," to show I was paying attention, but I couldn't stop thinking of my mother. What will she do? How will she bear it. Divorce is rare. It must be the first in her family, in my father's family, or among their friends for that matter. A subtle disgrace: the woman can't hold her man, the man can't curb his desire. No one talks about it in front of children.

When at last we turned down the oil lamp and blew out the diminished flame and went to bed, I said to Jimmy, "It's too late for her." Jimmy was almost asleep. "She could marry again . . ." He drifted off. Never. She would never marry again. She never opened herself to another man. She's a one-man woman, like the Blues songs. All her phrases, her cries through my childhood, sound in the night. She kept hoping for revelation: One day "the scales would fall from his eyes, he would recognize the pure loving heart he had so bruised, always beside him, through thick and thin, hard times and good times." He would say "What a fool I've been!" and, turning from his dissolute life, see her at last.

Before Eduardo and Jimmy went off in the morning to follow real estate leads, Jimmy stopped to write a note to my mother. Just a line, "Dear Betty, I hope you will come and stay with us, Love, Jimmy." Jimmy is all sympathy; forgotten, her early hostility when we married and she said "Blanche is dead" or "My daughter committed suicide"; forgotten her uneasiness and suspicion of him now "Do you go to Church on Sunday?" she asks when we are alone. She is my mother, his children's grandmother. He wants to help her, he thinks he can. He can't imagine how lost she would be in the country, how exiled she would feel; he doesn't know what a city woman she is.

———

Guarding against disappointment, braced for catastrophe, ready for bliss: my balancing act in life with Jimmy. Driving over Nash Hill from Williamsburg I was in the back seat with Eduardo and Deirdre and Michael. Jimmy sat in front with the driver, Silas Snow—A perfect name for a Yankee farmer who produces maple syrup, keeps a few cows, and sells real estate part-time. Nash Hill is a gravel road, narrow, wooded, and dark; we didn't meet another car. Out of the forest suddenly, over an iron bridge, and we were in a clearing, a changed landscape. On that fine late summer day in 1943, a great expanse of almost cloudless blue sky arched over green fields rising out of the hollow: a curtain going up, an eye opening wide. I was all attention.

"We're in West Whately," said Silas Snow, "a little hamlet, a crossroads. Five roads meet here." And we climb the one that goes up the steep hill that leads to the farm Silas has taken us to see. The cluster of houses, four or five modest eighteenth- and nineteenth-century structures, thins out; the dirt road goes up, up, a series of thank-you-marms. Silas Snow names them, "rests for the horses pulling carriages or wagons," the respite for teams, cut into the old roads: up a grade, level out, rest, "thank-you-marm," and then up again. At the top we appear to have reached another hamlet, there are so many buildings; dominant is a large Georgian Colonial with a tower on top, facing the long view to the east.

"The house needs paint," Silas says, "it's too bad, this was a show place" conjuring a lost time, "a famous farm. Gone downhill since Victor Bardwell's widow died . . ."

Downhill was lucky for us; we could never have touched it in its heyday. Silas would like, he tells us, to see this farm flourish again. He doesn't so much want to make a sale as effect a rescue. Uniquely private, this two-hundred-acre tract is the end of the road; the road goes on through the woods, becomes impassable; discontinued by the town of Whately it has reverted to the farm. There is a barway across the road that goes on up out of the farmyard to make that clear. To the east the fields stretched, dropped to a ravine, rose to a forest on densely covered hills. Beyond was the valley, and the Connecticut River, the University of Massachusetts, the Hadley church steeple—"On a clear day you can tell the time on the clock in the Hadley church steeple"—and in the far distance the blue range of mountains.

There are so many buildings. In the farmyard alone, the hay barn and the dairy barn; a separate milk house, garage, horse stalls, blacksmith shop. Jimmy and I and Eduardo and the children follow

Silas Snow through the barway, up the road, past the ice house, past tobacco barns: how many? each as long as a railroad train it seemed to me. Silas does not condescend to the novices he shepherds, he is straightforward, low-keyed. When he says "They grew fine onion crops in this upper field" and "Tobacco was always high quality," he is believable.

"Let's go up as far as the pond," says Silas, "it's a spring-fed pond, big enough to paddle a canoe," perfect for swimming, useful for cutting ice in winter. Skating.

I keep glancing back at the house down the road, the Georgian Colonial in the farmyard. I don't want to be overwhelmed; it can't be as big as it looks. When we finally get to tour the house it *is* as big as it looks. Seventeen rooms, grand for a farmhouse, with its classic proportions and crown of a cupola. Impressive for a farmhouse off the beaten track, with electricity, central heating, steam radiators in every room, hot and cold running water plumbed to the kitchen downstairs and the bathroom upstairs.

Far from being overwhelmed, Jimmy was excited. He forced himself to ask sensible farmer-like questions of Silas Snow, but I knew this was it: at the end of a dirt road, miles from the main arteries, a principality, our own country.

"This is the place we've been looking for, Silas," said Jimmy. No games, no bargaining.

Silas Snow, the rugged, white-haired man with a clear direct gaze, matched Jimmy's honesty and said, "I believe you are the people who are right for this farm," giving us his confidence in a way that had nothing to do with a real estate transaction.

Silas Snow drove us back to Williamsburg where we had left our car. The Snows' Colonial brick house was elegant, not in detail but in atmosphere. It was Silas Snow's wife, for one thing. Frances Clary Snow was a tall, spare woman with fine bones; composed yet shy, her speculative glance could kindle to surprising warmth. She was literate, cultivated; her family had links to the Concord Transcendentalists.

"I always thought," she said to me, "the Victor Bardwell farm a most felicitous place."

"I don't know what I will do with such a big house."

Mrs. Snow asked me to consider paying guests. "It would be your cash crop," a small contribution to the daunting prospect before us.

I thought about it. "How do you do 'Guests,' Mrs. Snow?" Is there a policy? A protocol?

"I have only one rule, Blanche," she replied serenely, "the guest is always right. I am flexible—breakfast in bed, pack a picnic for lunch." Breakfast in bed? We didn't even own a tray. "Still," she added, "it is not always easy to know if it has been a success. Last summer, for instance, Wystan Auden and Chester Kallman spent a month with us. Auden had been visiting professor at Smith for a semester, and he had grown fond of the area. I thought their stay with us went very well, we all became friends. Auden sent me his last book of poems and there was a line: 'the summer / was worse than we expected,'" and she smiled her baffled amusement.

———

The weaver's madness—it is an addiction, I admit that. A thread appears, almost invisible, the merest hint; it is about to slip away. I retrieve the thread, grasp it, follow it, pull it toward me; combine it with another, change its color and strength and tension. A disproportionate delight. One more coup for synchronicity. I don't care that friends consider me a little obsessive in this regard. They indulge me; after all, am I not in all other ways balanced, reasonable? "Oh Blanche and her connections," they will say, but they listen as I spin a recent or long-ago story. I watch for the wandering attention, the eyelids' involuntary closing, my story too convoluted to follow. I raise my voice, or use a shocking word to bring them back to me. I think of Aunt Magda and how relentless she was when she had an audience; I must be like her. I search for other reasons for my peculiar appetite: my life was so isolated, so confined, I didn't even drive a car for the first seventeen years of my life in rural countryside. It relieved my isolation if I could surprise a link between a stranger in my present with a person or place from the past. In the natural flow, in the casual revelations between strangers, antennae raised, I explore. Note cardinal facts of geography: "Where did you grow up? How did you get from there to here?" Accent, national origin, education; tied, or single. I do not rush in, I keep my distance, circle the quarry. Move the antennae; I'm not looking for anything special, I'm just ready if I see it. A small pleasure. I have a collection of responses, from the unsatisfactory "What a coincidence" and "It's a small world" to "There are two hundred people in the world and they all know each other," and best of all, "Stand in a certain section in a book shop in Rio de Janeiro, enter into conversation with the person reaching for a book on those shelves, and you are sure to know someone in common."

Sometimes a connection will just drop in my lap without any warning, as it did when Mrs. Snow said "Chester Kallman." How could Chester's path cross mine in the old New England house hundreds of miles from the beach in Brighton where Chester and I walked in winter when we were eleven and twelve years old, two odd children who made common cause. His stepmother was my cousin; his father was my first adult friend. Chester was already a poet, a slight boy with fair hair and large grey eyes. We spent a lot of time together when he stayed with his father, and we wrote to each other when he left. We lost touch. Years later and in another country, Auden died and left his estate to Chester, his long-time companion. When Chester died soon after, Edward, his father, my first adult friend, who gave me the run of his good library without censorship or condescension, found himself heir to the Auden papers, and he eighty years old.

———

The plunge into a fully functioning dairy and tobacco and paying-guest farm was abrupt. I signed every paper put before me. Deeds, mortgages, long-term loans for cattle and equipment, short-term crop loans for planting through harvest. We had magically acquired credit as owners of these two hundred acres; a famous farm, known in the thirties, a friendly banker told us, as the WPA of West Whately. Any farm worker who needed a day's work could apply to the prosperous Victor Bardwell and would never be turned away; if nothing else was pressing, he would be set to prune the pastures of juniper. We, raggle taggle bohemians, now talked to bankers and bureaucrats; made commitments for five years, ten years; mortgaged our future. I didn't worry. Jimmy could do anything. Eduardo was not going to stay forever, I knew that before he did, but there would always be someone, someone Jimmy could ignite, fire with his eloquence, his boldness, his swings from rage to tenderness. Someone he could challenge with his vision of this farm as an outpost, involved in nonviolent resistance to injustice anywhere, a place of art and ferment and hard work, a place of sanity in a world crashing and burning.

————

My mother telephones from New York, she longs to see me, the children. ". . . only for a few days, I must get back, some business to attend . . ." I know there is no business, nothing and nobody needs her; I see her seated at her "escritoire," one of the few pieces she saved from her nine-room apartment to console her in the lonely decency of the residence hotel. I give her the reassurance she won't ask for, "This is a good time, mother, please come. You could take the train at Grand Central," I tell her, "get a ticket for Northampton . . ." "No," Jimmy calls, "South Deerfield. Closer." I didn't argue. There was a real railway station in Northampton: a waiting room, benches, restrooms. Late to meet the train as Jimmy always was, nothing at the whistle-stop in South Deerfield could give her comfort, no place under cover she could wait if it rained. Jimmy's thinking of the six miles to South Deerfield instead of the twelve to Northampton; Jimmy's thinking gas rationing, the time he must take from haying, the rain that might come and ruin it. I know, I know. "South Deerfield, mother. Jimmy will meet you." The children go with him; it makes it easier for Jimmy, bearable for my mother. She is the only passenger to get off the northbound train, a conspicuous city person at the country railroad crossing; Jimmy greets her "How was the trip, Betty?" and reaches for her bags. Both carefully avoid the sham of embrace.

In the kitchen, in her city clothes, my mother sat at the table watching me, her eyes filled with worry and question. She watched me wrestle with the Medusa head of the milking machine, inserting the long-handled brush into each black hose. Standing at the black slate sink, in blue jeans and a man's shirt, slaving away in this old-fashioned kitchen: her daughter. A farmer's wife. I scrub the milk buckets and scald them, we must keep the bacteria count down—up-end the buckets on the rack in the shed, ready for evening milking. In the shed off the kitchen there is also an icebox, filled with blocks cut from our pond in winter. "You need a refrigerator," she says sadly. "Oh, this is an improved icebox," I say cheerfully, "no pan to empty, a pipe carries the water to a hole in the floor and empties under the house." She is not amused. She sees the paint that's needed, the furniture we don't have; what didn't I need? We make small talk on the run, I must keep going. My mother can't help, I can't stop. I run upstairs, gather bed linen, children's clothes, bring the heaped basket to the sink, the black slate sink I praise (one more puzzle for my mother), fetch the scrub board from the shed. This task must be done daily, in the morning, after breakfast, after the milking machine, after I make the beds; before I prepare lunch for the children, then the paying guests. My mother watches in disbelief. I who never washed the smallest garment at home; everything sent out: sheets and towels to the commercial laundry, shirts and blouses and delicate lingerie to the neighborhood French hand laundry. I now tell her, filling the silence of her disapproval, how wonderful not to have to heat water, to have hot water always on tap. "Do you have a good hand cream? I could leave you mine, don't neglect yourself; hot water and rough work are terrible for the skin, you'll be old before your time." I know better than to tell her how scrubbing and wringing strengthens my wrists, makes supple my hands; how hanging clothes on the line is my art form. Sometimes in color, sometimes in shape; punctuate with socks, stretch it out with sheets. Walk away. Go into the garden. View it from a distance.

A gulf separates us. The gulf widens when Jimmy appears. The Irish Catholic, working in barns, with dumb beasts; ploughing the fields, tramping into the house, bringing dirt on his heavy work shoes for her daughter to sweep up. What did she care about the impassioned speeches she heard in this house, the richness and life-giving et ceteras of life on the land. She closed her ears to laments for the suffering, jeremiads against the powerful.

For relief she turns to the children; blameless and beautiful, they touch her heart. She is careful with her claims: "Come, kiss your grandmother," but the children are generous. Deirdre moves into the circle of my mother's arms, admires her scarf, her blouse, her rings; Deirdre is so feminine, how my mother wished she could show her off to her friends, her family; that thick dark hair and high color and grey green eyes, she could be a child model. Michael, fair in contrast, still underground, waits for his sister to take the lead. He's shy. My mother is gently attentive, draws him out; she tries not to be partial to the little girl. But in an unguarded moment when we are alone she says, "It's not his fault that he is not circumcised, that his Christian father did this to spite me, to make sure he would grow up on their side," and I say only, "No, nothing to do with you." How can she think that, spite is not in him.

There is a story in Genesis of rape and vengeance. I can see why it haunted Jimmy all his life. Dinah, daughter of Jacob, walked into the land of the Hivites; Shechem, son of Hamor, the chief of that country, saw her, and took her by force. ". . . he took her, and lay with her and defiled her." That's the first bad part, the rape. Then, inexplicably, ". . . his soul clave unto Dinah, and he loved the damsel, and spake kindly unto her." He couldn't live without her, she must be his wife. He asked his father's help. Hamor went to Jacob. "The soul of my son Shechem longeth for your daughter," please give her to him in marriage; give us your daughters, take our daughters, intermarry with us; dwell among us, share our land, our cattle. Jacob held his peace until Dinah's brothers came out of the field; when they heard it "they were very wroth because Shechem had wrought folly in Israel in lying with Jacob's daughter." Shechem said, "Let me find grace in your eyes and I will give you any gift or dowry," anything you say, "but give me the damsel to wife." Then the sons of Jacob said "We cannot do this thing, to give our sister to one who is uncircumcised, for that were a reproach unto us, but if ye will be as we be, that every male of you be circumcised, then we will give our daughters unto you, and we will take your daughters to us, and we will dwell with you, and we will become one people." Shechem and his father lost no time in returning to their tribe; they didn't see the guile that covered the anger in Dinah's brothers. They came to the gate of the city and told the assembled men of the union they had been offered; Shechem told the men of his tribe how much the merging would mean to him. And because he was respected and loved, he persuaded the Hivites to accept Dinah's brothers' harsh condition: all the men agreed to be circumcised. On the third day, when they lay sore and in pain, the sons of Jacob "came upon the city boldly and slew all the males." And they took their sheep and their oxen, and all their wealth, and all their little ones, and their wives: they spoiled the city. And they took Dinah home. Jacob said to his sons "You have brought trouble on me, making me odious among the inhabitants of the land, the Canaanites and the Perizzites." But they answered, "Should our sister be treated as a whore?"

When I read that chapter in Genesis I could see the boy Jimmy, urgent in his sexual awakening, as he read that brutal story. The language of the Old Testament was so potent, so searing, how could the literal boy not be affected. His hands flew to cover and protect; he felt the pain, the betrayal. I could understand that. It was a cruel story, and unforgettable. What about Dinah, defiled? No voice; a puppet, an object of desire, an object of vengeance. Hopeless. Ancient tribal claims held fast in Jimmy, in my mother; roots so deep they were obstacles insurmountable.

Still, we managed to thread our way through the visit. Jimmy was considerate, circumspect; she couldn't help but see what was between us. She couldn't help opening herself to the children. I stored the anthropological nugget: children of mixed marriages have a special beauty. When she left after a few days, she paused in the doorway and looked out over the hills. A mist lay in the valley. Her eyes were filled. She said, "Write to him." There was only one "him" for her. "I know he wants to hear from you, maybe he'll help . . ." It was the only time in her visit that she said anything about my father.

In her next letter she wrote: "I don't really think he married that woman. I'm sure he'll come back." And she wrote: "I get up early every morning, I look out of the window on Eighty-sixth Street to see what kind of day it is. I take a bath, I dress, I take two hours to dress, carefully. And then there is nowhere to go. This is not self-pity . . ."

And then she was dead, at fifty-three, of a sudden heart attack. I never stop thinking of how I might have held her, consoled her, helped her find again a way to be alive. Useless, impossible thought; her heart was really broken. Like the blues songs.

Chapter Twelve

A SHOCK DELAYED. THIRD CHILD

– 1946-1947 –

THE WEST SIDE FUNERAL chapel on that bleak December day in 1946 held a small gathering of my mother's mourners: her sisters, her nieces and nephews, a few friends; little knots of people who cried and whispered and rocked, and, as I entered, came to me, enfolded me, "Your mother, your poor mother . . ." Aunt Clara took my arm and led me to the open casket. It is not my mother. I turn away "Look at her," Aunt Clara wept, "look at her, beautiful as a bride—" It was a good thing my father was in far-off California; Aunt Clara wanted to tear him apart, hit him with anything. See him bleed. Ravaged by some secret disappointment, bony and fierce, nothing she could think of was too terrible for the man who had destroyed her beloved baby sister. It was a good thing she didn't hear his voice when he called me at the farm. Without emotion, as if he were closing a business deal, he said, "I'll take care of the funeral expenses." Say something, Daddy, I'm waiting, say "I'm sorry you lost your mother" or just say "I'm sorry . . ." Was his second wife listening? Was she relieved by my mother's death? "You know I can't be there," of course he could not face my mother's family; a long silence, and then he said, "What happened to the Oriental rugs?" Unbelievable. How can he mention her pitiful property, trying to sound practical; it must be fear, he must be filled with terror. I want to shock him as he had shocked me, I wanted to say she's dead, she's gone, and you talk about rugs! I wanted to say calmly, Yes, the rugs; we wrapped her in them, they will be buried with her. I didn't say that; I didn't say anything. I felt shame for him.

I am the only child to bury our parent, an added sorrow for the small huddle of black-clad mourners. "Where is your sister?" She could not be here; she made the funeral arrangements and now, she's sorry, she can't face it. They murmur to each other. Paul, my brother? He is in prison, the whisper goes around, he's a conscientious objector. What's that? Prison is shameful, there has never been a lawbreaker in the family; Paul is a young man, only twenty-five, torn from his wife and child for a whole year. A year and a day, someone says. Still, it is brave, they say, for a principle, and it is a comfort to know that his wife and baby live at the farm with us. Does he even know of his mother's death? Yes. He knew. My father called the Warden at McNeil Island Federal Penitentiary in the state of Washington and asked him to tell Paul his mother died. "Is there a way," my father asked, "he could be at her funeral in New York City?" "Yes," the Warden said there was: "Travel expenses paid for the prisoner and two guards, round trip, prisoner handcuffed." My father agreed to pay travel expenses. The Warden himself went to the cell block; Paul was in solitary, doing extra punishment for protesting segregation within the prison. "I'm sorry to tell you your mother died yesterday"—and so Paul heard of her sudden death, "if you want to go to the funeral, your father will pay"—and he repeated the conditions. Paul gave no sign, he was silent. Then he said "No," he would not cross the country and appear at his mother's burial handcuffed to prison guards.

It is the outsider, the stranger, Jimmy, who is with me; who stands on the edges, speaks when he's spoken to, doesn't intrude. But oh he is noticeable, the Gentile, the shagetz in his country clothes. Poor Betty and her unhappy life, they think; discarded by her husband, her son in prison, her daughter married to a Christian. They can't know how deep is Jimmy's sympathy for their bereavement; he need only hear, or read, of suffering anywhere and he enters into it, feels the pain. Now he watches me, my key is low, unnatural, I am too numb; he's worried.

After the burial at the cemetery and before we return to the farm I am persuaded by the aunts and cousins to stop at my mother's apartment. Take something, take everything they urge, they entreat. Don't leave it for strangers. In her desk I find my letters, Michael and Deirdre's drawings, their sweet scrawled notes. In another drawer I find pages written to herself in times of despair. I put the papers in one of her leather bags without looking. "Take her mink coat, her silver fox," they say. Her bits of jewelry. "She would want you to have it." I say all right, I take the coat. I am suffocated. I slip off to the bathroom, and shut the door. On a hook behind the door hangs her nightgown, ivory silk, still in folds with the impress of her body. It was so alive, so affecting. I am convulsed with grief.

———

At home again, the reunion is fervent, the relief immense; I never want to leave our children, this place. We're ready for sleep, Jimmy is in the cellar, banking the furnace for the night; I slip under the covers, and suddenly, I don't know why, I think: She's free. She's herself again. Free. Her ardent spirit released, in a rush she is stripped of suffering, rejection; of being unloved, unwanted, misunderstood. Discarded. I don't know why I am flooded with that thought. I don't give her a heavenly place; I don't have the dogma, the discipline, the spiritual otherworldliness; but I am sure, it is a conviction. Not to be argued.

In death, herself again, she is more real to me, more present; in unexpected moments I catch myself in a gesture, a wave of the hand, and I think: "I *am* my mother." I rub my temples absently when I am tired, as she did: she is there. I speak to no one of these eerie flashes.

Not even Jimmy.

Nor did I tell him of the lead cap that now sat on the back of my head, that pressed the base of my skull, that was with me in the morning when I woke and through the day and into the night. What else could it be, I decided, but a brain tumor? Morbid, Jimmy always said, to dwell on disease; we made it a point not to read layman's medicine. So I had only fragments of information, all that a woman who lived as far apart from civilization's poisons could need. Blessed with health, we rarely went to doctors; when we did, it was only after discussion: is this vaccine safe? Do we want this serum coursing through the veins of our precious child? Who do we trust in establishment medicine; who do we trust in established anything. Even the Folk Medicine folk were not accepted without question.

So I was quiet about my brain tumor. I distracted myself with zealous housekeeping; I complicated my cooking; I was patient with the children when I asked them to remember that our paying guest

Otto was working on his book. The stranger, the waif, the poet at the door was welcomed. I was dependably in charge.

In the night I turned to Jimmy. He was always there for me, ready to take me away. Transported by the yea-sayer, I was too soon on shore again, as anxious, as sleepless, as before.

"What's wrong? Tell me."

I saw now I couldn't be silently martyred. It was not fair. I described a cap of lead, pressing in my skull.

"Since when?"

"Two weeks? Since she died. It may be a brain tumor." I shocked myself, hearing the words.

"Why? What makes you think so?" He took it seriously. He was frightened; he was worried. He thought I might know something he didn't. Jimmy was wide awake now, out of bed. "I'll be right back." He went down the stairs, quietly, quietly, in his bare feet; he switched on the light near the wall of books. I could identify every sound in this house. I lay still, suspended; I waited for his return. The book replaced, the light switched off, Jimmy was back upstairs. He sat beside me, like a doctor, and, like a patient, I submitted to his catechism.

"Do you have blinding pain behind your eyes? Frequent shooting pain?" His voice was hushed, not to wake the sleeping house, but somehow stern.

"No," I considered. "No, I don't."

"Well," he pronounced with certainty, "then you do *not* have a brain tumor," he thought I believed him. All he had to do was say it to make it true. "What you have is a neurasthenic headache."

The old-fashioned word, neurasthenic, from the discredited *Family Medical Encyclopedia* we consulted only for minor first aid, was intended to dissolve the brain tumor, annihilate fear—his and mine. Jimmy got under the covers, put his arms around me, whispered, "Get some sleep." I knew him. I didn't trust his report, but I slept.

In the morning I couldn't wait until Jimmy went to the barn. I couldn't wait to pull the book out and see for myself. I knew he had edited his version, and so he had. I read, under neurasthenic headache, of the complex spinal cord, the long cord of nervous tissue extending from the brain along the back in the spinal canal, and how its disturbance can variously affect the body. I read carefully, reread it, and shut the book.

In and out of the house from the barn, Jimmy watched me. Now with a bucket of milk, then back in a while with the milking machine for me to scrub, I caught his glance, checking me, checking the effect of his benign diagnosis. He didn't know I read the full text.

The next morning I couldn't get out of bed, I must get out of bed. I forced myself up; every step was pain. I couldn't stand straight. Bent over, I forced myself, through the morning, through taking care of the children, the guests, the house. Urged to take it easy, go to bed, I refused. It would work itself out. Everything just took longer; every move must be planned. Making a bed was a major feat, mounting the stairs a journey of pain. And humiliating. How could I have so taken for granted, so accepted without thought all the years of miraculous movement, all that complexity at my command. Frightened, and awed, I kept thinking: I did it myself. I read the symptoms and made it happen. And, more unnerving, Jimmy knew I would.

There was a doctor in Hatfield. He agreed to see me during visiting hours that afternoon. Jimmy drove me the eight miles to the doctor's office in a Victorian house on the main street. A gentle, sympathetic man, Dr. Byrne. I described my symptoms, head, back. He examined me for obvious disorders, took my pulse, stethoscope to my heart; flashed a light, peered into my eyes. I didn't tell him of Jimmy's doctoring or the voodoo that bent my spine in pain. I did tell him of my mother's recent death; he saw its relevance. His diagnosis: "You are suffering from delayed shock." And he sounded right. His prescription: coddle yourself. Take a walk each day without fail. A glass of wine before dinner. Warm bath at night. That kind of thing. A couple of aspirin if the pain was too bad, but he prescribed no other medicine. I would be all right. Let him know.

Jimmy was vindicated. Was I not relieved?

In a way. Never had the soma so forcibly directed me to the psyche: Pay attention; you have had a serious wound.

The palliatives prescribed by the kind country doctor were too easy. But every afternoon, after lunch was over for the family and the guests and the dishes done and dinner started, I pulled on my boots. In my mother's mink-lined coat over my blue jeans I walked down the road muddied with January thaw, past bare brown fields under gray skies, and searched the hills for the almost visible flush that touches the woods as winter recedes. Every evening I sipped the wine Jimmy poured, and every night, all chores done, Jimmy filled the tub at just the right temperature. He'd kneel by the tub and rub my back with his strong hands; he would read to me. My healer. My nurse, my lover. My anchor.

Let me give him a gift; something he longed for that I had refused: I would have another child.

Chapter Thirteen

EDUARDO

I NEVER CRIED EASILY, now hardly at all, but last week a convulsion of weeping seized me for a loss I cannot really understand. On an impulse, at high-toll telephone time, I called Dallas, Texas, from West Whately, Massachusetts. I had a possible phone number for Eduardo given me by a visiting researcher a few years ago. I was alone in my room, a memory led me to him, and I, ordinarily careful pincher of pennies, simply picked up the phone and dialed. The phone rang in Dallas, was answered after the second ring, and a voice that could be Eduardo said hello. "Eduardo?" "Yes." Pause. "Who is calling?" His voice is higher than I remembered, and light, but it's not an old man's voice. High but firm. "This is Blanche," I say. Silence. Maybe he didn't hear. Maybe he had a cat that was at this moment asking to be let out, or in. "Blanche Cooney." "I'm sorry. I don't . . ." That voice. Thin and silver and very courteous. "Eduardo . . ." I'm trying to think of what I must say next. Something's wrong. "Jimmy Cooney. Do you remember? His name?" "It sounds familiar," he really wants to help, I feel he considers it my problem. He repeats "Jimmy Cooney." Then, "Where are you calling from, did you say?" "Massachusetts, Eduardo. The farm. Where you lived with us—for five years. We're still here. . ." "Did you say a farm? In Massachusetts? I—I don't know." "Yes, a farm, Eduardo," maybe if I keep using his name this imposter will go away. "You brought the cows in from pasture. You kept bees. Remember the mushrooms you gathered? Lady? The mare you rode?" I hear my words coming out in a rush, pitched at him to force the gates open. I must keep it conversational. "Tell me more," he is polite, the old grace. "It sounds so interesting." Hopeless. Abandon it. I laugh. I must laugh, as though we were having a joke. "How are you, Eduardo?" "I'm fine," he assures me. "I live in the present. One can't have both, can one? The past, and the present," I can't answer that. I'm wondering if in that utterance he is trying to console my pain. As he did long ago. "Why Dallas? Why are you living in Texas?" "It's very pleasant, my dear. I have my friends, I never leave. My sister Graciella lives in New York, I speak to her once a month on the telephone. She's married, you know. I don't remember her married name . . ." I am in turmoil. I want to hold onto him. I want to get rid of him. I say something, anything, and goodbye. He thanks me for calling, so good of me, calls me "my dear." I replace the phone. He is gone, and now I know he has been gone all these years. In all these years he has never ceased to be a presence. Sometimes faint, a distant hum: I see four volumes of Charles Lamb's *Letters* on the top shelf, where did they come from? Then I remember Eduardo brought them for me. Why? And sometimes an oriole flies straight into the blossoming nectarine Eduardo planted and his name flashes in its wake.

And all those years, after he drifted away, and we didn't see his face or hear his voice, I imagined him, thinking of us, stirred by a nectarine tree in blossom, or the smell of honey, or the sound of a mourning dove. And giving himself to the same longing and regret for those days when we were all young and fervent. And being there, somewhere, if I reached for him.

Wrong. Dead wrong. I wish he were dead. I look around my room; everything has a history. I need it. Hold me; save me. I was not connected to Dallas by electronic whatever; it was a diabolic thread, spun in the Black Hole, pulling me to the edge, forcing me to look in.

———

Until we met Eduardo and he came to live with us I didn't know how much I had missed him. Someone like him. I didn't know how hard it was to be married to Jimmy, so principled, so intense, and he the only adult for miles around and months on end. Of course there was no one like Eduardo. In his slightly accented English, Spanish was detectable, but he looked Scandinavian, tall, fair. And elegant always. He was a rare bird, sui generis, an exotic.

Eduardo returned from Paris to New York that year, following his cousin Anaïs, "Anaïs l' incomparable." When he told her he wanted to publish his book, and set the seal on his last "twelve-year cycle," she suggested: "Why not print it yourself? Jimmy has a hand press, he could teach you. You would learn quickly." Her encouragment was essential. "They're poor. They could use the money." So he came up to the farm to talk it over.

We all intended it to be a temporary arrangement, no more than the summer, limited to the printing of the book. Like any man of independent means, Eduardo was cautious. "I can contribute. Forty-five dollars a month, if that's agreeable . . ." We did agree. Jimmy said, "Tell us about your book," sliding away from the subject of money, avoiding my eyes so that we could not exchange our joy at this princely prospect.

He had evolved a thesis, Eduardo told us, fruit of his studies of the lives of the poets, particularly Blake, and genius, notably Nietzsche, that turned on twelve-year planetary cycles. His investigations had taken him from record repositories in Germany, to the British Museum, to the Bibliothèque Nationale, where he examined relevant dates and ephemerides. He looked at his own chart in the light of his theory, the results were astonishing.

Raised as a Catholic in a large Cuban-Danish family, his intimates were their West Indian servants, and his brothers and sisters. His parents were remote, and demanding. He was sent to prep school in the States, then to Harvard, and then on to the obligatory gentleman's year abroad. That year stretched on and on, to twelve years, the significant number for the cycle's span. He lived chiefly in Paris, near Anaïs, among the surrealists. He lived on their fringe: not a writer nor a painter nor a poet, and too modest to fake it, he offered himself as audience. Occasionally he bought a canvas, or took a poet to dinner. A minor patron. There was something in him, though, that made him uneasy among the decadents. Besides, there was a fever in the air, a suppressed terror. The climate of chaos encouraged the smashing of taboos and the exploration of the perverse. Tarot cards were read, the psychoanalyzed formed camps: the Freudians, the Jungians; ancient discredited laws of planetary influence were studied, horoscopes cast and interpreted. No credo was too arcane.

In the study of astrology Eduardo found his work: an acceptable Dada pursuit in the circle of friends in Paris, an embarrassment to the family. Yet his family was grateful, in Cuba, for Eduardo's restrained deviations. Eduardo did not need to tell me how the researcher's life appeased him: the silence and dimness of libraries, the green-shaded lamps over long tables, the dusty stacks holding secrets and the faint smell of mold; the whole apparatus of scholarship was precious to him. His maps were meticulous, annotated in his fine hand, but, he confessed ruefully, he did not have the intuitive flair, that creative elixir, that could give an inspired reading. What you do not have, I thought, Eduardo, my friend, is hubris.

Odd material to bear the imprimatur of our press, used until now only for the literature of rebellion and protest. None of that mattered. We all knew we had found an inexplicable friendship, nothing to do with ideology. We liked to look at each other, to talk and laugh and eat and drink together. There was no time to lose. Eduardo went back to New York to pack his books and papers and clothes. He returned to the farm that same week.

Eduardo worked at a table that served as his desk in the room intended as parlor in our eighteenth-century farmhouse. We were proud of what we had done with Victorian junk in creating a literary gentleman's chamber, impromptu as a set in summer stock. The centerpiece was the sofa. I painted the voluptuously curved frame black, and I did my first upholstery job in bold red corduroy, secured by brass-headed tacks. I sat back on my heels when I was finished and called, "Come and see." Jimmy and Eduardo and our two small children, Deirdre and Michael, were at once in the doorway. Jimmy approved; Eduardo applauded. Deirdre was four, and she thought it grandeur, especially because Eduardo's room was out of bounds. The press was set up in the adjoining alcove. There was a cupboard in that alcove beside the central chimney, a hiding place, it was said, for runaway slaves on the underground railroad. We all thought it an auspicious spot for the press.

How happy we were together. Eduardo was interested in everything: our improvisations, our stratagems, our small triumphs as, that first year on the farm, we infiltrated the customs of the country. He accommodated himself without fuss to the outhouse, and the oil lamp. He churned butter, he helped Jimmy in the barn, he was attentive to the children. He wanted a family, and he chose us. He promoted himself prematurely to elderly benevolence, though he was, at thirty-eight, only five years older than Jimmy, and fifteen years older than I. It was the distance, the lack of tension between us, combined with our intimacy, that gave our life together its unusual flavor. The distance was not unbridgeable, but we ran well on our parallel track; the summer was golden, the light was green as far as we could see. Why would we want to change it. We loved each other without needing to possess, with complete acceptance. Without sex. I thought: we love each other so calmly, this must be how it is with old married couples.

I don't know how it was for Jimmy, but his pleasure in Eduardo's company was undeniable. They would set off together to cut wood, walking west across the meadow and into the forest, talking, gesturing. Late in the afternoon they would return, still talking, about the Church, or Spengler, or Otto Rank, who had last year analyzed Eduardo. They would bring the talk to me, we would sit around the table into the night after the children were in bed. When Jimmy pronounced outrageously, Eduardo would urge: "Jimmy. *Try* to be fair." The light of the oil lamp was benign, Eduardo's entreaty made Jimmy smile. Reason prevailed.

On a clear night, the children long asleep, we stretched out on the lawn. No other lights visible, the hilltop and the heavens ours alone, the silken summer air enveloped us. We lay, not touching, instructed in the stars by Eduardo. A long silence from Jimmy. We realized he was asleep. He missed the thrilling plummet of a falling star and we woke him to tell him so.

The printing of the book progressed. Eduardo was an adept student. Jimmy said he had a natural affinity for the craft. A bibliophile, a collector in a small way, Eduardo enjoyed the process: the setting of type in the stick, the shape of the characters, their look on the page. The smell of the ink. He bought fine rag paper—Worthy Hand and Arrow, procured cuts from fifteenth-century woodblocks of St. Christopher for endpapers. He designed a two-color title page. He found a binder in New York City with a reputation for fine work. Black boards, Eduardo specified, stamped in gold, with an astrological device in red. He could not wait to give his family in Cuba their bound and inscribed copy. It would justify their support. It would be, after his Harvard diploma, and his name in a *Playbill* during his one year in New York theater, tangible evidence of his seriousness. He took such pains; he wanted his book to be flawless. "Let us read proof, Eduardo," I said. "No, my sweet. This must be mine entirely." Printing finished, he read it through once more before packing it off to the binder. I heard ominous groans from his Victorian sanctum. Typos, terrible typos. There was no help for it, there would be a delay; he must print an errata:

> Since I have type-set these pages, I am supposed to be responsible for the errata. I query this. There are some "slips" that tax one's vigilance. Other, Puck-like, or fiendishly, elude it. For these, the author/typesetter should not be responsible. It's the OTHER who is to blame: p. 12: "Horrowing"—I am rather pleased with this portmanteau word. On p. 45: "holding the tip in your sharp mouth." The original text is: "holding the tip of your tail in your sharp mouth." But I prefer to make no further comment. P. 42: "Apocatastasis." When I think how hard I tried to make this a book without errors, it was a stupefying blow, indeed, to realize that the most important word in the book was misspelled. The most important word in the text, and the most conspicuous; the running head on each page. Anyway, Apocastasis is a better sounding word, and a more fitting pendant to "Apocalypse." I hope it "takes," in spite of the saturnian eye of Philology.

Such chagrin; poor Eduardo. We reassured him, his "errata" demonstrated grace and responsibility, the book was not ruined—on the contrary. Anyway, I thought, who would read it? We knew, and Eduardo knew, that it was a symbol, a contract with himself. Off he went on the train to New York, to the binder, and to take care of "other business." He would be back in ten days, at the most; we were his family.

There were letters from Eduardo, in one a hint of a minor Fall, a failure of will. From my green enclave, secured by Jimmy, and the innocence of our babies, I followed Eduardo in my thoughts as he went about his "other business": the world of fever and desire and danger in the gay bars of the city. He knew he should be casual. Cruising, pickups, rough trade: all in a night's possibilities. But each time he entered a bar, took a seat, ordered his rum, he deliberately withheld a slow survey of the room while he opened his cigarette case and extracted a cigarette, flicked his lighter, took the first deep drag. Then he raised his glass and sipped the rum and ran his eye around the room. He couldn't help the unreasonable hope that tonight he would meet The One. The mate of his soul, the mate of his body,

who would free him from this hateful life of promiscuity and humiliation. It was hateful, but it was irresistible. Tonight nothing mattered but that he should find an answering eye, an assenting signal in
the dark bar; and then to make the moves, the ritual abc's. Out the
door they would go, his brotherly guiding hand on the stranger's
shoulder. The first touch. Then the stroll to the Santa Lucia, the
modest hotel in the Village that was Eduardo's pied à terre. Pick up
the key at the desk, the clerk so bored he appeared discreet, and up in
the lift, into the room, restraints off, he was urgent and avid and
beside himself. Afterward, he might never see the stranger again, yet
he did not neglect the amenities. His companion was invited for a
nightcap in the hotel's Latin American restaurant, the Jai Alai.

Apocatastasis: the doctrine of final restoration of all sinful beings
to God and to the state of blessedness.

Origen preached the doctrine of final restoration; he believed in
the freedom of will in its struggle with the forces of good and evil.
But Origen castrated himself in early manhood, and with this drastic
act removed himself from the common struggle.

Never mind, it was just a lapse, a switch triggered by Eighth
Street temptation. Eduardo's planetary signs were in position for a
new cycle. He would put his life in order; at last he would take
control. All that went before, he told us, led to the farm, to a life of
usefulness, a balanced life of work and contemplation. He would not
return to Cuba, Eduardo wrote his father and mother. His dear
friends had a farm in New England; he planned to accept their
invitation to join them. He would "pursue agriculture," become a
U.S. citizen; he asked their blessing. Incomprehensible to Anaïs, his
longing for a rural life of hard work. "It sounds romantic," she kindly
said. She knew it wouldn't last. He met his old friend Claude at
Caresse Crosby's party: "Hand-set type and home baked bread? Too
medieval," casually deflating. Eduardo was impervious. How would
they understand? During our brief separation, he in Sodom, Eduardo begged news of the farm. He was anxious if the haying was
threatened by a rainy spell. He worried about the beautiful Jersey
calf, his Columbine, who refused to be weaned.

Eduardo wrote Jimmy:

> After reading your long letter, I lay on my bed paralyzed by
> the intensity of my feelings toward you and Blanche and the

Morning Star Farm. The age of innocent and serene relation-
ship with you is over. I suffer now, and I wish it were otherwise. I love you beyond the rationality of my affection for you.
It is a great pity. Only last evening I was telling Anaïs that
astrologically you both had your ascendants in Sagittarius, and
since my ascendant was in your Seventh House, I was therefore
to each of you, a husband and a wife and a partner. But since I
can never be, or should never be, your wife and husband, let me
be your partner.

If Eduardo's need for cosmic indicators must be satisfied, if he
sought parental blessing, and Anaïs' approval, Jimmy and I entered
our partnership consulting only each other. It would be a beginning,
Jimmy said, the nucleus of a community of loving friends.

Maybe. That was a silent reservation. I knew how bitterly Jimmy
resented my caution. But for now, for as long as it lasted, I couldn't
imagine a companion more sympathetic to both of us. Who but
Eduardo could stretch out on the bed beside me in the mornings, ask
me my dreams, tell me his, and have Jimmy's approval. And who
but Eduardo would formally cut in as I danced around the house
with the baby in my arms because I couldn't sit still when I heard
"A Slow Boat to China"? Jimmy didn't dance, Eduardo loved to, and
I thought I couldn't live without it.

Eduardo's homecoming was a festival. When I heard our car in the
driveway I put a match to the kindling in the fireplace, put the needle
on the record of Handel's "Entrance of the Queen of Sheba," lit the
candles. Both Jimmy and Eduardo came through the door laden with
suitcases and packages. Eduardo freed himself to open his arms to
the children. To the music and the laughter, to the firelight, to all the
sights and sounds of celebration, was added the implicit solemnity of
our new bond. Presents for the children first: A. A. Milne's *When We
Were Very Young* for Deirdre. A Paddington bear for Michael. The
champagne cork popped, glasses were filled, and Eduardo presented
a copy of his book to us, inscribed "from their debtor forever." We
teased Eduardo for the laughable collection of "necessities for the
farm" he bought at Hammacher Schlemmer. He unpacked the big
box and produced a small "but excellent" scrub board—"I will do
my own laundry," he assured me; a special wax for the runners of the
drawers of his pine chest; an ice cream freezer, maple bucket and

dashers—"Clever Eduardo"; an insect repellent "for my delicate skin" he primly mocked; a ZigZag corkscrew from France, "really the best in the world," and he demonstrated on the cork in the bottle of Madeira, my special gift.

And so the courtship ended, the partnership began, and the visiting sybarite was subdued. A sober Eduardo emerged. He would confound the sceptics, he would prove himself capable of sacrifice and austerity. I watched him, applying pressure, adding one more turn of the screw each day. "I must get into shape," he told me when he came in for lunch, winded from chasing a cow. He must keep pace with Jimmy, be as strong, be a man, match Jimmy's stubborn endurance. They went to cattle auctions, buying carefully, not to be cheated because they were "book farmers." They bought to balance quality Guernsey stock with productive Holstein. Baucis and Sheba. We spent evenings naming the creatures, Jimmy and Eduardo boasting of their triumphs over crafty country characters, telling me of their "deals," their "steals." Eduardo bought a pretty Morgan mare, an amazing bargain. She was to be a riding horse for him. Lady Una Woodford. Lady was not indulgence; she could pull a farm wagon, or a sleigh in winter. We would certainly not change *her* name. It was perfect.

The balance shifted, it could not be otherwise. Eduardo and Jimmy were in the barns or in the woods or in the fields together. I worked in and around the house and cared for the children. Eduardo was ready as ever with sweet consideration and civilized gallantry. I could count on him. I would offer a new dish at lunch; he would taste it, pause, and by saying thoughtfully, "Interesting," let me down gently, tell me it was a failure. We banded together, he and I, we defended ourselves and each other against Jimmy's heat even as we leaned into it. Jimmy and I clashed when we were alone, often. Afterward, Eduardo could see I avoided him, not trusting my eyes, or my voice, to hide my anger and pain. And the next day, I tried to dim the glow of our imperative reconciliation. Healing sex. Not available to Eduardo.

But the strain of hard work and ascetic denial was evident to me. Eduardo fumed at setbacks he would formerly have viewed philosophically. He snapped, and apologized. He got migraines. No more lingering at table with visitors. He surprised his nephew Augustico, at the farm during school vacation to "help," by the commanding no-

nonsense way he stood up, cleared his dishes, and said: "Oyez, Chico, vamos atraer las vacas"—Come on, boy, let's go get the cows. And Augustico went, immediately.

Time for a trip to the city.

The occasion this time was filial duty. Eduardo's mother was flying in to New York from France, he must be on hand, his reassuring figure moving swiftly toward her in the airport, taking charge of customs and baggage. What a comfort. He arranged for her room at the Plaza and checked with the maitre d' for imperious mother's particular table, near a window overlooking the Park. He wasn't gone long, and he said "Thank goodness, there was no crisis" of barn or field to make him feel worse about deserting us. But nevertheless he brought peace offerings. "What about bees? Shall we keep them?" Out of his bag came Maeterlinck's *Life of the Bee*. We all read it, amazed. The orchard, the garden, would benefit, and even we in our mythical arthritic old age would be better for an occasional bee sting. Eduardo ordered Italian bees, material for building hives, helmets and veils and gauntlets. We thought about labels for our jars of honey.

Departures and returns. He received frequent summons. The Cuban family was large. Eduardo, the black sheep, the younger son, who was useless in the family's banking, investment, industrial interests, was dependable, even skillful, with admissions officers in prep schools and universities. He secured transcripts, groomed the nephews for interviews, celebrated acceptances with avuncular pride and small but significant gifts.

Sublimation served during Eduardo's months at the farm. Then controlled longing became bitter frustration, and off to the city. I came to realize that Jimmy was the object of his longing, and the source of frustration. Gradually the departures were more frequent, the returns more routine. Without a final break, no scenes, no wounds inflicted, Eduardo just left. "You ask too much of yourself," I said, and he thought that was true.

Chapter Fourteen

JEALOUSY

AS SOON as they were in the door I could feel it, the charge; the excitement came down the hall, into the kitchen, to me. Surprise: Jimmy's summer help is an eighteen-year-old wonder. It is Jimmy who carries the charge. Jimmy, one look at him is all I need; he can barely take his eyes off her, as though she were his creation, his discovery. He's showing her to me: See what came off the train in South Deerfield! But he won't meet my eye. I *do* see: I see her hair, thick and curly and black, the way it springs from her head, its ordered disorder, its fine condition; her clear dark eyes, their open intelligence; her glowing skin, her breasts insistent, the way she moved. Tall and lithe, a horsewoman, a tennis player. "What a great place, I love this part of Massachusetts," she looks around. "What a great old house. I'm so glad I could come, and thank you for having me." In her voice, a little husky, I hear the ex cathedra sound of privilege.

Around the table in our farmhouse kitchen is Michael, our seven-year-old, Deirdre, our ten-year-old, Jimmy, and Jeness; I've just put the baby Gabriel to bed in his crib upstairs, and now I join them. Jeness appreciates the buckwheat groats and ceci beans. "I've never had this before, it is *so* good" and "Is this your own butter? And bread, did you bake it? Eduardo told me your farm food is delicious." Jimmy has not spoken; he passes the salad, the pitcher of milk, then, smiling into the young girl's eyes —a bit of mischief, that's all it is,—says, "Mary Farrick told me she wouldn't have a young girl working in their barn alone with Vic . . ."

Why is he saying that? Why? Out of nowhere, bringing sex and intimacy to the table, to our first meal, our first meeting? Just as disconcerting is Jeness: "Oh, you needn't worry about me, I'm solid as a rock." I look at her. She's oblivious, unaware of how insulting her assurance is. She's solid as a rock. It's in her hands, is it?

Jimmy removes himself from womanly crosscurrents; he's suddenly attentive to the children, passing this, urging that, making a little joke; Michael giggles. It's not that he isn't always attentive to the children. They were precious; he adored them. But this was in a different key: patient, sweet.

I'm being unreasonable.

Jeness' parents were Eduardo's friends. Her father, Hamilton Eames, was his classmate at Harvard; her mother, Marne, the daughter of Nina Bull, a figure in Paris among the expatriates in the twenties; Jeness' uncle, Harry Bull, edited *Town and Country*. Her great aunt was the famous mezzo-soprano Emma Eames. So what was the well-connected knowing nymph doing here on a poor farm in West Whately as unpaid barn and field hand. Jeness had just graduated Rosemary Hall; accepted at Vassar, but her parents thought she was distracted by a young man who wanted to marry her and work his family's ranch in Montana with Jeness as his partner. Eduardo, back in the city, guilty in his desertion of us in the country, suggested she try farm life for a summer. Jimmy desperately needed help. Good idea, said Hamilton, said Marne; she's capable, strong, she'll learn fast; she needs a taste of rural life and hard work. She'll earn her keep, said Eduardo, and Jimmy loves an audience.

She brought jeans and sturdy work shoes, Basque jerseys and Shetland sweaters for cool days, halter tops for hot days. She woke early; she was cheerful and tireless. She looked great in the evening, glowing from her day in the sun, from the strenuous work, and the company of Jimmy, the teacher, by her side. What went on in the mowing, on the haywagon? In the hayloft in the barn, the vast old three-tiered barn, its darkness lit by shafts of light that came through the boards, its darkness filled with sweet smells of grass dried in the sun, cut in the sun, pitched into the aromatic animal dark.

What is going on? In me.

It's the fever I thought I was free of, the fever I thought I had conquered when our first child was born and at last, at last, Jimmy stopped living with Anne. That was in Woodstock, Greenwich Village in the country, an art colony. Now we're living in New England with high purpose and hard work and long stretches of isolation. We had reached this place, after eleven years together. Nothing could separate us, part us. Indissoluble; always, in all ways. I knew that. So now in this golden summer on the hill in West Whately, through what fissure had the serpent crept? Why did I feed it? What could I do about it?

We all slept on the second floor of the big old farmhouse. That summer, for our privacy, Jimmy and I took the room under the eaves at the west end of the house, the baby Gabriel's crib at the foot of our bed. Then Michael's room, then Deirdre's room, and on to the east where the two best bedrooms were kept for guests. No paying guests that summer; I awarded myself a sabbatical from paying guests because of the new baby, so Jeness had one of the large rooms facing east. There we were, strung out on the second floor, west to east, Jimmy spooned around me obliviously sleeping away the strenuous day in field and barn, the baby in contented baby slumber. Through the house, Michael in his room, Deirdre in hers, to the bedroom at the other end facing east where, also restoring energy, the perfect young woman's body lay in guiltless abandon: the focus of my obsession.

Within Jimmy's arms at night, waking in the morning, all through the day, I feed the viper. Jimmy's up before six, no groaning, no reluctance to leave our bed; instantly awake he throws the covers back, good morning, bends over the baby Gabriel's crib, wraps and brings the baby to my side for nursing. "Do I have clean jeans?" Clean shirt, clean socks, clean underwear? Clean everything. No more pulling on stained and sweated garments, real farmer's work clothes good for another real farmer's workday. Quietly to the bathroom, not to wake the still sleeping children, to carefully wash and shave and brush his shaggy goldish reddish hair before she sees him. Then down to the kitchen and he had the coffee percolating, oranges squeezed on the reamer and a pitcher full of fresh orange juice before anyone appears.

Accustomed to life among the rich and privileged, Jeness was immediately at home in our shabby farmhouse with effortless noblesse oblige. She cleared her dishes from the table, kept her room in order, did her own laundry; played checkers with Michael, let Deirdre use her Mason Pearson hairbrush, gave the baby her key ring—"What a cherub." And out the door with Jimmy, just the two of them in the morning, up the long lane to the top pasture; just the two of them in the evening to drive the cows down, the slow amble, cowbells sounding, and into the barn. Into the barn, the cows in their stanchions; Jeness was learning to milk. Sitting on the low stool, her dark curly head pressed against the cow's flank, she was quick to learn from Jimmy, who crouched beside her, as close as need be; she found the rhythm, the gentle pressure, the alternate tug at the teats of the patient beast, the milk streaming into the bucket.

I'm not there; I'm in the house, with the children, or at the clothesline or in the vegetable garden. I am there, with Jimmy, tantalized by the closeness of her delectable breasts rising half-naked from her brief top, tantalized by the brush of her silky wild hair. I'm with them when they're haying, on the wagon when they're pitching it, in the barn when they stored it. I am with them, I can choose the scene: in the filtered light in the forest, in the hot sun of the hay field, in the dark of the barn. Irresistible scenes, fast-forward, slow motion, frozen in stills, when desire resisted doubles intensity.

And when they came in from field or barn the actual me had my house in order: my voice pitched just right in welcome; peach pie baked, bread on the rise, soup on the simmer. I diverted Jimmy and Jeness with stories of my day, stories of the children, the letter from a friend; I told a joke. I was allowing Jeness to know who I am. In a life I could not alter, and would not if I could, I would not be defined as mother and wife. Anyone could see I didn't spring from this Yankee country. I needed color, decoration, harmless theatre; I needed it; vanity lived. Hand-me-downs, once-splendid rich-relatives' garments, patched and cobbled: cut down a coat and make a jacket; take the sleeves off a jacket and have a vest. Wear any old rag with verve and assurance even if there is no one to see it. What am I saying, no one? There's Jimmy, always aware of me.

Perfectly conscious of her power, Jeness wore it as a matter of fact: there it was; she wouldn't deny it, nor would she take unfair advantage. She knew she stirred men: her father, her father's friends, her girlfriends' boyfriends, the clerk in the drugstore, the conductor on the bus. Not a tease, nor a flirt, but available. How could she not be, so close to Jimmy, all day, every day. Jimmy in his full power: the writer-farmer, the compelling, audacious talker, the loving father, considerate husband. That summer, when Jeness lived with us, he was definitely husband. No imperative touching, or intimate glances. No more, not in public. Jeness was public.

The nights were different, more intense, more complicated, we were not alone; if only a vapor, a breath, the serpent found Jeness a place in our bed. A many-sided torment.

The spy in the service of the serpent is vigilant. If Jimmy passed a dish to Jeness, did his hand brush hers? Did he keep his eyes lowered to hide the light of excitement? The spy noted well that he was never surly, or sullen, or moody. He brought his new discovery, Herman Hesse, to the table; read from *Demian*. He was persuasive; Jeness would like to borrow it. When he told her, before he put Beethoven's *Kreutzer* Sonata on the record player, that Tolstoy considered it so nakedly erotic it should not be played in mixed company, he avoided my eyes.

In our kitchen there is a fireplace, on either side there is a cupboard; one holds wood, the other household supplies. This pantry closet is narrow but big enough for one person to step in, to get a bag of flour, a box of raisins. Time for milking; Jeness steps in, reaches for the milk strainer filters third shelf up on the right. At that very moment Jimmy remembers he needs matches, kept on a shelf on the left. He squeezes in back to back. They emerge face to face, laughing, extricating themselves from the absurd tangle. I can't believe it. He is so besotted he doesn't even care that I am in the room.

The serpent can slide away, its work over. The toxin secretly coursing through me these weeks, through veins and arteries, bursts now in livid anger. As soon as we are alone in our room under the eaves I turn on Jimmy. "What's happened to you? Do you know how transparent you are?" I am angry; it's rare; he's the one for whom anger is always available. Jimmy is uncomfortable, he says "Hush. You'll wake the baby." What do I care? I don't lower my voice. "Can you imagine how I feel? Outside, left outside of your excitement?" "It's nothing darling. Nothing . . ." "Nothing? Am I blind? You are smitten. A forty-year-old adolescent," I cry. I am so exposed, so ashamed; where is my pride. "You know I would do nothing to hurt you," he's distressed; he's never seen me so angry. "Have you—" He assures me, "No, no." Not only is it of no importance, he says, but it has not gone beyond the most casual . . . ; he can't say the word. "It's your lesser self speaking," he says gently, lovingly. He reminds me of how rich we are, how fortunate; our babies, or life: the litany of good fortune. Be generous, he implies. "You cast a shadow," he says.

I subside.

We began to talk at night, in our room under the eaves; a catharsis. The old talk of marriage, and its possessiveness, its exclusiveness; the possibility of variations within. No taboos. Old unlikely scenarios, Jimmy urging imaginary deviation, "do it, it will please me . . ." Did he know he perfectly insured I wouldn't when he said, "There is nothing you can do, nowhere you can go, that I am not with you." He is safe; I am isolated, immobilized, and my appetites are impossibly particular. Yet when he unexpectedly answered the telephone at a friend's house and I ask in surprise, "What are *you* doing there?" and he said, "Don't you know we have a direct connection? I am at the other end of any line you call," I loved it. I laugh but I love the idea.

And one night, before I lose myself in sleep, I *do* see the shadow I cast. It's the duality of jealousy I must wrestle with. Blessing and boon for Jimmy is curse and pain for me. The very thing that makes his summer a pleasure makes mine a torment. Hadn't I wished he would find someone to relieve his lonely drudgery, find the help he always needs, so that he could remember why he chose to live here, with me, and our children, keeping the prospect of community alive. And there Jeness was, this summer's someone. Literate, intelligent, an eager apprentice; with her the barn chores go like the wind, weedy fields become orderly gardens. He's happy, he's stirred.

How could I not be glad for him?

Chapter Fifteen

Tobacco

JIMMY RAISED his glass of Jameson's Irish. "A shot glass like this filled with seed will grow an acre of tobacco." In three languages—Nicht wahr! Fantastic! Figurez-vous!—the magician had his audience's attention. It was early spring. The paying guests were emigrés staying with us on our farm in the hills of Western Massachusetts. "Like the Black Forest," Hertha said, moved by what she saw and what she remembered. It was Hertha who opened the floodgates when she said in her warm, deep Austrian accent "It must be such hard work, Jim." Then he raised his glass, tossed off the whiskey, and he took them the course. "There is no crop so demanding, no crop that needs so many separate, painstaking, crucial steps. That can perish in an instant . . ." "How can that happen!" Hertha was the one who responded. Jimmy addressed her, his leader's instinct finding the follower. "The seedlings can be blighted by disease in the tobacco beds. Cutworms can destroy young plants in the field. Hail, big as golf balls, can come out of nowhere just when the plants are ready to harvest and tear the leaves to shreds!" "No insurance?" "Ha. The rates are prohibitive. Small farmers could never afford it. No, farmers are at the mercy of the elements." The range of Jimmy's voice was so effective, from grim to exultant, it filled the room.

I cleared the table. His voice followed me into the kitchen, rose above the water running from the tap as I scraped the dishes into the bucket for compost and rinsed and stacked. Ernst asked the question about insurance. Ernst was civilized, so civilized he was almost extinguished; he gasped as he spoke; smiled, small muscle adjustments around his mouth. Hunched shoulders protected his chest, a silk paisley scarf guarded his throat, the gasp muffled his voice, yet

there was a great sweetness and courtesy in him. He met Hertha
when he was her editor at Scribner's. Born in Munich, educated at
Oxford, he was a distinguished translator of Karl Jaspers. Hertha,
well, Hertha's persistence, and enthusiasm, her canniness in choosing salable themes for children's books in her adopted country:
Statue of Liberty, the Christmas Tree, made her not only a published writer but anthologized, dramatized, digested. A skier, a
swimmer, a fast-moving woman with short cropped auburn hair and
eyes that flashed gold and green, she was Ernst's lifeline, he lived
through her, she infused him with breath, the exclamation point to
his parentheses, he was uxorious to a degree. Ernst was the friendly
observer; he was well-disposed to the American, if only to please
Hertha. He was not interested in farming or its history or its
problems, but he followed the tobacco-raising description with academic alertness. "It's like champagne, made more precious for the
human toil involved. A royal crop, tobacco. King of the Valley,"
Jimmy went on. "Not so long ago men were persecuted, imprisoned,
their noses were cut off, for using tobacco!" Hertha's cry of horror,
"What! Why?" She was ready to champion the cause of any victim.
"Early in the spring you build the cold frames for the tobacco beds in
a place where they will get full sun. So many feet of frame to an acre.
You fertilize the soil in the bed, rake it, pulverize it, make it as fine as
possible. Remember how small the seed that must germinate there?
Like poppy seed." Poppy seed rolls. Jimmy loses his attentive audience for a moment; they long for the fragrance of the Viennese
bakery on Seventy-eighth Street. "After you sow the seed, it must be
well watered, soaked, then the beds are entirely covered with sash
made to fit frames closely. Sash? "Like our windows only bigger.
Very heavy and, of course, fragile. All that glass."

It takes two people to move those heavy covers and moved they
must be. When the sun is too hot, off! when the temperature falls,
back on; when there is a gentle rain take the sash off; a pelting deluge,
on again. I stop what I am doing and run out when I am called. It's an
awkward operation. If you drop your end, glass all over; if you
stumble, disaster. Make no jokes, curse no curses; a blank mind and
a sure foot for that job.

"While the seedlings are growing in the beds you must prepare the
land," I could hear the patience now in Jimmy's voice, invoking toil
immemorial. "Plowing, harrowing, fertilizing, and harrowing again

until the tilth is made fine . . ." He would race through barn chores, deny himself the talk he loved around the kitchen table, deny himself the last sweet minutes of morning sleep.

"More coffee?" I asked Heinrich. He was showing signs of restlessness. "Thank you, yes."

What did he care about all this plowing and planting? He was Heinrich Lessing, a poet known well in his native Berlin. His career was at a standstill; there was nothing for him in this country. He lived for the day he could return, when the madness was over in Europe. Meanwhile he must beg refugee committees for crumbs. Put up with noble fools like this primitive American. He shifted his narrow, bony bottom on the wooden kitchen chair: a very small man, more like an old child, in a shabby brown suit, a shirt and tie. When he went out the door he wore his Fedora. He approached the pasture fence in the mornings after milking, and as the cows ambled out of the barn, two or three of the curious stopped to look at Heinrich. They mooed. He doffed his hat. "Lessing," he said. No levity. This was a dignified exchange. He continued his morning walk, and they went on to the upper pasture.

"Why don't you use a machine?" Heinrich asked Jimmy out of boredom.

"Tractor," Ernst murmured.

"Wouldn't it be faster?" a small light of mischief in Heinrich's ferret face. "Horses are more romantic, but after all, Jim, you are growing for big business, yes?" Heinrich didn't know yet that Jimmy thrived on baiting.

"Is it romantic to prefer the company of sentient beasts to a stinking noisy metal machine? Can you imagine a living connection with a tractor? Compare filling a tank with gas from a pump to climbing into the haymow and forking hay to your horse . . ." Jimmy switched from patient teaching to rhetorical mockery. He avoided Heinrich's reference to our crop as "business." That was an uneasy dilemma, a sore point. Anyway, he didn't owe Heinrich Lessing an explanation. Cerebral little worm. Jimmy masked his contempt for the poet with brusque politeness. Not only because Heinrich was a friend of Ernst and Hertha, but also because we needed the income from paying guests. Under cover of a child's cry from upstairs Heinrich said, "Compare a horse's fart to a tractor's backfire . . ." He was not afraid of Jimmy, who was, after all, a convinced pacifist, but there was something definitely intimidating about him. Heinrich did not feel quite safe. If Jimmy heard him he gave no sign. A gnat's bite. He lit a cigarette, took a deep, lung-filling drag. "Then the plants are ready, and again there's the scramble to find help. To pull plants . . ."

––––

I ran up the stairs, changed the baby, urged a nap, crooned promises, all the while following the sound of Jimmy's voice. I am his true appreciative audience although invisible. Not only did we need the income from paying guests, but we—I—needed the world they brought to our hilltop. It was my theatre, my seminar, rich and tantalizing with names of people and places until now only literary. Toller, Von Horvath, Werfel. Stories of their friends and colleagues destroyed by the Nazi terror. Or stories of the lucky ones who escaped, who were at our table. We sat around the fire far into the night, Hertha's cigarette in the corner of her mouth, her eyes narrowed against the smoke: a mock-tough Brechtian character, sipping brandy, rum, vodka, whatever was brought in, and talk, talk, feverish talk. I loved it; I fed on it. The small warning reminder of early-rising children and duties of the day didn't have a chance. I'd catch up. I had trained myself to find a quiet room during a quiet time, stretch out, close my eyes, be instantly asleep, and in exactly ten minutes up again and back to work, refreshed. We never advertised for paying guests. They were friends, or friends of friends passed on to us through the dense network of sympathetic connections, American and European. There were disappointments; sometimes expectations on both sides were wide of the mark. It wasn't just an Inn, they were not only guests, they were also a source of erotic tension between us. A flicker of my interest in any man put Jimmy on alert, raised his specific awareness, awakened an unexpressed tremor of anxiety: Did I long to escape my life with him, our life of insecurity and isolation? Did I regret a life of luxury and irresponsibility and city excitement? And I, I always knew when he would find a particular woman appealing. It was easy. I simply used his eyes. He was so direct, so transparent; I was familiar with the signals. I knew his predilections, his discriminations, his seriousness. No signals and no flares from our early summer European guests, but they were fast becoming warm friends. Hertha and Ernst would leave next week, but Hertha was already making excited plans to return for an extended stay, "maybe six months," so that they could work on their books in "the room with the so-beautiful light." She liked our children, too, in a grave, formal way, and she was generous enough to find indisputable evidence of genius in the shape of Michael's thumb.

———

I covered the baby, tiptoed out of the room, and closed the door soundlessly. I stripped the guest beds and changed the linen. He wouldn't tell them about another hard job that is part of growing tobacco, I thought. Jimmy wouldn't tell them about last week when he forced himself into the despised role of supplicant. Hat in hand, knot in stomach, he had applied to the bank for a crop loan to pay for fertilizer and field help. He shaved and trimmed his mustache; his hair was glinting gold and not too shaggy. In his worn, clean work clothes he hoped the bank officer would see him as a prudent man, a credible risk, even though the odds were against him. He petitioned in the right mix of firmness and respect. Nevertheless, Mr. Holden's response was, "It's a gamble for us, Jim. Are you going to be able to get help?" Jimmy swallowed his retort, "Your astronomical interest will pay you for your gamble you bastard." He imitated instead a confident young grower who was at the same time not too irritatingly cocky. He got his loan, with chattel mortgage attached. "Chattel" had a ring of doom. It conjured the sheriff, the eviction; the children clinging to us in tears as cows and furniture were trucked off.

———

Jimmy was incapable of living without drama and poetry. If our life was not the ancient idyll of Hesiod's *Work and Days*, it was still far from the corruption of the marketplace. He would never change places with the man behind the desk who drew up the instrument for our loan. He chose the precarious position. He chose to swim against the tide, towing me and the children, defending us, protecting us against sharks and treacherous currents. And sharks and piranha were sighted with regularity. Crises and alarms took their toll, frayed my control; silent protest could be silent no longer and my deflating barb would be in the air. Jimmy caught it, gave it an effective twist, and shot it right back. Always after these wounding exchanges I was sorry for the damage. The longer we were together the more accurate was our aim.

————

Charlie was the only worker we could find this season to help us set. He was sorry for us, with our antiquated horse-drawn setter. He was disgusted with the smug talk in the local bar of our imminent failure: "They won't last long." But we need someone to partner him. It was he who suggested, "Blanche can do it. Hell, she'll catch on after the first few plants." "You really think so?" Charlie's confidence gave me new status. I thought setting tobacco was a skill that could only be acquired after years of teamwork. I felt honored, and anxious. I fixed a meal for the children. Jimmy and I were too keyed up for more than a bit of bread and cheese. The garb for this job was cover: blue jeans and a long-sleeved shirt buttoned to the neck, a cotton scarf to cover my head, all hair tucked in. Charlie watched me lower myself into the metal seat, it was right down in the furrow; he checked the footrest to see if it was long enough for legs extended, put a box of plants in my lap, and then got into his seat beside me. "When you hear the click, that means the water gushes from the drum and you drop your plant. The next click is mine and you're getting another plant ready. And so on. Your turn. My turn. We try not to skip. If you do, don't panic. The setter won't stop. We'll get it when we stock over." He could say don't panic; I was going on cold, no rehearsal, and my heart was beating wildly.

It was Jimmy's job to keep the horse's pace slow and steady. Viewed across the new tilled field, bordered by woods in tender tremulous poplar green, I could see us as a stately procession: the powerful Percheron leading, then Jimmy holding the lines, sitting alertly straight; lastly the setters, absorbed, heads bent to the planting and just visible above the furrow. We established a rhythm. The only sounds were the click of the spout on the water drum, the step of the horse, the quiet urging from Jimmy. Charlie and I so concentrated that it was only in the turnaround at the end of the row that he could say, "You're doin' good. Sure this is your first time?" A gallantry I appreciate. The clouds of fine dust settled on me, my clothes, my face; grit in my mouth. It didn't bother Charlie, I would not let it bother me. We set a two-acre piece and when I got out of the setter and stretched and turned and looked back on row upon row of bright green upstanding plants I thought: I did it! Early the next morning as soon as it was light, even before the cows came down from the pasture, Jimmy was up and out and walking the field Charlie and I had set. "Very few missed," he reported. He knew I was waiting for reassurance, "but the cutworms . . ." The enemy cutworm. Caterpillar of the noctuid moth. In the spring its fat worminess found tender cabbage plants or new corn shoots; these were acceptable but tobacco plants were far preferred. Suck the life from the plant, fasten on the stem just at ground level and then curl up to rest, replete. Cutworms were a phenomenon that would bring out the anthropomorph in anyone. So Jimmy, for whom the forces of good and evil were manifest, had no hesitation in assigning to the cutworm vicious intentional destructiveness. With the lifeless plant marking center, searching fingers would uncover the killer. "Aha!" Pick it up and squeeze between thumb and forefinger. Hard. Pop and squish, and green ooze seeped. Disgusting and gratifying. Wipe your fingers in the hot soil and on to the next victim, plant, and the next quarry, worm. The squeamish could use two stones for the execution. I didn't care if it was effete, or slower. I used two stones. Even the cutworm's late summer metamorphosis to white moth fluttering around the table lamp did not earn philosophical forgiveness for its cyclical beginnings. Jimmy damned the moth for its sneaky escape from righteous destruction in cutworm days. Our Polish neighbors who had worked in tobacco since they were little kids hated the spoilers as much as we did but they didn't waste their breath cursing them. "You want to farm Jim, that's the way it is." Privately they called him the "Professor." Although he dropped his g's to, he thought, slip inconspicuously into their company, he could not help his peculiar eloquence in praise or outrage. His voice was its instrument and ranged from whisper to bellow to the consternation or delight of his listeners. There were no forbidden subjects: the Pope, the President; prisons, corporations.

———

The Kuzontkowskis were weary, sitting with their backs against the milk house, legs outstretched, having a beer, telling Jimmy they'd seen worse years for cutworms. "The top field is devastated," Jimmy said bitterly. "Hey, Jim, gimme a bucket. I'm goin' t'take a walk,"

Carl Finkowski was restless. Now in his forties, he was the oldest of Alec's seven children: Alec, the most prosperous, and the stingiest farmer in the hills. Carl had a failed marriage and lived off by himself in the flats near the railroad, rarely sober and mostly miserable. Back he came after a while, just as the men were getting ready to leave, and showed his horrid haul: the bucket was filled with squirming live cutworms. "Carl you crazy bastard! What are you goin' t'do with them?" "Spread them on the old man's field. That's what." It was so grotesque a punishment for the despised father, such an unthinkable criminal transgression—and to announce it!—that they all hooted with delight. They rolled on the grass, held their sides, imagining Carl's father's rage, forgetting their sore backs and grime and beer all gone. So buried was the source of the irrepressible bubble of laughter, so secret was the shared pool of humiliation and hard work and the harsh authority of their own fathers that it would never reach daylight. But Carl would do it for them.

——

"And that's only the beginning," Jimmy would tell our friends from the city. They appeared to give him their attention, but it was plain to me they were thinking "Gott sei dank," Thank God for the city life they would return to: their emigré's existence in seedy upper West Side rooming houses; their rounds of publishers, casting agents, galleries; pooling leads, guarding connections. Weaving desperate intrigues. "Once your crop is in, and stocked over, then you must cultivate." Jimmy did not trust the new Percheron team. They were not trained to cultivate; he chose the gelding he judged more tractable and intelligent, but when he stopped for lunch Jimmy said, "Impossible. He won't stay in the path. Steps on plants." His horse had failed. We sympathized. He sat across the table from Patricia Wilkinson, our early summer guest. He looked at her: a possible solution. "You ride, Patricia." "Sure." Junior League in English habit around Central Park. "How about sitting on the horse and guiding it?" "After lunch okay?" Patricia was willing. Jimmy contrived some comfort between horse's back and Patricia's bottom with a pillow folded in a blanket, and with a wide-brimmed straw hat on her well-groomed patrician head she bumped and rocked all afternoon up and down the tobacco rows. No longer the useless darling of privilege, she was determined no complaint would pass her lips; she would endure the hot sun and the maddening midges and the soreness of her stretched limbs. "Get *over*, you fucker." She could not help flinching at Jimmy's command to the horse. She distracted herself from the sound, and the heat, and the persistent bugs by whispering encouraging French phrases remembered from Vassar classes. Percheron *was* French. When Jimmy thanked her— "It's a great help. Really went better"—she was rewarded; her fine skin flushed.

————

Hot days and cool nights, the combination that made the Connecticut Valley ideal for growing cigar leaf tobacco, produced a luxuriant wonder in our fields: the broad-leaved brilliant green plant, so viscid any contact left a sticky residue. It grew tall as a man, a tropical forest transplanted to a New England hillside. Tall as a man, it became vulnerable to wind and storm, to the sudden violence of late-summer barometric plunges. To minimize the vulnerability, to give it secure purchase in the earth, the plant must be topped. The top, the spire, was the tubular flower, nicotiana. Reach into the plant, stretch for it, break it off in one swift snap. The taproot was then mysteriously strengthened, and the plant would have a chance to withstand sudden squalls. A messy job, topping; the juices came spurting out; great care must be taken not to damage a leaf yet we must move fast. Jimmy worked opposite me. "What an erotic plant this is," he said. We milked it for analogies: deflowering sends the taproot down; the flower could only be reached by passing the barriers with care; even the language: juices, suckers, stripping. The teasing talk made the work go better; before we knew it we had done another row. The smell was wonderful, aromatic, and the blossoms, how could I toss them away? We wanted the broadest leaf for market. Frustrate the seed and the growth should go into leaf. Not at once. Nature, the Force, sent shoots between stalk and leaf, each shoot carrying seed, each shoot stealing nutrients from the leaf. Suckers. So once again, a few days after topping, we went through the rows, the acres of rows, stopping at each plant, spotting the suckers, reaching in and snapping them off. I stole time from guests and children, an hour, even half an hour to do two or three rows, then back to the house to bathe and start dinner. At night, those August nights, so still, so hot; the milky mist hanging in the valley, rolling right up and into our windows. The children asleep. The house silent at last. We are alone, we closed the door on the day, on the tobacco in the field and the cows in the pasture. Shedding clothes, duty and distraction bathed away, our hot skin slippery; exploring, taking our time. The last thing I saw behind eyes closed on my way to oblivion was tobacco plants, row on row, imprinted on my lids.

———

That was August; heat and high hope. Now in November it was cold and news of the tobacco market was ominous. Gone was the exhilaration of other years when the price was soaring and Jimmy converted all barn and shed space to hang plants to cure, anyplace under cover and off the ground that could be vented and fitted with beams and planks. The golden leaf then at eighty cents a pound or more and Jimmy the "book farmer" savoring the buyers' verdict: "beautiful leaf." The markets in the Indies, cut off during the war, were producing and shipping again. The price had plummeted. Thirty cents was what we were hearing. Thirty cents would not even cover the cost of raising a pound of tobacco. There would be nothing for payments on bank loans, personal debts, clamorous merchants. Not one buyer had yet come up the hill to look at our crop. There was dark and bitter talk of conspiracy. Representatives of rival companies met in secret cabal at the Hotel Warren in South Deerfield. The price was set there, and they agreed firmly among themselves not to pay one cent above it. Any grower foolhardy enough to hold out, to hope for a better price from a buyer-come-lately would be taught a harsh lesson. He would be shut out, black-listed: his tobacco could rot.

"Car coming!" Lights over the hill, Michael counted: two, three, four cars. They came up fast, wheeled into the barnyard. It was the Kuzontkowski stripping crew. This past summer the Kuzontkowski brothers rented six of our eleven acres of tobacco tillage and space to hang it. They took their crop down during the damp last week. They climbed high on the beams, up to the peak, nimble and surefooted as goats, handing down from level to level the slats of cured tobacco plants. The men in dark clothes, their faces the only light in the long dark of the barn festooned with the hanging brown, gold, copper, brass of the great leaf; I suffered sympathetic vertigo watching them up there. The shadows thrown by the dim bulbs in temporary loops of extension cords around the barn were grotesque and dramatic; the geometry, the dark and the light, a Piranesi. The Kuzontkowski gang, joking, cursing. "Hey Zack! Catch me" "Jesus Mary and Joseph this is one slippery bitch of a beam." Their language is mild when I am around. Mike to Joe, Zack and Leon to Stefan, the shouts traveled. Anthony is the older brother, responsible for renting our land, for organizing the work crews; he had the final decision in closing with the buyers. He responded to the rough cheerful mood, but his heart wasn't in it. He was sober and worried. The need to take down fast, while the damp lasted, was tempered by the need to watch for careless handling of the tobacco, to watch for reckless climbing. Some of the kids were crazy. No one had insurance that would cover a broken neck. Each day after harvest the crop curing in the barn had been checked; vents were opened; vents were closed. The plants, stalks speared by slats and hanging head-down, were checked as green leaf gave ground to brown. The natural curing process was slow; trusting to seasonal damps was tricky. Rich growers—Consolidated Cigar, for instance—steamed their cured tobacco on schedule. We gave weather reports close attention, scanned the heavens for signs, waited for a damp, rainy spell, when the tobacco could be handled without crumbling. Now that it was down it was imperative to work fast, before the plants rotted in the heat and moisture generated in the pile. Jimmy had exhausted every possibility for stripping help. A maze of old ties: "we're cousins, we're neighbors, we were in third grade together" bound them in mutual aid. We couldn't get in.

———

"Shoot me! Somebody shoot me if I ever grow another leaf of the filthy stuff!" The children raised startled eyes to their father, struck mute by the fierce intensity in his voice. Eight-year-old Michael lowered his eyes to his plate, his appetite for gingerbread suddenly lost, the worry bump on his forehead instantly visible. His older sister watched their father, Deirdre wanted Jimmy to see her devotion, to know she would help if she were allowed. She was almost eleven. Her eyes filled: "Shoot me"; she could already see him before a firing squad, refusing the blindfold. Jimmy pushed away from the table, buttoned his denim jacket, pulled his navy watch cap to the right angle; he looked around the kitchen distractedly. "Where's my flashlight?" he demanded. Deirdre jumped up to search for the hiding flashlight; at last she could do something. I lifted the baby Gabriel out of his highchair. I slowed down, I spoke quietly, "Come sweetie, to bed," as if by my example I could change the turbulence in the air. To Jimmy, in neutral, I said, "Try the bench in the hallway." There he found it. He nuzzled the baby in my arms, kissed Deirdre and Michael goodnight, and trying not to sound importunate or pleading he asked me "Do you think you could come out for a while?" "As soon as I get them to bed . . ." He went out the door, shutting it quickly to keep the frosty air out, the precious heat in. I stood at the window, obscurely comforted by the baby I held, watching Jimmy cross the farmyard to the barn. The moon was rising, full, and awesome: its light touched the crown of the forest in the ravine and beyond, in the valley the pure clarity of the night transformed the lights of Amherst ten miles off. Brilliant winking lights signaling happenings of unbelievable excitement. I pushed that nonsense away. Hurry, get out to the barn I told myself. I heard Deirdre's peremptory, "Michael. Finish your gingerbread. I am clearing the table for Mother." "Do you have to be so *bossy*?" No time for the wounded, indignant boy, I started up the stairs and called down, "Stop bickering. Michael, get ready for bed."

I pulled on black wool pants, found an old lovat green shetland sweater to go over my jersey. The shetland was so stretched out its sleeves covered half my hands, and that made it perfect because gloves could not be worn for stripping. Two pairs of socks, oversize lace-up boots somebody left behind, and roomy enough for flexing toes when you stand in one cold damp spot for hours. A black jersey helmet that covered my head and came down around my neck; I could pull it over my chin and mouth, breathe out and be my own instant furnace. And finally, to top it all, a hand-me-down coat of French loomed wool in jewel colors of crimson, purple, and blue; the warmest thing I had and a private emblem of courage in the gloom and bad luck. I stopped in the hallway for one last check. I heard a thin wail. Baby? I listened and I heard it again: steam escaping from the radiator valve. Relieved, I looked into the study. "I'm going," pitching my voice away from the children upstairs to Deirdre reading. She raised her head, damp-eyed and sorrowful. "*Little Women* again?" She nodded with a quivering smile. "Tch," I gave her hasty sympathy, whispered, "I must hurry—I can't breathe in this mountain of stuff." I slipped out onto the porch; the cold air was a relief. I crossed the road to the barn. The four Kuzontkowski crew cars were parked near the ramp; lights and noise up there. Jimmy was visible in the window, alone in the lower level. I pushed aside the rug in the doorway, pushed aside the heavy silence that surrounded him. I took my place on the other side of the waist-high pile he had uncovered, a small portion of the mammoth stretch to the end of the barn. He kicked a plank over: "Stand on that." He stamped his feet, reached for another stalk, continued stripping. "Are they all in bed?" "All except Deirdre," I said, pulling loose a heap of stalks, taking one, starting it slowly, my hands remembering: turn from side to side, hold the stalk in the left hand, pick with the right. "She's with *Little Women*." "Weeping?" "Mm." A burst of laughter from the crowd above, and we both looked up, following the sound. Our eyes met in commiseration as we stripped the limp brown leaves from the stalks. I was still warm. I picked up speed, plucking dexterously, quickly ascending the stalk as I turned it. "What a difference it would make, a gang like that . . ." "All the difference in the world," he agreed. And how many times have we said that I wondered.

———

The crew up there, mostly men, a few spunky women, were fresh from warm rooms and good kielbasa and golompki. After taking down in a damp, the word went on: Kuzontkowski needs strippers. No question. Pile into the cars, drive up into the hills, into the freezing barn: Get that leaf stripped! Bring your bottle. The whiskey was passed only to take the edge off the cold; it was a party anyway. The times I had stripped tobacco with our Polish neighbors' big gangs, elbow to elbow all around the huge barn-long pile, I thought I might have inhibited them, but not much. I could learn a lot in one evening. Sophie was "expecting." "Must have good neighbors, Mike," said Roman to Sophie's husband. Innocently. This was such a routine tease no one paid much attention. There was a general air of affectionate good nature. They shared a family look and a family sound. Those stressed consonants. "He's a touch-hole cousin . . ." I heard on my left. What is a touch-hole cousin? I wondered and didn't ask. But a remark in Polish causes such an explosion of laughter I begged a translation. I was refused, kept outside, but they closed the door softly: "Aah, Blanche, you don't want to hear it. Nice girl like you." I passed my hand of tobacco to Sophie on its way down the line to the packer. "Do you speak Polish at home?" "Sure. Everybody. It's the first language for the kids. That way they never forget." Our first autumn here when the call went out for strippers, Jimmy volunteered. To be neighborly, to learn about tobacco. He went down the hill and up the next to a ten-bent barn. Two big piles, a gang around each. Room was made for him, basic instruction briefly given, and he picked up his first stalk with a spurious air of confidence. He was doing all right, fine in fact, gaining speed, picking up useful tips on "making a crop." Learning the names of the people near him, first names only; last names were unpronounceable and interchangeable. A man opposite him, a distinct Yankee, no smiles, no jokes, no nips at the bottle, a man named Dexter, cleared his throat and asked, "Did you hear the one about the Roosevelts? Eleanor said to Franklin: 'You kiss the niggers, and I'll kiss the Jews and we'll stay in the White House as long as we choose . . .'" Jimmy instantly threw his stalk across the pile, said, "I won't listen to that garbage. My wife is a Jew," turned on his heel and left the barn. That must have been an unexpected diversion. The "book farmer" had declared himself, and although many of the Polish farmers didn't like Jews either, they liked Dexter less. It was a story told at the bars that week, then forgotten.

––––––

I hated to see Jimmy disconsolate. I so depended on his invincible optimism. It was too much, the hard work, the wretched return, the responsibility for me and the children. The inevitable borrowings. Who could I ask? Who hadn't heard it before? How could I help? Tonight, I said, as though it really didn't matter, "Did you ask up there if anyone wanted to work?" "No one bit. They all want to go deer hunting. Season opens tomorrow. It's a ritual; they wouldn't miss it. Give me your tobacco." I passed the fistful I held, thrusting my freed hand inside my coat for a moment; the tips of my fingers were growing numb. He began stamping his feet slowly, heavily, in his big clumsy boots. "What do you suppose the temperature is?" I asked. "Never mind that." It's true. He's right. It's as cold as we are. What's the difference if it's 15° above or 5° below. Silence. I kept stripping. Jimmy carried the stripped stalks out of our way; he uncovered another small section of our tobacco pile. What time is it.

I think I've been here all my life. We've barely begun, barely made a dent, but I can't wait for eleven o'clock, the time we set for quitting.

"Tell me something," he said. It was a command. "What?" "Anything. Tell me about"—I knew what was coming—"the one at the hotel that summer." "Oh, it's all a blur. So long ago." He had hold of it again. "Oh come, you must remember something. What was he like?" Coaxing. Pretending detachment. I was silent, frozen inside as well now. I listened to the shout in Polish that came from the loft and wished myself there. "Was he mechanical? Was he casual? Did he astonish you? You do remember." The inquisitor is loose. How can I answer, answer briefly, and appease him. "How did he approach you? How did it start?" "We danced." "Come. Dance with me." He extended his hand and pulled me up on the tobacco box. We jumped on the packed leaf, compacting it, pressing it, facing each other, his arm around my waist. He grinned in mock lasciviousness, pulling me close. We hopped off, back to our stations, momentarily warmed. He was engaged in the struggle for that past, for that one year I was free of my parents and not yet tied to him. Tonight, to leave the dusty pile of tobacco and the boring grind of repetitious work he was willing to suffer the pain and excitement of jealousy. "Where's your total recall?" he gibed. "Where's that photographic memory you boast about?" I smiled faintly. I would not help him. I continued stripping the tobacco, tossing the stalks behind me. Think of something else, be unavailable, don't collaborate. So I thought: There will be wagonloads of the stripped stalks carted out to the fields and spread to decompose and become fertilizer. And I thought: When these leaves are rolled into cigars who will cut the ends and light up and where will the smoke rise. And—how quickly I am cold again. Bitter, implacably frigid air. I'm made for the desert. Hot, dry places. Sun. "The one on the Island. What about him? You wept, you said. What made you?" "I felt lost." "How do you mean, lost?" I shrugged. "What did he do? How did he react?" "I don't remember." "Oh God—" He flung his finished stalk on the pile behind him. I am sorry for him but I won't hand him his weapons.

I passed my hand of stripped leaves to him. He pressed them on top of the packing box, folded the paper lining, and tied the bundle's three strings, one at either end and one in the middle. Pulling and tugging so it would be tight, so that no air would get in to further dry it and take away the precious weight. He lifted the fifty-pound bundle out of the packing box and lined it for the next one, moving deliberately; I could see his breath in the frosty air, his heavy clothes slowing him, his attention to the task automatic. His pursuit absorbed his thoughts. He shifted direction. He asked me now, with simple reasonableness, "Why can't you talk? I do, to you. About things much further back in time." "It's vivid to you, I guess." I was caught by the changed line. I felt myself thawing, recognizing the fairness of his assertion, disarmed by the switch from demand to entreaty. "It's far away and nothing. They're nothing, those people." "Not Vincent. You never said he was nothing." How cunning he was, sensing my guard lowered he returned to attack. "Only by comparison. He had no center. Sweet, warm. Fun to be with. No more." He hated this shorthand description. His imagination could not take hold anywhere. Too bland a ghost. "Tell me what Mr. Nothing looked like," he jeered. "You can remember that." "He was, tall . . ." I considered serving up the phantom of the gentle debonair Southerner to the insatiable Jimmy. I saw the South Carolinian, blameless man, at this moment seated at the bar in the Algonquin: he was drawn to such obvious spots. How could I have been so stupid and trusting in those early days with Jimmy. I had no thought then of handing him arrows for his quiver, no thought of protecting anything or anyone. We were in a rush to discover each other, to uncover each other, to fill in the years before we met: an unending revelation of life before union of our disparate tribes. Since then we were never parted. We lived and worked together, our friends, our books, our music, our highs, and our lows all shared. The faintest inflection, the merest frown, the shadow of a smile: everything affected our climate. Tonight, during the catechism across the divide of tobacco leaves, a thought that until now had been formless took shape, a calculating and treacherous thought. From now on I would have a zone marked "Private." Do not enter. Don't touch. "Look, darling . . ." He knew I meant stop, please stop. "Why do you care?" "Why?" His voice was low and level, there were elements of pain and scorn. "I resent their coarseness of spirit—that they didn't recognize you . . ."

Oh Jimmy now the whole dark barn glows with the gift you give me. I will have my subversive chamber but we will live together always.

Caught in our struggle the sounds of the work gang above were an unheeded background hum. Suddenly there were shouts and the thunder of clomping booted feet and Anthony's voice calling "Jim! Uncover your pile! We're coming down." We looked at each other, stunned by joy, pure joy. Jimmy rushed off to turn on the big bare bulbs that illuminated the whole pile, then began hastily pulling off the canvases, the rugs, the blankets and old quilts and tarpaulins that covered the tobacco that was waist high and ran the length of the barn. The Polish workers were full of high spirits, wonderfully noisy, they sounded like angels. When they climbed over the barrier of discarded stalks and took their places elbow to elbow around the pile they looked like angels too. There were a few women, the mother of Joe opposite me, the sister of Jose beside me. I counted the rest dizzily: fourteen, no eighteen. Two men packing now. Jimmy pretended no surprise when Anthony, who was packing, said, "Where are your stones, Jim?" Anthony was only half-joking; almost everyone buried a couple of good-sized stones in odd bundles to add to the weight. "And wet it down before you deliver" to further add to the weight. As if Jimmy would jeopardize the marketing of our crop by so petty a cheat. He stripped and packed and heaved and stacked with nervous urgency. We did not exchange a glance. We had one thought: we would finish stripping tonight.

What is this subversive chamber? In the beginning, I am silent inside it. I lean against the walls thick with mist of dreams, old yearnings, wild ambition, sudden desires. They yield, cover me with amorphous dark, envelop me with chimera, dissolve, form again. And again. Until, after ten years of life with Jimmy, I grow up. When I grow up, the walls of my subversive chamber are stone, a trap; the quartz glints in the words early inscribed: This is where I choose to be. Still silent, inside it I confine rage and restlessness and discontent. I am immobilized, dependent. Possessed. Outside my subversive chamber I am busy making the trap fast, inescapable. I never stop working on my collaboration, my fate. Constructing the myth.

Chapter Sixteen

THE FARM FAILS; FOURTH CHILD

- 1951 -

SOMETHING important is happening at the big barn across the road. The dairy herd has been sold, all nineteen head, to Sam August our friendly cattle dealer; three-year-old Gabriel and I sit on the front step, watching the departure of the cows. Jimmy leads each cow out of the barn, Sam takes the halter from him and walks the cow up the ramp and into the van. "Why Columbine go?" Gabriel's voice is low and sad. "Why Sheba go?" his voice raises; I hold his hand. But when Jimmy follows the last Guernsey heifer into the van Gabriel clutches me and cries in alarm "Jimmy go too?" I reassure him, "No, no. Never." Poor baby.

It has become clear to me that the goal of farming and living in community may never come to pass. From time to time someone appears, a likely person to cast his life with ours. After the courtship, the seduction, and the surrender, there is disillusion: regretful or cold or bitter. Jimmy fights finally with everyone, no one can measure up, his demands are total. Even in Jimmy the idea of imperative community grows distant, though it never disappears. Without that vision, I know farming is not for him, not for Jimmy's temperament. Patience, patience; the willingness to endure monotony, loneliness, drudgery; the fatalism to accept hail, drought, the tyranny of the market. "Where else," he demands, "where else does the buyer set the price? Who but the farmer will take what is offered for his milk, his tobacco, his grain? Imagine," he says with scorn, "telling the grocer you will give him twenty-five cents for his five-pound bag of sugar and he must accept." "Organize?" an innocent radical from New York City asks. "What, Yankee farmers?? Impossible," says Jimmy.

I am no more a farmer's wife than he is a farmer. Even the word "wife" troubles me. I avoid "I am his wife" or "He is my husband." We are lovers and comrades. Losing the farm would be an unthinkable defeat for him, not for me.

It is a wonderful place. I know it gives me balance, solace, surrounds me with beauty, delights all senses, but I can live anywhere. I can imagine living in a town, like Northampton, or even back in New York City, in the Village. I can imagine living anywhere unregimented, where I would be free to compose and invent my life with Jimmy. Oh he knew it, but as long as I kept it out of sight, in my subversive chamber, as long as my faithlessness was silent and secret and did not challenge his resolve, he could ignore it. He could count on me. As we thrash about, we present to our world a couple united, determined to keep the farm, to keep the vision; not to get mired in the ordinary, the humdrum; not to let the glow fade, the myth, the fairy tale. He could count on me to write placating letters to dunning creditors. Reluctant to see me go into the city to beg and borrow from our sympathetic friends, from my rich relations, I assure Jimmy it's nothing to me, a game, a role I play of respectful petitioner. A small loan, to tide us over? A second mortgage? In city clothes, falsely presenting a blithe confidence, I am greeted affectionately, treated to meals in elegant restaurants, gently let down. Discreetly slipped a check for a few hundred dollars. "I wish it could be more," murmurs our benefactor apologetically.

Stopgaps until we can find "capital." Capital was different from money. We are never poor, we are "broke," it is capital that can make the difference. Capital for schemes, inventions: a fuel-saving chimney cap, a filter cigarette, a telephone with buttons to press instead of a dial to spin.

"Our troubles are over." Jimmy's down from the upper field; he's been planting the three-acre piece in cucumbers, a lowly crop, but it's ready money; we must diversify, the bottom is dropping out of the tobacco market. "I have a million dollar idea." He brings in the sun and the heat, the flush suffuses his skin, his eyes shine triumphantly blue. What is it this time? I make myself receptive, I sit down at the table along with the children. "Tell me." He pours a drink, whiskey straight, he lights a cigarette, he paces around the room. He's too excited for lunch. "Take carrot seed, for instance. How tiny they are, how the seedlings must be thinned, how painstaking the job is. If the seed could be fixed to a tape, spaced just right, on a tape impregnated with fertilizer, it could be wound on a spool that would be unrolled in the furrow, the spool could be attached to a tractor, or a horse-drawn planter. Just think of it! Never need thinning, never need fertilizing, the tape would disintegrate! Precision planting, labor saving." He spins on "Suburban gardeners. They could buy it by the yard." The children are caught by their father's excitement; Michael appreciates Jimmy's ingenuity, Gabriel likes the look and sound of Jimmy's jubilation, Deirdre is doubtful of untold riches, but she tries not to show it. Say nothing negative, say nothing to puncture the bubble; with every word it expands, grows more brilliant, iridescent. "Sounds good." I give him my full attention, "amazing no one has thought of it." He's relieved that I see it his way. "Isn't it?" But now that it's in the air, Jimmy's thinking, it's on the wind, every current ready to whisper into a receptive ear; they're out there, just waiting to snatch the pot of gold. "First thing I must do is to send myself a registered letter"—describing and dating his original idea; that done, he must find a patent lawyer, then we need capital, to pay that lawyer, finance his travel to interest seed companies.

It did sound good. Better than the Log-of-the-Month, last week's idea. The Log-of-the-Month. Hardwood: oak, maple, beech trees, chopped in our woodlot, cut to fireplace length, seasoned; delivered to apartment-dwellers in New York City. A brochure to go with the month's supply of firewood: the botanical, literary, mythological properties of each particular tree. A truck, a decent secondhand truck would be needed to make the 180-mile trip to grateful subscribers generated by our network. Jimmy was excited last week too. Last week, although I didn't stop preparing dinner, I was careful. Don't let him see my dubious look, don't utter the obvious, "Isn't it seasonal?" I see him in an old truck, the platform loaded with firewood in neat bundles; he's headed across the Tappan Zee Bridge into Manhattan; he pays no attention to the curious who stare into the cab: farmer? logger? artist? I follow him to the street in the East Seventies; he double-parks, the doorman directs him to the service entrance, to the service elevator. I can't arrange in my imaginings the logistics of unloading and delivering, but I see Jimmy, the transaction concluded, admiring the Bechstein piano, the Modigliani canvas in the elegant apartment, having a drink with the happy, satisfied customer, friend of a friend.

Then the search for "capital" was displaced by the search for "endowment." What better use for publishers' profits, for patrons-of-the-arts largesse, than a writers' colony? We had the ideal place; in the natural beauty of this two-hundred-acre hilltop farm we would build simple studios, renovate one tobacco barn for lectures, readings; another for dormitories; build a wing on our house for a larger dining room. An income for us, a boon and a blessing for the city-trapped writer; a seedbed for community. Not I, nor anyone, said, "Too ambitious," or "This may take years." Our friends suggested useful contacts, offered introductions; Jimmy even made a trip to the city, his own bold idea, to see the mysterious entrepreneur Ben Sonnenberg.

Double First Person

Now Jimmy was back at the typewriter; he had a story to tell, our story; a direction to point, a warning to give. He knew he would be able to get an advance on his second novel. He had no doubt that with fifty pages and an outline he could get a contract. Every morning he fired up the furnace, drove Deirdre and Michael eleven miles to Northampton, to Smith College Day School, and returned to fill his coffee cup and go to his study. The door was never closed. I heard the typewriter going full speed; I heard it stop; I heard the page ripped through the rollers, the crunch and crumple of the sheet discarded. He could hear, and listens, to everything going on in the house; *that's* why he kept his door open. He would seize on anything, any distraction. The mailman drove up the hill; before he turned, Jimmy was out the door to take the mail from his hand before he could put it in the box. In again, curses for bills and final notices; more promising distraction in a letter: could I manage a paying guest for three weeks? The baby bumped his head and wailed; Jimmy was out of the study, bounding up the stairs: What happened? Where? How? He wanted to deny it, reverse it, or at least find a culprit for the assault on our baby; Jimmy picked him up, kissed the hurt, found a cookie. Or, at the other end of the house he heard murmurous indistinguishable words running on in story, punctuated by laughter. I was telling it; our guest laughed. He was missing something.

Even when there was a pause between guests and we were alone and he worked at night after the children were asleep and the house was quiet, he struggled; he couldn't get into it. How could it be, he was such a talker, a spell-binder, never at a loss for words. Maybe he had dissipated it in talk; lost in the air, it wouldn't translate to the page. I thought, in my subversive chamber, he needed a congregation, a platform, a mountaintop.

———

"What would you be doing, Jimmy, if you didn't have us?" Us: three children, me. This big place and debts and bills. No hesitation. "I'd be sitting in a hovel somewhere, writing about how I didn't have you," he said soberly. How can I help? I know how I can help. Believe in him. Don't move away. In no way collude, by eye or word, with a critical visitor in the house, with a challenger, an adversary. In no way confuse our children by showing sympathy for their disappointment when Jimmy thwarted one more urgent desire, for their own good. Keep an even background hum of diligent domesticity. Be available.

———

"Listen," Jimmy says, and while I cut corn off the cob for a chowder he reads a long passage from Hermann Hesse's *Demian*; he's trying to convert me to his new discovery. I'd rather read it myself, pause, re-read; hear the author's voice. He knows it, and ignores it, he so wants the words to come through him to me. And it's true, he is a wonderful reader. Sometimes I tune out, I'm not entirely selfless. I turn to my journal, I've always kept a journal but now I cover pages and pages recording and speculating about our life. I write long letters to the world outside. I use a significant incident to shape a story. I show Jimmy a piece I'm working on, he groans, he wishes for my facility. I think I have the key, the key that will unlock Jimmy and open the door for me, and one morning I say, "Let's do it together." He was just waiting for me; he said "Yes," and the excitement begins.

———

Double first person, alternating voices, our very different voices, describing the same scenes, or the same time, from our separate views.

Jimmy scraps his manuscript.

We pace ourselves: writing in snatches in the day, saving concentrated work for the night, the quiet, uninterrupted night. Jimmy is at the typewriter in the study, I write with pen on pad in the kitchen; we stay up until three or four in the morning, fall into bed for a few hours of sleep, and we're never tired. It works, we're growing in it, it's growing in us; it is so intense. Living now both in the light of the present and the shadow of the past we enter each other in all possible ways.

When we had a hundred pages and an outline we were off to the city to find a publisher—all five of us, the whole family, together in the city for the first time. Jimmy believed so completely in what we were doing he was untouched by doubt, almost serene. He could disregard advice from our published writer friends. Agent? We didn't need an agent. Jimmy could walk into John Hall Wheelock's office, formerly Maxwell Perkins' office at Scribner's, and ask for, and get, an overnight reading. This venerable publishing house was interested in our manuscript, but cautious. Can we sustain the double first person? Wheelock would have to see more before he could offer a contract. Not everything we hoped for, but enough. Enough to go back to the farm, knowing we were on track, not to be deflected. Scribner's was right to be cautious; we couldn't sustain it. Up against the charge to write truly, nakedly, to be in the illustrious train of the literary continuum, Jimmy failed. He could not finally face exposing himself—the break from Anne; the pain he inflicted; the lies he told, to her, to me, to himself. I couldn't believe he had not through the years of our marriage examined, re-examined, taken it out, turned it over, offered atonement.

The hundred pages went into a desk drawer.

I could not go on alone then, it wouldn't be decent, it would be heartless to see Jimmy go off each day, doing who knows what, so that I could stay in our lighthouse, writing.

———

For the first time, the first time since we were together, Jimmy went off each morning, like other men, leaving me at home with small children, like other women. Jimmy had this ambivalence: champion of freedom in all its aspects, he was in thrall, tied to his family. He was willing to go into the marketplace and sell anything, take any job, as long as it was not respectable. Selling bibles door to door, storm windows, franchises for convenience stores. The underbelly of the economy. "While there are losers I want to be among them"— a line I found on a scrap of paper in his pocket. Not for him the nine-to-five clock-punching security, "gray security," foot firmly on the bottom rung of the famous ladder. He would use his wits, tilt his free lance. Concealing the cracks in his confidence, hiding his defiant rejection of convention in a look more acceptable, each morning he left the house with Deirdre and Michael. Although there was a Whately school bus that stopped at the bottom of our hill, Jimmy was their only transport to the private school in Northampton. One more mystification for our creditors, the private school; one more affront that further isolated us from the people who lived in this hilltown—"Too good for our schools." After Jimmy dropped the children—he was always late, and they were always anxious—he went on to Springfield to follow leads culled from classified ads. By three o'clock he must be back in Northampton to pick up Deirdre and Michael; often deceived by his optimist's sense of time, he would find them waiting in the deserted school driveway, half an hour, an hour; worried, almost in tears. Home again to me, the slayer of dragons had tales to tell, of the Flats in Holyoke, of Hungry Hill in Springfield, of the pathetic, the hopeless, the brave; Jimmy brought me the trophies of the heart of his day, sparing me his humiliations I could only imagine.

Sometimes he appears unexpectedly, early in the afternoon. Has he forgotten something? No, no. He was in Williamsburg, so close, he just came over Nash Hill; he looks at the mail, glances at the book I'm reading. Restless, he wanders away, puts a record on the turntable. What is it? Whatever it is, he takes over the air; I pay attention. "Keep it down, Jimmy; the baby's napping." Just right for him, it's too loud for me; he wants the instruments *in* the room, the sound filling his head. Listening to the Schumann, I stand at the window. He comes up behind me, close, but not touching. "How long will the baby sleep?" "An hour . . ." He takes my hand: "Come upstairs," his voice is low, almost a whisper. I meet his eyes, their special light; the look, the touch, the sound of his voice is all I need. I head for the stairs, Jimmy close behind me, quietly, quietly; we are in our room, the door shut. No children, no guests, only the innocent sleeping baby at the other end of the house. We find the other nothing can change;—not years of killing intimacy, not dreams stillborn; outside time.

———

Pregnant with our fourth child, I say "No more," after this baby, no more. Jimmy's not daunted: another angelic spirit chose us as entry into our world. The moment of ecstacy made flesh. How blessed we were to be the channel for these children; from our disparate pools of race and history, such souls would emerge; Jimmy was willing to go on and on. Why couldn't he be mother?? My rebel cry. Jimmy is not daunted, but he agrees: there will be no more babies. Tubes tied, abortion, anything; he promises he will offer no objection. The womb is holy, these interventions offend him, but he agrees.

———

Thirty-three years old, motherhood is not my destiny, raising children is not my destiny. There is more, more. I need a life of my own.

First Person Singular

Only if there is a visitor who will watch over the sleeping baby and the wide-awake small boy can I leave the house and walk off alone. Today there is such a visitor, Edith Noble Warner. Married to a man in LaGuardia's administration, she frequently escapes her Madison Avenue apartment and New York social life for a week or two as our paying guest. An acute, subtle observer, an explorer, she is all tawny and amber and moves like a cat. And she is profoundly deaf. When she sits at the table she slowly, imperceptibly, slides on her elbow toward the speaker, cupping her ear to the conversation. She refuses to wear a hearing aid. Edith has a funny crooked smile and a large wise tolerance and never clashes with Jimmy.

Now she sends me on my way, assures me, reassures me; it is no imposition. Out of the house, I turn left and walk up the dirt road into the November woods. The road is narrow; I pass stone walls, slipping, sinking, growing formless, connecting me to the eighteenth century when new settlers cleared this land and built the walls with stones they unearthed and the stage coach to Boston traveled over Poplar Hill. Sometimes an artifact, a real object, will conjure those long-gone people. A glint of glass catches my eye as I walk past an old cellar hole; I turn back, climb down, and uncover and bring to light a pale blue narrow bottle as long as my hand. Dirt-encrusted but in perfect condition, not a nick or a crack, the raised, molded letters perfectly legible: Healy and Bigelow's Kickapoo Indian Cough Cure. A find. The old nostrum, a potent mix of alcohol, morphine, cocaine, heroin, would not cure anything, but when stoicism failed the homesick and frightened early settler, it was this bottled euphoria that eased a bad night. The bottle went into a pocket of Jimmy's old denim jacket; I would take it home and soak it in vinegar and water; when it was clear and sparkling I would pass it around and make a story, and then keep it on the kitchen windowsill.

The woods are alive: the rustle, leap, dash of the small creatures; I sidestep the sudden silent black wet line of moving snake in front of me; I hope to see a fox, I could see a bear, it was possible—there have been recent sightings of black bear. The floor of the forest is covered with fallen leaves in scarlet and russet, ochre and copper and gold; a survivor lets go and comes drifting, like a live thing, turning as it falls, leaving the bare black limbs; the floating descent of a single leaf, distinct from all others. After another mile the forest crosses the road, forms a barrier; overgrown, it is impenetrable. The end of the road. I turn back.

Edith and Gabriel are sitting on the front steps. They like each other, the five-year-old boy and the fifty-year-old woman. Edith is amiable about any game Gabriel proposes and he doesn't exploit her. Now I can see all is well; no crisis in my absence. I sit beside them, I empty my pockets: two smooth stones with interesting markings; a couple of mushrooms I amuse Edith by identifying as Perplexing Hypholoma, though the name is ambiguous they are edible. And the prize: the Kickapoo Indian Cough Cure bottle. Edith turns it in her hand, appreciates my pleasure, shares it.

Clouds darken the sky, a chill in the air, we go indoors. I put a match to the kindling in the fire I laid, pour a glass of sherry for Edith, for me. "How long have you been married, Blanche?" "Fifteen years." I smile, the numbers are unreal. "It's really twice as long, Edith. We've never been separated, Jimmy was always here . . ." I pitched my voice louder, toward the ear she says is her good one. "It's really thirty." She smiles her crooked smile, she understands I can't measure in calendar time. I won't talk to her or anyone of Jimmy's twenty-four-hour silences that are like a month of exile. "The baby's awake, I just heard her," Gabriel runs up the stairs, he's sure he's his baby sister's favorite, he is the one who "can get a smile out of her." The baby is Eliza; it was Jimmy's idea to name her a version of Betty in memory of my mother, to please me. And it does. And she pleases me, this last baby. Sweet to hold close, content when she's on her own, she seems glad to be with us. It is with guilt and regret that I stop nursing her before I need to. I want my body to be my own. First person singular.

Preparing for War

Slipping away; Jimmy knew I was slipping away. I love the time when I am on my own and he suspects it. He looks for reasons. He says "You're disappointed in me"; "You didn't bargain for this." "You're dismayed, disgusted." He's off the mark, he has it all wrong. He thinks he has lost something in my eyes: moral stature, principle. Not so. I am mystified that he chooses so seamy a road to money but I think he's brave, I think he's Don Quixote. I am moved even by his stubbornness; I can't bear it when he says "I don't know where to turn."

It's his control I am slipping away from. It is not only injustice in the world that evokes his thunder, he has something to say about everything. Cosmic, international, domestic; the food on our table, the clothes on our backs, the way we cut our hair. His disapproval is withering, his applause is balm. Immoderate, he will never change. And I will never abandon him. He is not sure.

He wakes me out of deep sleep. I want to stay there, way down, I struggle up, Jimmy has turned on the bed lamp, bending over me he whispers "What are you dreaming? What were you dreaming?" and I try to answer, obediently, then "no, no," I moan, "let me sleep," I turn my back, put my head under the cover, to tunnel my way back. I fail, my rage has waked me completely. I can't believe it. He can't

let go; he must possess the waking me, the sleeping me, the uncon-
scious. And yet, when I recorded this in my journal, I add "my poor
darling."

Jimmy didn't fool me with talk of chess moves, the adroit softsell,
competing with old pros, outwitting greedy bosses, having a beer,
pretending to be one of the boys. I am sorry for him, but it's only a
detour. Selling any product Jimmy can convince himself is useful,
not toxic, not a fraud, we are paying our way. Discharging past
debts, keeping afloat. Better than that, advancing. It is not an
important compromise, we decide, if we exchange the kerosene
cookstove for a gas range, the icebox for a refrigerator. It would not
be a serious capitulation if I gave up the scrub board for a washing
machine. Now that the last baby is out of diapers, the house is wired
for increased voltage and I have a laundry room. "It's about time,"
friends say. Black and white tiles cover the floor, wicker baskets, and
the ironing board always ready. On the wall a Degas print of women
ironing. It's not the riverbank where women gather to scrub the
family's handwoven garments, to exchange remedies and recipes,
wisdom and wit. I give up the riverbank—I never saw myself there
anyway—for the machine that whirs and throbs on command.

All of Western Massachusetts is his territory and it is harder and
harder for Jimmy to get back to Northampton to pick up the children
when school was dismissed. Now there were three children waiting,
Deirdre, Michael and Gabriel, and though Deirdre was as good as
she was beautiful, little mother to her younger brothers, I heard
panic when she called. "Mother, it's almost five o'clock. It's getting
dark. Where's Jimmy?"

Where was he? I was helpless. I couldn't drive. "What for?"
Jimmy always said, "I'm here. I'll take you anywhere you need to
go." Our cars were eccentric, he said; the back roads tricky. Besides,
what could possibly pull me away? What was missing? What was out
there?

He was out there. Jimmy went off with our only car, a raffish old
wooden-bodied station wagon, and now our children were stranded,
miles from home, and no way for me to come to their rescue.
Unavoidable, Jimmy said when he brought them home that night;
he was sorry. The children forgave him, and I, I decided to leap over
the wall. It wasn't easy for him, I knew that, but Jimmy agreed to
help me. He would find me a car; I would go to a driving school; it

would take pressure off him, I would be there dependably for the children. I knew it wasn't easy for him to let go, fracturing the image he held of me safe at home, keeping the fire, tending the baby, reading and writing and listening to the birds. Now, like any suburban housewife, I would do the afternoon school pickup, and he, he must put our children in other hands than his, even though those other hands were mine. Jimmy would think of me, a novice at the wheel, on the deserted back roads in all weather, maybe unplowed, unsanded; no street lights. No streets.

Instructed, encouraged, then praised by my driving teacher, a young man I instantly love, I am licensed to drive. My car is a 1950 De Soto sedan, neat, solid, cream-colored. It looks ordinary to the casual observer, I suppose. Not to me. A golden chariot, a magic carpet, I will take care of its body and penetrate the function of all its parts: piston, rings, carburetor; valves and alternator. I might even learn to change a tire. For the first time in all these years, seventeen years of country living with Jimmy, I could come and go on my own. It didn't matter at all that the coming and going was domestic routine, school pickup, and marketing in the service of the family. It was bliss; it was heady. Every day, down the hill, round the curves, past the reservoir, the pine woods, into the town. Everything looked different from the driver's seat. My hands on the wheel, my foot on the brake, I could negotiate the deserted country roads, the traffic in city streets, the novice growing confident, skillful; granting right of way at an intersection, waving a driver on with a sweet swell of majesty, passing another in a powerful burst of speed.

———

He wore a tie; it was a noose. He had an office; it was a cage.

The older children were at college, away, Deirdre at Bennington in Vermont, Michael at Earlham in Indiana. The younger Gabriel and Eliza were still at home, testing security locks.

Jimmy was fifty years old. It was rushing by: stop time.

Driving home, headed for the hills, Jimmy began to shed his day. He listened to the evening news, mocked the newscaster, argued with the radio voice. I knew he put a curb on his tongue in his daily rounds—not that he dissembled; he wouldn't do that—but with prospective buyers his judgments on the state of the world were tempered, more reasonable. We got the full flood. When he came in the door he had a live audience. "Those bastards!" he said. It didn't matter who was at the table: old friends who knew what to expect, new friends unprepared, the children's overnight guests, intimidated. Jimmy was never a spectator, or one of the company; small talk made him restless. The young must be set on the right path; the old must see the error of their ways. Jimmy is alert for a word, a phrase to challenge; escalation is swift, is outrageous. I see signs of distress, will the school friend dare to come again, will the old friend bring a new friend and chance insult. Another day, another mood, and Jimmy joins the laughter, tells stories: Greenwich Village days, Woodstock, tobacco-farming days; stories of his strict Catholic boyhood, fascinates the company.

I had heard it all before, I had moderated, collaborated, been the balance wheel. Explained, excused, defended, protected. Sometimes the wound is too deep. Let the friend go.

The main thing always is us.

Chapter Seventeen

My war with Jimmy.

Second series *Phoenix*

– 1970 –

I AM THE ONE who should be out there. I am in all ways more
suited. Hungry for the world, I can be a player; I can bend, I
am resilient, flexible. I can amuse myself, change costume, present
myself as a woman free, without impediments. Not mother of four
grown men and women, not grandmother. Not Jimmy's wife. Not
chatelaine of this big shabby house, arena of intensities. I look
around, consider the possible, speak to no one. Certainly not Jimmy.
I want a sanctum, a refuge, a place where I can exchange a piece of
my day for a small check. Nothing to do with food, or babies.
Nothing domestic. Nothing to sell, no worldly ambition, no threat
to Jimmy.

Vain hope. Everything was a threat to Jimmy. When I found a job
in the Smith College library he hated it, of course he hated it.
Working for an institution, sullying my days; serving in the world of
bourgeois privilege among arid academics. Every day, from eight to
four, gone, out of sight; what did I do? who did I talk to? He found a
reason to interrupt his rounds, to come to the library; there was
something he must tell me. He stopped at the main desk; I was not
there. "Will you tell me where I can find Blanche Cooney?" Helen
hesitated. I was new. She checked the desk schedule. "She should be
back here in twenty minutes." "I'm her husband, I can't wait."
Husbands didn't usually appear; there was something about him,
there was something about his assurance that set up a little flutter of
interest in Helen and Alice and Caroline. Maybe they could hear

beneath his civil manner "Where are you hiding her? She doesn't belong here!" and other fierce expressions of his disapproval. "Take the main stairs to the third level," said Helen. "Turn right into the north wing. You should find her there."

Down the dim corridors to the stack aisle where he found me sitting on a low stool with a shelf list drawer in my lap, checking the records against the holdings. I looked up. Surprise. What was wrong? Nothing, and nothing that couldn't wait. He must tell me Lucy and Karl were coming for the weekend; Michael was bringing a friend; Gabriel was going to Boston. Someone wanted to rent the wing and we needed to talk about it. He left; he remembered one more thing. He didn't want to leave. Or he wanted to take me with him. Nothing that couldn't wait, just a reminder that I had left my true post for work of no importance.

Jimmy disappears. Students, faculty, library staff, all disappear. I am alone in the stacks of the library. From floor to ceiling, row on row, I take possession of my retreat, my refuge. A sanctuary of thought, art, history. An accumulation of voices. Imperative genius, ambitious talent. Relentless pedant. Dedicated scholar. Forgotten failure. All these voices, preserved in type, bound in boards, waiting for release. My hand reaches high, searches low; I open each book to the title page. I am not only checking the condition, the edition, the number of copies against the record, discarding superfluous multiples bought for courses now obsolete. I am not only custodian and caretaker. I hear echoes. In the nineteenth century, serious binding, old typefaces; the paper, full of clay, often brittle and crumbling. In early twentieth century novels with their dated faintly jazzy bindings. Old familiars, new discoveries. I even find Jimmy's novel. I'm back in New York City in the Fourth Avenue secondhand bookshops where I started to buy books when I was fourteen, fifteen, and I remember the smell, the dust, and the promise.

Finite, yet limitless, my life in the library; orderly and civilized, my life in the library. And a small check, a regular small check, the "gray security" Jimmy so despised. The money was nothing. It went into the maw of common expenses: tuition, utilities, taxes and mortgage payments, groceries and gas. It was the freedom; it was the choice. Free to drive down the hill every morning, loving it. It was not a job; no detail or routine could obscure the grand intention of the library; it was a way for me to live in another country without giving up my own. Antennae out, I brought Jimmy gifts, prizes of my day: this book, this person. Woman, man; student, professor. I could show my new friend my own country.

Any gathering at the farm in the late sixties was dominated by talk of the Vietnam war and the growing opposition on college campuses across the country. A vigil in protest was forming in Northampton, and we would be part of it. Standing on the vigil became our Sunday ritual. No matter what the weather we were there, from eleven in the morning until noon, standing on the sidewalk in front of Pulaski Park, near Northampton's City Hall. There were twenty or twenty-five regulars: old radicals, Independents, Quakers, a few Smith College students, a couple of young faculty. No leaders, not really organized at all; whoever got there first fetched the signs from the Unitarian Church basement. "U.S. Out of Vietnam," "Stop the Killing." We spaced ourselves to stretch as far down the street as possible; at either end a sign was held. Our greetings were subdued, no laughter, the tone was solemn; it was our church service. A newcomer was silently welcomed when the line moved to open a space; a newcomer raised our spirits. Northampton on a Sunday morning in 1968 was a quiet, almost deserted town, a decent New England town where families kept the Sabbath and no business was transacted, where demonstrators and placards on their Main Street, in front of their City Hall, were disturbing, distressing. Foreign. Passersby, dressed for church, hurried along, looking straight ahead, or crossed the street to avoid us. Cars coming up to the light slowed down; adults glanced at us, then away, but their children pressed against the window until they were out of sight. Shambling along, barely awake, a rare derelict dared himself to mutter, "Commies, all of you, bunch of Commies" with a look of disgust. I knew it was hard for Jimmy, hard to hold his tongue. "Moron," he said under his breath, so that only I could hear. No talking back to hecklers, no talking; it was a silent vigil, dignified. In a common impulse we circled our stand and returned to position, careful not to obstruct the pavement, keeping within the rules of our permit; even this small ritual heartened us as we passed each other and our eyes met. If, during the hour, a car slowed to read our signs, sound the horn; if a hand was raised in salute, a fist in approval, then a current of joy ran through the line.

"Next week," we said at noon as we parted and headed for the hills. The vigil in Northampton was prelude to the Sunday gatherings at the farm: students, faculty—my library pickups—houseguests, old friends from New York City. Eliza and her friends; Gabriel and Elizabeth, married last year, who live here now. A feast, music live, and talk, talk. Jimmy pulled out old *Phoenix* issues, read anti-World War II essays, stories, as valid today as they were thirty years ago.

After months of Sundays, autumn into winter into spring, Jimmy chafed. Too passive, this silent protest, too polite. Nothing in jeopardy. A town like Northampton could absorb dissent; the College flew the banner of the humanities, and the Town's economy depended on the College. Safe. The *Daily Hampshire Gazette* even carried a notice of the weekly vigil, something between a listing on the calendar of events and a small news item.

"I want to find someone who will picket the Northampton Draft Board with me," said Jimmy to Eddie standing beside him on the Sunday vigil, "make these men show their faces, be known to the whole town before they send men off to be killed." "I'm your man," said Eddie. Eddie Felien was a new friend. I picked him up in the library and brought him home, a tall, blonde, curly-haired Swede from a blue-collar Minneapolis family; an academically unambitious Ph.D. on the faculty of the theatre department. Reckless, loving, he even smiled at unfriendly passersby.

Placards lettered, permission secured, every weekday, from noon to one, a small band, rarely more than fifteen, picketed the entrance to Northampton's City Hall where the Draft Board met. Jimmy, Eddie, four or five Smith College students, several Sunday vigilers, Gabriel and Elizabeth and Eliza. Walking out of the College gates to Main Street, I joined the line during my lunch hour.

Northampton Commercial College students begin to show up. They stood at the edge of our small demonstration and chanted taunts and insults. "Hippies." "Reds." "Go back to Russia." They carried American flags and poked them provocatively; they lit matches and waved them with menace. A music major started to sing "America"; her voice, pure and fervent, was joined by others. We kept our discipline. Other Smith faculty, Ken Stern in Philosophy, Myron Glazer in Sociology, Phil Green in Government, walked down at noon to "observe." To protect "our girls." Until one day at the end of the second week, they, our hecklers, waded in, knocked

Gabriel to the ground, opened a gash in Eddie Felien's head. The Northampton Police car was standing by and Eddie was taken to Cooley Dickinson Hospital where Emergency stitched him up. The *Daily Hampshire Gazette* and the *Springfield Union* and the *Amherst Student* carried the story, and on the weekend we heard of support growing throughout the valley.

On Monday when I walked out of the College Gates and down the hill I saw not only the Northampton Police but also the College cruisers parked on Main Street. The attack and the attention changed the mood of the demonstrators: more determined, and yes, more cheerful. There was Eddie with his bandaged head, and there in the background were the patriots from Northampton Commercial College. A movement across the street, the Northampton Police were joined by the Fire Department, and suddenly the stream started. Pouring into Northampton from Amherst, Mount Holyoke, the University of Massachusetts, from the hill towns: students and faculty, ministers and doctors, supporting the right of assembly. The stream was a river that flowed up the street to the Grecourt Gates and onto the campus. It was thrilling; it was marvelous. We couldn't believe it. Tom Mendenhall, Smith College president, emerged from College Hall and addressed the crowds of hundreds. Maybe a thousand. Our hecklers, the patriots, had been carried along. They were at the edge of the crowd. Town boys, from Agawam, Springfield, Holyoke, they had never before been through the Gates of the Castle. Subdued, overwhelmed, they were ripe for Sociology's Mickey Glazer and Psychology's Dietrich Snoek, who found them and proposed a series of meetings with Smith College students, right there on campus, in Seelye Hall. They could talk about free speech and Vietnam, one to one. They agreed, it came to pass, and, wonderful to relate, our most aggressive heckler became a leader in the Springfield Peace group.

———

In this ferment of protest, Jimmy was excited. The need was urgent; the time was right: *The Phoenix* must rise again, fly from the valley, through the country, across the sea to Europe, Asia. There was no time to lose. In the cellar of our old farmhouse a print shop grew: a secondhand press, type stands. From the aroused college community help was volunteered. The mix of family intimacy, the big old house, the New England hills, and burning purpose was hard to resist. Tonic to the man who waited all these years to revive the little magazine. Elixir to the man who wrote one morning not long before:

> Last night I really went into a panic. I saw the looming ruin of my life. My heart so constricted, I was terrified, the anguish was intolerable. I felt myself slipping into an abyss. I wanted to groan, cry out, just to relieve the pent-up agony, but I shrank from disturbing my wife, my dearest darling love asleep beside me. I don't know how I found my way back into the refuge of sleep. Now it's day again and my courage has revived. And I tell myself it would be a major relief to be ruined, wiped out. Oh I really screwed up. And I don't have that much time left. I'm fifty-nine. And I'm at an impasse.

No longer divided, no longer disguised as farmer, business man, he could be the self he kept alive through all those years. He need never wear a suit again. In his preferred artist-worker garb he presided over the print shop, the symposium at the kitchen table, compelling the receptive young with candor and thunder and poetry and music.

———

So why does the monster stir? It's after me, Jimmy's dearest darling love.

———

Imagine enemies, girded for combat; rage in the heart, thunder in the voice, blood in the eye. Towering over reason, oblivious of pain, Jimmy follows me, upstairs and downstairs, into the garden, up the road. He follows me, jeering, insulting: fierce and inventive and cruel. His face is changed; his mouth is shaped for hatefulness; beside himself he becomes the monster. Cry, shriek, scream my pain, Jimmy pursues me until I break, lose control.

The monster vanishes, the lover appears, numinous, luminous. Be grateful, inside and out; heal the air; be careful. No angry sound allowed; no banging, no slamming, no stamping. Glide into and around, step lightly. Open all doors, all passages, the very pores of your skin. Let your hair be unconfined, your eyes shine. Cook something delicious, wear a color he likes, get into bed naked.

A long time ago, before we began our life together, Jimmy warned, "You don't know me. You would turn away if you knew how stubborn, moody . . . how impatient, rude, short-tempered . . ." How could he imagine, I thought then, I would care about such imps of temperament. How could I know the imps were the monster incubating. Would it have made any difference? Where did it come from, how did it get so strong, so destructive. So abominable. How could Jimmy love beauty, the body, the mind illuminated; be so tender, passionate, compassionate, and harbor the monster. Insatiable, it will not be deflected; it is not satisfied with strangers and friends of our children. They can leave. But the monster has privileged information: I will not leave, and it is inspired to go to dangerous lengths, to the very edge, to find my breaking point.

――――

After a terrible fight and a three-day silence, I left this page written in quick heat on Jimmy's desk:

Hysteria from me. Righteous wrath from you. All right. The insults and contempt and hatred you fling at people are "just words, they don't kill." But my words are not just words, they so wound that you break up our lives. Even suggest it. It is the mechanical man in you I cry out against. Never mind how hysterically. Mechanical. A drink, a certain face, and you're off. Nothing can stop you. Not my stricken silent begging you to remember this is our Michael's birthday, not his misery. Nothing can stop you. No occasion, or celebration; no reunion with old friend or anticipated meeting with a stranger. There's that George's face, despicable thing. What comes out of it that you can jump on. Anything. You can find an opening for attack even in our talk of dinosaurs and prehistoric beasts. In the name of love, humanity, you exhibit the face of hatred. You wrong yourself, you defeat yourself, you negate yourself, you, the most remarkable man any of these people have ever met. Who fights you? Jehovah, thundering scourge and jolter? No one. Just me, when I am less accepting and begin to resist you.

No answer, no acknowledgment from Jimmy, but a partial thaw.

――――

The monster moves in its subterranean depths, out of sight, temporarily vanquished by fine weather and an excess of beauty. Our children are beautiful, men and women now with loves more immediate, but Jimmy is still their touchstone, they seek his approval. He is the grandfather ready to play, to tease; he is the friend who offers intimacy and shelter; the editor tough and strict, rewarding the writer not only with publication but with hospitality. That means me.

I come home from a day at the library, a stop at the market, laden with sacks of groceries, to find three or four or six strangers at the table. Poets, pilgrims, potential printers. Jimmy is talking, his voice in a crescendo of persuasion, they listen, attentively, eyes on him, chin in hand. My entrance interrupts. Jimmy says, "My wife, Blanche," they turn to me, "why don't you introduce yourselves" because he can't remember their names, and they do. One polite visitor overturns his chair in his eagerness to help me with the heavy bags. I can manage, but I don't want to deny him and I smile my thanks. "Set it here on the counter." I refrigerate perishables. The pause is closed, and Jimmy resumes, he finds the dramatic peak he was approaching before I came in. The subject is punishment and prisons, the wisdom of primitive cultures and the barbarism of civilized man. I run upstairs, change from city clothes to farm blue jean skirt, wash my face, run a comb through my hair, and smile into the mirror. They don't sound as though they are winding down; Jimmy has probably asked them to stay for dinner, and he has.

I look for a voice, a face appealing, and as I finish unpacking the groceries I plan a meal; quick, simple, something from the garden. At the table Jimmy can be quiet; I move the conversation. From the abstract to the personal, from the cosmic to the particular, I ask what do you do, where do you come from, where do you want to go? Easy, slow; resting where it is safe, moving fast where the ice is thin. Byzantine in my indirection, I am a foil for Jimmy's hammer and tongs.

———

"I'd like you to read this," and Jimmy hands me a manuscript that came in the morning mail. I can tell by his neutral tone that he intends to print it. He wants me to say Yes. He challenges me to say No. I read it through; "interesting," I say; he hears my reservation. Jimmy brusquely takes the typescript from my hand, gathers his correspondence spread on the kitchen table, and limps off down the hall to his study. The limp tells me he has much to bear, not only an arthritic twinge. He shuts the door. Silence for a week. He will keep out of my way; if he encounters me he averts his eyes, tightens his mouth; we pass as strangers in our house. If it is necessary there will be a communiqué; amnesty when others are near. To save our friends the embarrassment of witnessing us at the barricades, we conceal our weapons.

––––––

Although the print shop had outgrown the cellar and was now in an outbuilding formed by cannibalizing the chicken house, the black-smith shop, the horse stalls, and although in this shop Jimmy had a desk and worktables and files, and although he also had a roomy study in front of the house, he began to establish a post at the kitchen table. Deliberately putting himself in my path was a variation in Jimmy's hostilities. The kitchen table, an old hutch, is the main dining surface; the kitchen was the principal room, the center of the house; the kitchen was my design, my creation of order and ritual.

It is a Sunday morning in early autumn; the kitchen is filled with the rich aroma of lentil soup simmering, a cauldron to feed the after-vigil visitors. I slice cheese, cut carrots and celery, open a tin of black olives. "Jimmy," I say, "you'll have to clear the table. We'll need it when we get back." Cold, remote, he doesn't answer, he doesn't look at me, but he begins to assemble his papers. "Where are the pear seeds I saved?" he demands. "Where were they?" I ask neutrally. "On the table. I left them on the table and they disappeared." The past rises; he accuses, I mollify. It's suddenly all there and I'm out of control. In an angry choking rush: "How am I to know what you want saved in all that *garbage* I must clear from this table!" "Oh. Seeds are garbage. That's right." This rejoinder is weary, sad. He sees in those little black seeds he saved from the misshapen pear, the tree in blossom; he smells its scent; he tastes next year's fruit. He is weary and sad because I am so unfeeling, because such a chasm yawns between us.

————

Journal entry:

This month, Lent, another terrible scourging period with Jimmy. It is different, in a desperate way different. There is no wild reconciliation possible. I think now that the family, domesticity, was wrong for him and he knows it and I must be punished for conspiring to build the prison. The embrace that in sorrow, contrition, healed and comforted, no longer seems possible. He takes risks with me that take us beyond that, to a nowhere place. A glance back in this journal, same period, same discovery: "Domesticity and the backwater are tragedy for him." I can do nothing. The only steps possible, to release him from serving the money needs, I have taken, and he hates that along with so much else. And finally, I have the disease of sanity, and he has the gift of madness.

Three days later I opened my journal to find it invaded. One entire page, covered in Jimmy's large, strong handwriting, black, black ink, broad-nibbed pen:

You are a delightful idiot. You are the very center of my life, which had no center until I found you. And you will always be the center of my life. I am incapable of not loving you, of not having you as the center of all meaning in this hilariously tragic world. I was *imprinted* by your image before I was born.

Jimmy

I can't believe it. I run downstairs to find him in the study. "How could you do this! It's my own private place; it's mine! you ruined it." I rip the red-leather-bound volume down the center and fling it to the floor. "It's worthless" I cry. I could see he considered my reaction extreme. What was it? Only a message of his love, left where I would find it when I was alone and quiet. I couldn't part with my journal. I retrieved it, mended it; the scars would remind me of a dangerous passage.

At every turn there was a dangerous passage. No red lights, no signals, and suddenly the black hole. This time, during a friendly stretch, we both read Sybille Bedford's biography of Aldous Huxley. I liked it. He did not. Somehow it was a personal offense, symbolic of many of my offenses. Six weeks of silent coldness.

In that six weeks I went from disgust to pity, and I wrote to Jimmy as honestly as I could:

> The miracle of my life has been the intensity of the mingling of our souls. In that alternating balm and fever I knew you were the only serious man for me. The trouble is you paid no attention to the way our rhythm changed; you would not or could not adapt. You demand violent reconciliation. You allow no tenderness, no daily, hourly consideration to build between us; you allow no comradely salute, no touch or gesture, no token of all we have loved in our time together. You will not recognize that we are separate, and in many ways far apart. Not a new thought. Well Jimmy, if we really can't work at it, the rest of our life threatens to be as grotesque as this siege. I can't believe you want that.

"If we really can't work at it, the rest of our life threatens to be as grotesque as this siege": Jimmy couldn't hear words like "work at it," as though we were a couple in an encounter group or counseling or therapy, earnest and reasonable. I found this note:

> Blanche,
>
> Because I feel, during these wounded days and nights between us, that you are unaware of it, I have the need to remind you that you are far dearer to me than my own life and that I love you beyond all words and all telling. That you have drifted so far from me that I have to remind you of this is sadder to me than all else.
>
> Jimmy

He was aggrieved. I was angry. I left this letter on his desk:

> I don't think, for all your searching, that you can know what it is to give love *and* freedom. We are all afflicted and flawed. We try to help each other. What are you doing? Not writing or editing or printing, or sending warm encouraging letters far and wide, speaking your credo with passion to strangers. What are you doing in the orbit of your life? "In the orbit of your life" is another phrase you have always used to define the first circle

of responsibility. Do you recognize yourself in the man whose mood needs to be carefully determined each day, it is so changeable; who needs to be stepped around, petitioned in just the right way; who needs to be avoided with care when the black cloud descends. Who may answer, or not; rebuff you or not; dismiss you or give you his sympathetic attention. We can't count on you. Is there anyone else, in the orbit of our lives, who needs such special care?

Journal entry:

Another sick spell. This time almost three months. Jimmy spends hours in the garden, or in his study, emerging only when he is sure he will find me alone. Deceptively reasonable, he will begin "We must have a talk" and then he's gone, he's off, on his bitter recital of accusations, scoldings, insults; grievances ancient and current. His myth of our history is fixed. I sit there in disbelief. He permits himself words, not whispered in his darkness but lies shouted to me: "You triumphed in your Jewishness. You influenced Deirdre and Eliza to circumcise their sons!"

Letter to Jimmy's study:

I oh vastly prefer my erotic dreams of you to your cruel actuality. Bullying insulting wretch, destroyer of hope. How can you justify your public face and commit these vile private butcheries. Each time I have written during your imposed punishments I have tried to fling a bridge, to connect again. You issue *warnings*. When will you recognize and seize the beast in you. And what's wrong with Jew, revolutionary?

———

A genetic fault, rooted in his family? His fanatic father, Catholic, anti-Semitic; his brother who died insane; his only sister in and out of institutions. Or possession? Possessed by a doppelgänger, an alter ego. Or schizophrenia; a chemical imbalance? Exorcism by therapy, psychoanalysis, mind-altering drugs?

No. He is responsible. He is, more than anyone, the victim, but he is responsible.

———

For my birthday in December Jimmy brings a vase full of brilliant anemones to the breakfast table. He always buys anemones for my birthday, no matter what our weather. The house is noisy and lively with visiting family and friends; I turn aside to read his card.

> Through all incarnations may I be your husband or your brother or your son, or your wife or your sister or your daughter, and failing that, may I still ever glimpse you as you pass through the long reign of time.

What can I say about such messages from Jimmy. He sends non-answers to my cries, transcends the temporal, the merely daily, with the eternal. What can I say, when I am so honored.

Above ground, in the day, in the sun, oblivious of our war, life on the hill in West Whately came as close to community as it ever could. No rules, no tests, in this community. It's fluid, it's transient; distinctions of age and generation are blurred. Who stays, who goes, is all in the winnowing, the sifting and sorting. Everything signifies: the sound of your voice, the music you listen to, the books you read; what makes you laugh, what rouses your passion. It's love or hate, all or nothing. The judicious and pragmatic move on.

It was Charles who came closest to making his life here. He was economics faculty at Smith; he and his wife Pat, and their three children Bill and John and Ponteir, came up from Northampton whenever they could and soon decided they never wanted to leave. Transplanted Texans, they would build their own house on the farm; Charles would teach part-time, write, work in the print shop, the garden. Pat, too, would garden, but her main work was in the Women's Movement. Feminism and women's liberation had triumphantly come to the Valley, and Pat was a natural leader. In the wake of that wave of militant emotion, the masthead of *The Phoenix* carried three new associate editors: Rosa Luxemburg, Louise Michel, and Emma Goldman. All women, all revolutionaries, and all dead.

The Sackreys built the house, a wonderful little house, sited so that from its privacy in the woods there would still be the sweep of hills and fields and valley before their eyes. Three months after they moved in the marriage dissolved.

Charles remains a family intimate.

——

Wherever they were, our four children stayed close, close to each other and close to us. Deirdre, Michael, Gabriel, and Eliza. After years of saying to myself and to others, in passing, with no particular emphasis, "My children and I are friends" I suddenly sounded smug. It wasn't true. Our children cannot be our friends; only equals can be friends, and we can never be equals. Our connection is ineffable; blood, arteries, the valves of the heart. Our connection is unnameable, unreasonable; is umbilical. They are very different, these four people, though they share aspects of beauty, a family look. Men and women whose skin is thin, whose conscience is keen, who remain vulnerable, and so keep a kind of innocence. A family affliction and blessing. The meddling and the jealousy, the shifting alliances peculiar to families, are true of ours, but at bedrock their love for each other is unconditional. I am sure of that.

Deirdre, firstborn, is married to Cristobal Bonifaz, a gentle Ecuadorian, research chemist with DuPont. They live in Pennsylvania with their children Margarita and John. Deirdre, dark-haired, fair-skinned, green-eyed, her Irish beauty dominates the Roumanian-Russian lines. She is immersed in seeking out, supporting, and marketing rural crafts. Although they travel—Europe, South America—they are always here for celebrations of marriages, birthdays, anniversaries; we talk often on the phone.

Early dominated by his confident older sister, and his demanding father, Michael surfaced, his own man. Uniquely without meanness, I think he is also without vanity. I don't think he knows how appealing he is, so open and genuine. All his life a wizard with motors, he has a shop in Concord and a reputation throughout the northeast. In an 1820 house in Plymouth, Michael and his wife Mary Randall, an Anglo-Saxon beauty, a woman at once enigmatic and warm, live with their sons Thomas and Nicholas. Visits to the farm from New Hampshire are infrequent; Mary and Michael, unable to deny their sons, travel with extensive paraphernalia: Lego parts and matchbox cars and special juice and peanut butter. The logistics are daunting. Though we don't see them often, our connection is constant.

Life with us was different for our younger children, Gabriel and

Eliza. Jimmy was always "Jimmy," but now they call me "Blanche." Born here on the farm in West Whately, they made their ritual escape to city life in Boston, New York; Gabriel went to Morocco, Eliza to San Francisco, but they came back and stayed to make their lives here.

Gabriel is a photographer. The camera in his hand is his paint brush, his violin, flute, cello. His senses are acute; he is a perfectionist. He also cuts our wood, keeps bees and goats, gardens, prunes the fruit trees, maintains the buildings. Gabriel was twenty years old when he found Elizabeth Bzura, a nineteen-year-old sophomore at Smith. They married and came here to live. Their two daughters, Isabel and Emily, are the resident children.

Elizabeth is a slight, dark-haired woman with distinctive beauty and a questing mind; she entered the circle of the family and without reservation became my ally, my friend. Not my child, she could be my friend. I can only imagine how hard it was to commit her young life to this tangle of family. To enter into my house, my kitchen, the ritualized domain of the older woman, the mother-in-law, and adapt, adopt, follow my ways, my aesthetic. To enter the house where her husband was born, and in the air, ingrained in the wood, are the old taboos, the jokes, the myths, the vendettas and alliances. I can only imagine what it was like, in the early years of her life here, before they moved into the wing, when she worked in the print shop with Jimmy, and suffered the tensions between father and son. I can only imagine her dismay when she must move around our skirmishes or silences.

It is Elizabeth who helps me with the revolving door of guests; the beds that never cool, the meals without end. One night after a notably thoughtless group—pigs, in fact—left after an interminable week, we decided we must protect ourselves. Elizabeth and I drew up a notice. Anarchy denied, in mock-formal severity, in careful calligraphy, it was headed:

Suggestions for Considerate Guests

- Keep common rooms clear of personal belongings.
- Place no commercial containers on the dining table.

- Remove your dishes from table and bring to sink.
- Do no harvesting of garden produce before checking with the management.
- Wipe shoes on mat provided before entering the house from the garden.
- Do not enter the print shop without a family member.
- Bring all your towels and bed linen to the designated area before leaving.

Posted conspicuously in the bathrooms, it helped.

Eliza, the youngest, lives in Northampton. Only fifteen minutes from her house to ours, she is here often on impromptu or long-planned visits, with her children and her friends. Eliza has two children, Annabel and Caleb. In and out of love and marriage, she is honest, impulsive; her life is never easy. She cares, she cares; without guile, her brown eyes shine, or fill with tears; her chin is set in determination or quivers with pain; open to joy, I think she is beautiful. A painter, she gives herself without reserve to the teaching of art to children.

———

It was New Year's Eve; the house was quiet, celebrations were elsewhere. I was quiet; I liked it that way, on New Year's eve. I sat by the fire, built it to a brightness, and I thought of Jimmy alone at his desk in the study. I ached for him, locked with the monster. I found my pen and a van Gogh card I had been saving and I wrote:

> Dear Jimmy, for this New Year I want to thank you for the ways you made my life so rich. You led me to love, to the delights of body and soul joined; you taught me to live in the day, without fruitless anxiety; to recognize essentials. You brought me to this place, and with your boundless hope and vision made it a magnet for so many. You taught me to make a fire, a garden, and where to find real nourishment. Through our life together I learned about limitless possibilities and limited choices and I try to be always aware of both. I thank you, and wish you to go on and on and on.

Chapter Eighteen

In one stroke

– 1981 –

FEBRUARY 11, 1981. I drove home, out of Northampton, up through the hills, on the back roads, past the reservoir: my track from the library at Smith College where I work. The night is black; the roads are icy, after the final steep climb I am relieved to be back at the farm where my real life is. Carrying my books, my bag, the champagne for our small celebration of Gabriel's thirty-fourth birthday, I make my way up the walk. Why is Elizabeth at the door?

"Jimmy had a stroke," she said in a rush, her voice urgent, careful, it held me. "Gabriel found him on the floor."

I move faster, "When?"

"About ten minutes ago."

"How do you know it is a stroke?"

"He can't speak. He can't move."

They had covered him with a blanket; I knelt beside him, he looked at me, a look of consternation and amazement. No sound. We called a doctor friend. I said "Jimmy would hate the hospital. Can you come?" "This is the twentieth century, Blanche. Call an ambulance. Get him to the hospital, right away."

———

Jimmy is diminished in his hospital gown; speechless and paralyzed, skilled strangers care for him. "Mr. Cooney is a good patient," the nurses say. Who would have thought it. They like him. I wonder if they can see the man he was. It is faint, barely flickering, yet I know somewhere in the cave he has started the struggle to return. Listening. Watching. Obeying. Obedience is hard but he has no choice.

Morning, noon, and evening, I stop at the hospital on my way to the library, I take my lunch in Jimmy's room, I stop again on my way home. The Hospital, grand central of healing and dying and birth, is my world now. Holy and blessed are the doctors and nurses, the people who sweep, who do the laundry, prepare the food, keep the records. Although the work here is at the very edge, the extreme edge of existence, I meet with nothing but kindness and patience. I help Jimmy with his meals; I bring him messages from friends, drawings from the grandchildren; the family is constantly in and out.

Soon there was a voice, sepulchral, from the cave; a word, a phrase incomprehensible. Soon he could be assisted to a chair. Soon he would be ready for physical therapy, speech therapy. No one who knew Jimmy failed to see the irony, the pathos, the cruel punishment for a man whose tongue was so fluent, so outrageous, to be suddenly silenced. For a man so physical to be immobilized. No one knew as I did how this cruel irony was compounded: that his weapon—silence—inflicted on me through the years as punishment, was finally turned on himself.

I met with the speech therapist. Aphasia, the Greeks named it. The therapist told me there were several kinds of aphasia; there was no way to know how much speech Jimmy might recover. Could I tell her anything about Mr. Cooney that might be helpful? And she showed me the wide-ruled paper, the large kindergarten printing, the primer words. "I supply a simple word, and the patient completes the sentence."

I, too, was in the hands of strangers. I absolved myself of treachery. I said, carefully, not to offend, or belittle her trained technique: "Try priming him with family names." Our children: Michael and Deirdre, Gabriel and Eliza; our grandchildren: Margarita, John, Annabel and Caleb and Isabel and Emily and Thomas and Nicholas. The stuff of his life. Music and writing and gardening, printing and protest.

At first he was at sea:

> Emily————likes potatoes.
> Next week————the potatoes will be cooking.
> I like to plant————potatoes.

What was all this about potatoes?

But soon the therapist was leaving notes for me—"a fantastic day"—and on the wide-ruled paper, in her careful printing.

The hospital is————a useful being.
The farm is————a castle.
Writing————deserves pristine precision.
Being sick————is like being possessed.
Communication————is authority.
When I get home————I will resume a statement.
I wish————to be alone.

With those last words he told the therapist he was tired of the necessary game.

Homecoming

Although the air is sharp, the sun warms the late March morning. There is no wind. In the doorway, and on the terrace of the house that stands alone on top of Poplar Hill, the bud and blossom, the fruit and flower, the fragrance and substance of Jimmy's life awaits his return. The grandchildren on either side of the terrace, eight of them, range from infant to youth; solemn or smiling all are quiet, it is an important occasion. They know that. When Jimmy arrives he will see them first.

The car comes up the hill; Michael is driving, Jimmy sits beside him, Gabriel is in the back seat. Jimmy raises his eyes as the car turns, he looks toward the valley, and away. When they stop in front of the house he doesn't look at us, he is gathering himself for the reentry. Michael opens the car door. Gabriel sets the walker before Jimmy, who turns in his seat, grasps the walker, pulls himself erect. Michael and Gabriel, on either side, support without touching their father as they make their way up the walk slowly, slowly. Jimmy's right leg drags along. He is once again in his familiar black beret and black corduroys, but his hair is suddenly very white. In the slow procession to the waiting family Jimmy knows we're there, but he keeps his eyes fixed on his task: to move from the road to the house without faltering.

I watch from the window; I want to be the last to greet him at the end of his passage. It is so moving: Tiresias, Oedipus at Colonus; the fallen father supported by his son, carried home—ceremonial, mythic, heartbreaking. He pauses there, on the terrace, to gaze at the grandchildren; his eyes pale, transparent, taking in the remarkable tableau. They call to him softly, they're shy of this different Jimmy. "Jimmy, hi." "Jimmy, I'm here"; he is silent, a slight twitch of a muscle near his mouth may be a smile; he resumes his careful deliberate entrance. The assembly in the doorway parts to receive him.

———

The sick old man is my dependent, my charge. He must depend on me for food, for comfort; sleeping or waking he must accept all my arrangements. He must accept, and I must assert. I am his history; because he knows every inflection in my voice, every thought reflected in my eyes, I must be careful. This house is his history; even where the spider webs and the dust drifts it is rich, warm; it pleases us, every corner speaks.

I sleep lightly; set on "Alert," I listen. In my room upstairs, my bedroom, study, retreat, I listen for the sound of the walker setting down, the dragging leg, I'm ready to spring up if there is a thump or a cry. I am the front line of emergency; in the wing in the north end of the house is my witness and essential help: the family who with me absorbs the inexorable dailiness of this new life with Jimmy. Elizabeth and Gabriel back me up, help me forgive myself when I lose balance. At bedtime their little girls lovingly kiss Jimmy and he with his good left hand holds them as they lean against him. Between Gabriel and his father, so often antagonists, a symbiosis takes place. Gabriel gives, and his father in his paralyzed silence accepts the help of bathing and shaving and combing and clipping and dressing. Tenderness and courtesy from son to father; from father to son silent cooperation. When Gabriel helps you out of the tub and carefully wraps your aged body in the bath sheet, when he holds the shaving mirror at just the right angle for your direction or approval, say Thank you. Say it! Only now do I realize Jimmy has never expressed a spoken thanks to me, or to our children; just as he would do anything for us, we of course would do anything for him, and for each other. The family, one body, extended parts; would you thank your arm for bringing the cup to your lip?

———

People who traveled a distance, California, Minnesota, Montana, Virginia, of course were put up. Habits of hospitality persist. Since

Jimmy is immobile and dependent here on the hill, I summon old friends and family, mixing and spacing so that he does not grow tired or confused. In this part of the house life is subdued, an almost twilight equilibrium prevails; when the young are here, when vivid thrusting irrepressible life comes in the door it is funneled into the wing, where Elizabeth and Gabriel absorb it. Here we keep the sound down, volume down on Mozart string quartets, put the mute on the horn. Along with the old friend and the beloved family I welcome an occasional stranger to differently stimulate. I sit in, to interpret, to translate; I am getting pretty good at this skill. It *is* a skill, sensing and responding to the needs of the other. Like caring for an infant. Or making love. But he is not my child, and only memory is potent. I am a devotional neutral: nun, nurse. For the visitor, family or old friend or stranger, it is hard to find a way to be with him. Raise your voice; speak distinctly. Say nothing disturbing. Some handle it better than others but everyone handles it differently.

Soon after Jimmy's return from the hospital my brother flew in from Chicago; Paul wanted to give me comfort, to show his sympathy. What did I need? What could he do? I know it pleases Jimmy that Paul has made the trip, but he sits silently at the table, listening, watching me as I move from stove to sink, talking about friends, family, Paul's building projects in Chicago, anything but death and decay. I left Paul on his own; it was not long before I heard him come down the hall and slowly, heavily up the stairs to find me at my desk. "I can't sit there," he said. "Am I supposed to talk to him? I can't tell if he hears me. Or if he hears, does he understand? I can't just sit there." "Don't." I couldn't spare any sympathy. "Do what you like." I was sorry; he had had a lot of pain, trouble and damage in his life, and in his dark eyes it was there. Mostly hidden. Tall, noticeably handsome, fit, Paul raced sailboats; he was sixty years old, a successful builder of urban housing. When he left, the scene at the farm haunted him; he kept in touch, called me frequently from Chicago, made a few trips, brought me rare brandy and Bols gin, and endured the uneasy meetings with Jimmy growing frail.

———

How to deal with this strange new Jimmy. There he was, near the abyss; no one was in danger of argument or insult or being called to account with, "Take a stand!" Little expression of any kind from Jimmy. But he watched; he listened, and once in a great while he would speak though he didn't like the sound of his uninflected voice. After hours of silent observing and listening he might surprise us and suddenly correct a date, a fact. He might say, out of nowhere, "What do you think of God?" A serious question, a vital, stern question. Who knew what prompted it? An answer was demanded, an answer was fumbled: no glibness would do. Some gifted friends, without effort, simply talked to him as they always had.

Our children, grown men and women with children of their own, each sought the Jimmy they knew. The magic man of their early childhood, the impossible, arbitrary man who made their growing up so arduous, so strenuous, in his uncompromising demands. Judged, scrutinized, criticized; everything in their lives, from the clothes they wore to the friends they brought home, the books they read, or didn't read when they should have—the music that surrounded them, or the music despised and banished; in their turn they accepted or resisted or resented or rebelled but never stopped loving him. Now they were here whenever they could be: vulnerable and generous men and women, facing the unthinkable. Jimmy, indomitable Jimmy, in this state. Autonomy, authority, power, all brought down.

Wait. Not altogether, not just yet.

"When I get home," Jimmy said in one of the hospital speech therapist's exercises, "I will resume a statement."

And he did. What could he use, what was left, what was lost, where were the boundaries? He could hear, he could see; his body was crippled, speech eluded him, his brain had faulty connections. But what could not be measured or seen or touched was intact, was indeed stronger, and fiercer. I'll call it courage. He assembled material from his files; his files—they were all over the house, attic and closet, desk drawer and trunk—but the main repository was an ancient metal double filing cabinet in his study. It stood about five feet tall, dark brown-green; the drawers were balky on their runners. Within these crowded drawers there was surprising order: manila folders marked, alphabet and chronology observed; from these overflowing papers Jimmy found material for the last issues of *The Phoenix*. Using his walker, propping himself against his desk as he sorted through papers with his one useful hand, Jimmy would not ask for and I would not offer help. The effort and the triumph were important; unless he was really thwarted, I kept my watchful distance. In 1982, a year after his stroke, Jimmy cannily chose Miller's letters to us 1937–40: a special Henry Miller issue. In 1983, and 1984, one issue each year: trophies of Jimmy's tenacity. Some of the contents were odd, and why not? Let it go, I told Dan, our young printer friend who now ran our Heidelberg press in a shop of his own; I edited only glaring blunders. Jimmy taught himself to type with his left hand, he typed all the mailing labels for the one thousand subscribers, stuffed all the envelopes; slowly, carefully, deliberately, he resumed his statement.

———

The little magazine had an unusual history. A small but international circulation received the opinions and editorial choices of stubborn and passionate Jimmy from 1938 to 1940, Volumes One and Two of the literary quarterly, handset and printed in our letter-press shop in Woodstock, New York. After a thirty-year gap, in 1970, the still stubborn and passionate Jimmy assembled a print shop again here on the farm in West Whately, and with Volume Three, picked up where he had left off, with the same format, the same editor, even continuing a serialized journal and novel from the last issue in 1940. Walter Grossman, director of University of Massachussetts' Boston library, proposed to mount an exhibit of the history of *The Phoenix*. His swan song, Walter called it; he was retiring from the post he had distinguished for so long. Through Walter, in the process of assembling our papers, putting them in significant exhibition order, I made new friends. They came to the farm, Elizabeth Mock, librarian for archival development, and Molly Matson, assistant director for public services; Nicholas Olsberg, a professor of archival history; his graduate student, the graduate student's actress wife. Jimmy was the interested observer, pleased; maybe he was delighted. I think he was delighted, why wouldn't he be, he who had never lined up for foundation or grant money, who was always outside the literary academy. Sweet recognition. He was alert to everything we discussed, the choices we made of manuscripts, letters, photographs; he answered questions in the minimal language available to him now. In his reduced condition he tried to help the strangers.

On the fifth floor of the Joseph P. Healy Library of the University of Massachusetts in Boston, early in April 1984, Jimmy sat in an armchair, his hands resting on his cane; in his black beret and black corduroys, his trimmed white beard, he had a natural distinction. The light, the view of the Harbor, the assembly of strangers and friends and family who traveled distances to honor Jimmy; they sipped wine and nibbled cheese and each one approached the man whose singular determination was manifest here. He acknowledged their words with a nod, a murmur; to a hand offered he gave his still-obedient good left hand, warm and firm. I watched him move slowly around the exhibit on his cane, from case to case, around the five double cases of the chronologically arranged and carefully labeled artifacts of his life, and I thought, for the indelibly Catholic Jimmy, it was a rite of confirmation.

———

My blessing-counting beads are worn thin; I cling to them; they cling to me. Even worn thin through years of rubbing, their luster glows, heals, affirms. Count your blessings my friends say, and I do, I do. I count even the privilege of seeing Jimmy through this time, here in this house, on this hill, where all the strength of his life was spent; where all the scenes of his manhood were played. It is getting harder, I keep losing the ritual and the grace it confers. The days are endless, featureless, gray; I am despondent; I fight depression. Food tastes of ashes, and mirrors are terrible. When I leave my bed in the morning there is no one to reach for me, to pull me back; no one to show coldness; no one with whom I am at war.

To Jimmy, to our world, I present a smooth imitation of the ordinary routine we never had, dispensing medication, preparing meals, arranging health-care help. Every evening I build a fire in the kitchen fireplace. No big blaze, a quiet fire: back log, kindling, then two small logs in pyramid, the rule of three. Jimmy sits in the rocker pulled up to the hearth; he holds the poker; I am ready to protect my fire from his poking. He's the master fire-builder, sign of Leo and all that; he taught me all I know, but I am in charge. He gazes at the fire, I sit on the rush-seated little chair we keep on the hearth; we're quiet, we're always quiet; some weeks we don't exchange more than five sentences. "What would you like for supper?" "I don't know," he says to the fire; he's uninterested. "Baked potato? Corn chowder?" "I don't know." I go through the list of the acceptable, the simple, the good-for-him-easy-to-fix: tuna fish, omelet, tomato soup, grilled cheese; I exhaust the usual menu. He is still not interested. "Well"— I'm not concerned; I'm not one to think you can't skip a meal— "I can't say anything else." "Then be quiet," he continues to gaze at the fire. I laugh. I laugh and go back to my book. I'll try again later. "Then be quiet" is better than nothing; it must stand in for the old autocrat.

Jimmy watches me as I read the Sunday *New York Times*; I passed the Book Review section to him, but he has not turned a page. He's watching me. An ad for the Hemlock Society caught my eye: send for our literature on "How to Make Your Own Death." I clip it, his eyes followed the scissors blade; his eyes question: what am I doing? I pass the clipping to him. "I'm sending for this," I say casually. I give him time to read the ad. "Do you want to see it when it comes?" "Yes."

———

Two weeks passed, and one morning at breakfast Jimmy asked, "Did you mail the letter?" "Letter? What letter?" Had he given me something to mail that I had forgotten? I didn't know what he was talking about. "The letter . . ." he gazed out of the window, his brow furrowed, he searched. "The letter to whom?" I persisted. He shifted slightly, his good left hand rubbed his useless right hand, he looked into the branches of the great maple. Finally he turned to me. He had it. "To Socrates." "The Hemlock Society!" I clapped. I cried, "Wonderful!" My extravagant appreciation made him smile. Victory.

Summer 1985

Although there was no marked change in Jimmy, Paul had the sudden impulse to make an unplanned trip, to say goodbye to him. As a boy my brother had been bowled over; as a man he was critical, then hostile, and now when all was said, and almost done, he wanted Jimmy to know that he loved him. Paul flew in from Chicago and spent a few days. At the kitchen table they played chess, as equals, no quarter asked, none given; they played to a draw. "Good game, Jimmy." Paul said it as though he meant it. "You're still tough to beat." Jimmy, replacing the pieces on the board, smiled to himself. There was something malfunctioning in the stereo in Jimmy's study. "Let me see if I can find the trouble," Paul said. While Jimmy sat at his desk and watched and supplied from the left-hand top drawer needle-nosed pliers, I left them. I didn't think Paul would find the words he had come to say. After my brother left and Jimmy and I were alone, I said, "Paul wanted to tell you he loves you. Did he?" Jimmy thought for a moment. "Sort of," he said and I knew Paul had made his farewell.

———

What's going on, as he sits in his silence, gazing out of the window in the mornings, sitting at his chosen place at the table, does he see the birds at the feeders Gabriel faithfully keeps filled? Sitting in the wing chair before the television at night, sometimes alone in the living room, sometimes I sit beside him, he closes his eyes when the picture is on, or stares at the blank screen turned off. What is passing through him, what is the process of letting go. How is he doing it? Because he is doing it. Relinquishing life—he so tenacious, so stubborn—leaving the world he fought to change, leaving his loves he sought to possess. Opening his hand, clenched for so long, letting it spill away.

Chapter Nineteen

DEATH

- 1985 -

September 1985

NOT AT THE TABLE, not in his bed. No sound. Where was Jimmy? I found him in the bathroom, just sitting, holding his cane. He looked at me, stunned; something had happened. "Have you had an accident?" Yes. I helped him. This was bad. He barely made it to the rocker in the kitchen. We got him to the hospital. He was in intensive care, tubes, drains. The family gathered. After two days of tests and doctors' reports we had a conference. In the dimly lit lounge outside the room where Jimmy had been intensively, invasively cared for, the doctors consulted the records on their clipboards. A bleeding aneurism, a growth quiescent until now, had burst. Considering other factors, regretfully, sadly, they summed up, "He could not survive surgery." I said, "Let him go, take those tubes and drains away." I said, "No more torment," and the family agreed.

Except Michael, who had to make a quick trip back to New Hampshire. Gabriel found a telephone; he gave Michael the doctors' report and told him how we felt. Yes, Michael agreed. Then he said, "Now you must ask Jimmy." No one, not the doctors, nor any of us, thought to ask Jimmy. It was Michael who gave the ultimate gift of love and respect, and it was Gabriel who went into the intensive care unit, to Jimmy's bed, and placed it before him: the gift to choose. In a few minutes Gabriel was back, his eyes filled to brimming. "Jimmy listened. He didn't say anything. And then he smiled, and he said,

'Wrap it up.'" Gabriel turned away. Elizabeth put her arms around him; they wept. Deirdre, Eliza, took my hand. Now we were all dissolved. The doctors gathered their papers, said "We'll move him to a quiet room; we'll make him as comfortable as possible. Valium, morphine. It can't be long," and they left us.

Wrap it up. The play is over.

Decisive, in charge. He was thinking of his travail. He was thinking of us, sparing us. Wrap it up.

My father, dying in Cedars of Lebanon Hospital in Los Angeles; his black housekeeper, his friend, leaned into the oxygen tent: "Boss, we're going to take you home, don't you worry." "Not this time, Mary. I hit the jackpot." Tolstoy, dying in the railway station in Russia: "This is checkmate."

The family kept vigil; for three days, around the clock, for the rest of his life, we said goodbye. He was never alone; Eliza spent the night, Gabriel brought tapes of Jimmy's favorite Mozart. There was always someone to hold his hand, touch his brow. Always a child came in the door, came up to his bed, a succession of grandchildren, a farewell feast for his eyes, for his heart: Michael and Mary, with their sons Thomas and Nicholas; Mary seven months pregnant with their third child. Jimmy saw Mary, close to term; he would never see that baby. Deirdre last year moved from Pennsylvania to nearby Conway. Her father was dying, dying; she wanted to be close, to be there. She and Cristobal and their daughter Margarita. Annabel, Isabel, Caleb, Emily. They were all there, careful to take their turn, not to overwhelm the small hospital room. We spelled each other; in the corridor wc murmured and consulted. We were careful, aware of the other's fragility. Valium kept pain at bay; the nurses ministered and discreetly vanished.

I wore the topaz stone on a gold chain, Jimmy's last gift to me. "See," I said "here's the yellow stone you gave me." I was close to him, at the head of the bed. He looked at the necklace. He was reminded of something, something yellow. Yellow. I leaned closer. His voice was so weak; he spoke in fragments, a word, a phrase: "In my desk—top drawer . . . a long pause; in his mind he opened the drawer, "My yellow bank book—" his voice was a little stronger— "give Margarita five hundred dollars." "Margarita?" "Yes," he said that firmly. Then I thought he would go on: five hundred to this one, five hundred to that one. There was something so classic about this leave-taking, this scene in the hospital room: our children, their children, the child unborn, the love of his life by his side. I think he wanted to fulfill the image of the dying patriarch, and this was the traditional bequest scene. He stopped. We all waited. Nothing more. I thought Jimmy stopped because he doesn't know his bank balance; I smiled at the private unsuitable thought. I knew I was right, but I kept it to myself.

Pain overwhelmed valium. Jimmy pressed my hand. I leaned closer. He breathed, "I love you." He whispered, "Kiss them for me." This was the hardest thing we had ever done together. I think I said it; I think he heard.

Goodbye, goodbye. Take the children away. He could no longer see them and his struggle was too terrible to witness. I must go out, Gabriel would stay until I returned. I needed air; I needed to walk. I must be alone. I couldn't really leave; even though Jimmy was on his way, far from me, I had to be there. When I walked slowly back to the hospital, I saw Gabriel outside, waiting for me. And I knew Jimmy was dead. "He's gone," Gabriel said, and he held me.

Back into the hospital I went, up to Jimmy's room. No one was there, no one. I was alone with Jimmy.

I shut the door. I found Mozart's clarinet quintet among our tapes, and for the last time I sat beside Jimmy, struggle over, glory over, listening to the music. He has just left, I thought, maybe he is able to take those sounds with him.

A few months before Jimmy died he typed the line, "I want my ashes to go into a river that leads to the sea." On a gray card, dated and signed "Jimmy" with his left hand, as formal as need be. He gave it to me without a word. I said, "Thank you. It's good to know what you want," and I put it back on his desk.

Jimmy's obituary, with his picture, on the front page of the *Daily Hampshire Gazette*, announced a memorial gathering to be held in the West Whately chapel. At the foot of our hill where four back country roads cross, the one-room wooden building had served the tiny hamlet in ways secular and worshipful since 1895. There were telephone calls, New York, Boston; there were encounters in town, and the family said the chapel was too small. "It will never hold them all," they said. This one's coming; that one's coming. The chaplain at Smith offered Helen Hills Hills Chapel on Elm Street. Too grand, I said, too institutional. No, no. Here. In West Whately.

Although I was consulted, considered, tenderly spared, this farewell was arranged with Jimmy very present in all decisions. Not only was the chapel small, but there was no electricity. We wanted a record. Smith College would lend audio equipment, and we could secure power through extension cords to the nearest dwelling. Gabriel's Marlboro College friend Jeff Turner would take charge of recording, mikes hung outside the chapel would carry the sound to the overflow. The string quartet Gabriel found was rehearsing the Dvorak; Sue Kurian has chosen to play a Bach flute sonata.

———

The weather was fierce, first week in October. Hurricane weather; winds blew, leaves torn from trees, it poured rain, a deluge, a gale. But on our memorial day, October 6th, the sun rose, the day was golden, still. Brilliant. In the morning we drove, just the family, the five miles to the Sunderland Bridge over the Connecticut River, all our children and their children. We walked to the middle of the bridge. We scattered Jimmy's ashes into the running current. Deirdre had a basket over her arm; we each took a flower and tossed it into the river after the ashes. Suddenly Isabel, twelve years old, who had lived with Jimmy all her life, broke from us and darted across the bridge to follow the passage of his ashes in the flow of the river, the Connecticut River that leads to Long Island Sound that leads to the open sea.

Appendix

THE FOLLOWING INTRODUCTION to *The Phoenix* is from
an editorial note by James Cooney published in the first issue
of the new series of *The Phoenix*, volume 3, number 1, Winter 1970. It
is reprinted here with permission.

The Phoenix last appeared in Autumn 1940. Since then the suffering
of this grim century has deepened. Freedom is withering. Tyranny
flourishes. Joy, gone underground, is led forth with a queerly frantic
air at festivals & celebrations taking place while far-off flashes of na-
palm transform remote peasant villages into instant crematoriums.

The Phoenix is appearing again to offer itself as a medium of
communion for those who keep faith in mankind and Creation—a
Promethean faith. Manuscripts are invited: completed novels, novels in progress, stories, poems, diaries, wood-blocks & line drawings. And letters from readers. Publication will be quarterly.

Little magazines come and go. *The Phoenix* first appeared on the
scene in Spring 1938 with Henry Miller, then living precariously in
Paris, serving as European editor. Miller, in those early days of his
struggle for recognition, had managed to have his first novel and a
collection of tales privately printed in France, but those editions
were banned in this country. Through *The Phoenix* Miller was published for the first time in the United States and his writings began to
reach his native audience. These works included some of his now
most famous stories (such as the long one *Max*—the cruelest and
most haunting of all his tales) and portions of his banned books as
well as critical evaluations of Proust, Joyce and D. H. Lawrence.
And his early essay on the unpublished *Diary of* Anaïs Nin. Excerpts
from Anaïs Nin's *Diary*, which ultimately found its way into commercial publication in 1966, first appeared in *The Phoenix* in 1939.

There were other obscure writers and poets, now widely recog-
nized, who appeared in *The Phoenix*: Robert Duncan, Dilys Bennett
Laing, Derek Savage, Kiedrich Rhys, Raynor Heppenstall, J. C.
Crews, Thomas McGrath, and William Everson known also as

Brother Antoninus. Kay Boyle's early novel *Big Fiddle*, which deserves transition into a classic film, was published in its entirety. Michael Fraenkel contributed his uncanny insights into the deathward drift of the Western nations. In his dispassionate essay *Beyond the Bread Principle* Fraenkel charted the deranged future courses of the rival Communist, Fascist and Democratic states as lucidly as Thucydides recorded the accomplished devastations and ruin of his era.

One of the most passionate voices in the pages of *The Phoenix* was that of the powerful French writer Jean Giono whose spirit was tempered under the anvil of his war experiences after his conscription as a nineteen-year-old into World War I. Decorated by the English for valor under fire in rescuing fallen comrades, Giono passed somnambulistically through the fiercest battles and carnage of that War without ever firing his rifle. Jean Giono died just two months ago in the night of October 8th, a night during which our press was printing pages of the final section of his novel *Refusal to Obey*. He was 75 years old. With over fifty volumes of his works published, he continued writing prodigiously on through to the last days of his life. Giono was regarded by eminent critics as one of Europe's greatest novelists. The opening portions of his war novel *Refusal To Obey* appeared in 1939 and 1940 issues.

And every one of our preceding issues, from the first in Spring of 1938 to the last in Autumn 1940, carried the blazing voice that evoked *The Phoenix*—the voice that attracted poets & writers to contribute unpaid to its pages: the intransigent voice of D. H. Lawrence. His furious stand against the vileness of conscription and War, his loathing of politicians and generals, his mockery of dictators and their debased masses of followers, his revulsion against private profit and the enslavements of Money and his exposure of the spreading blight of our automated society illuminated *The Phoenix* throughout its entire earlier course. Among Lawrence's writings published was his clairvoyant March 1924 *Letter From Germany*, warning men, long before Hitler & his Nazis had appeared on the horizon, of the approaching disaster; and his prophetic essay *The Good Man*, revealing the inner putrefactions and impending collapse of the American and Russian regimes. D. H. Lawrence's widow, Frieda, in a letter to the American editor of *The Phoenix*, said: "Lawrence's writings seem more powerful in your edition than ever before—it's because before they only published words, but you believe in the meaning."

Obscure and lost from general sight in the avant garde little magazine field, *The Phoenix* made its way around the world gathering readers in such unlikely places as Yugoslavia, Palestine, Africa and mainland China. It was the only serious literary journal in America during the late Thirties that opposed conscription and War; and it continued its opposition after World War II broke out. Pledged to non-violent resistance, it openly offered its support and allegiance to all those following this course of action. *The Phoenix* was also on the outposts of the Thirties in seeking a way out of the enslavements of modern society through the brotherhood of agrarian communes. Its American editor served as its pressman, often by foot-treadle operation of an old Colts Armory press when the electricity was cut off for non-payment of bills. Twenty-eight years old when *The Phoenix* was started, he had his nineteen-year-old wife for compositor. Their infant daughter spent most of her early life in the crude country print-shop in Woodstock, New York where the issues were hand-set, hand-printed & hand-bound with occasional help from visiting friends. Toward the close of its third year of publication, a year after World War II broke out, *The Phoenix* came to an end. Friends, contributors and subscribers were scattered and lost from one another in the vast chaos of those times. Funds to carry on had withered away. *The Phoenix* expired.

But in its fabled way *The Phoenix* is rising from its own ashes. A two-volume facsimile reprint of the entire original file of issues, long out of print, has been completed and is now available in a hard-cover limited edition priced at $55. Proceeds from this facsimile edition are funding the new *Phoenix* which has its original editor again serving as its pressman and its original compositor again handsetting type. But this time there are grown sons and daughters & young friends serving as loyal assistants.

Yet it's not been easy, this reappearance. To begin with there was all the work involved in converting the crude cellar of our almost two-centuries-old New England farmhouse into a print-shop. Along with months of search for second-hand type-stands, galleys, etc. as well as our central search for one of the few still existent but commercially obsolete Kelly B cylinder letter presses which we had decided would best suit our needs & finances. Most of these once famous units, after long standing idle and occupying needed floor space, had been given away for scrap iron or disposed of by paying junk dealers to dismantle & cart them off. Nevertheless that was the vanishing press we were determined to find. It would be large enough, at maximum capacity, to print eight pages at a time in our format (twice as many as our former old Colts Armory press) and it would just barely fit through the five-foot width of our cellar hatchway door. We finally located our Kelly B in New Haven—battered, poorly kept, much abused, yet still staunchly running in a small back alley print-shop that was closing and had been bought out completely by a second-hand printing-equipment dealer. He told us this Kelly B was one of the latest units made, a 1931 model, and asked $500 for it. We examined the factory serial number which revealed it had left the factory in 1921 or '22 and made a counter offer of $75. He shrewdly accepted.

And although it cost us twice that much to hire a large steel-platform truck rigged with a winch & manned by three husky movers to get it from New Haven into our cellar, we were jubilant. Several nights later with candles held aloft in the cavernous cob-webbed cellar, where new wiring & lights were not yet installed, our press received a blessing from two girls, music majors at Smith College who once sang with us on a far different occasion at a brutally assaulted demonstration against the Draft Board in front of Northampton's City Hall. Their voices were like voices of angels as they sang in Latin two ancient hymns over our press: *Not for our glory but Thine, O Lord* and *Dona nobis pacem.*

Index